I0760200

Inventing Baseball Heroes

Inventing Baseball Heroes

TY COBB, CHRISTY MATHEWSON, AND THE SPORTING PRESS IN AMERICA

AMBER ROESSNER

LOUISIANA STATE UNIVERSITY PRESS
BATON ROUGE

Published by Louisiana State University Press

Manufactured in the United States of America
First printing

Designer: Laura Roubique Gleason
Typeface: Minion Pro
Printer and binder: Maple Press

Library of Congress Cataloging-in-Publication Data
Roessner, Amber, 1980–
Inventing baseball heroes : Ty Cobb, Christy Mathewson, and the sporting press in America / Amber Roessner.
pages cm
Includes bibliographical references and index.
ISBN 978-0-8071-5611-7 (cloth : alk. paper) — ISBN 978-0-8071-5612-4 (pdf) — ISBN 978-0-8071-5613-1 (epub) — ISBN 978-0-8071-5614-8 (mobi) 1. Baseball—United States—Social aspects. 2. Baseball—United States—History. 3. Mass media and sports—United States. 4. Sports journalism—United States. 5. Athletes in mass media. 6. Cobb, Ty, 1886–1961. 7. Mathewson, Christy, 1880–1925. I. Title.
GV867.64.R64 2014
796.3570973—dc23

2013041468

The paper in this book meets the guidelines for permanence and durability of the Committee on Production Guidelines for Book Longevity of the Council on Library Resources. ♾

This
book is
dedicated to the
women who paved the way
for this southern gal to write about
baseball, communication, and American
culture—from Ella Black, one of the first female
sports journalists, to Melissa Ludtke, who fought her
way into the locker rooms of professional baseball clubs.
It also is for my family, especially my great-
grandmother, my grandmother, and my
mother, who taught me that I could
accomplish anything with a
measure of tenacity
and hard
work.

Contents

Acknowledgments

I began working on this book in January 2006 during my second semester of graduate school at the University of Georgia's Grady College of Journalism and Mass Communication. There, in the halls named for Henry W. Grady, the man who brought professional baseball to his New South, I began to grapple with the press's role in the production of sports heroes in Janice Hume's seminar. I became consumed with learning more about the practice of hero construction—"hero-crafting," as I liked to call it. That first study of the role of journalism in hero production evolved into a conference presentation, a journal article, a dissertation topic, a book, and a full-fledged research agenda. None of this would have been possible without the invaluable guidance of my mentor. Over the years, Professor Hume demonstrated unceasing faith not only in this work, but also in me. I want to thank her for her continual support—for knowing exactly what I needed to hear when I needed to hear it.

Of course, a project of this size does not come together without the assistance of numerous individuals. It does, after all, take an academic village to raise a scholar. With that in mind, I would like to thank Kathleen Clark, Jay Hamilton, Horace Newcomb, and Karen Russell for their assistance. I would be remiss not to express my heartfelt gratitude to Carolina Acosta-Alzuru, who oversaw the oral history that served as the foundation for the book's prologue and epilogue. Thanks also to my University of Tennessee colleagues Paul Ashdown and Jim Stovall and to my astute reviewers and editors at LSU Press for helping me polish the manuscript.

I also am grateful for the invaluable professors that I encountered along my academic journey, from communication scholars Leara Rhodes and Dean Krugman to historians Laura Mason and John Inscoe. Furthermore, I wish to thank the warm support team who traveled with me down this winding path. Thanks to my fellow graduate students at Grady College of Journalism and Mass Communication, especially Kristin English, Kimberly Davis, Brett Robinson, Curt Wanner, Noah Arceneaux, Kristen Heflin, Matt Corn, Mark Lashley, and Brian Creech, and to my friends and colleagues at the University of Tennessee. These kind folks supplied fresh insights, encouraging words, and more than a few laughs during a challenging period of my life. Thanks also to interested scholars at conferences such as the American Journalism Historians Association, the Association for Education in Journalism and Mass Communication, the International Communication Association, and the International Association for Literary Journalism Studies, who engaged with this topic, and to the Cooperstown Symposium, which published an early version of the research presented in one chapter in the *Cooperstown Symposium on Baseball and American Culture, 2009–2010* (McFarland Press, 2011).

I am indebted to the Society of American Baseball Research and the University of Georgia's Grady College of Journalism for their generous aid through the Anthony A. Yoseloff-SABR Research Grant and the Paul C. and Margaret Beasley Broun Student Support Fund. These two grants financed an extended visit to New York's National Baseball Hall of Fame Research Library and Columbia University in autumn 2009. I also am thankful for the knowledgeable librarians, archivists, and curators at the University of Georgia's Richard B. Russell Library in Athens; the Ty Cobb Museum in Royston, Georgia; the National Baseball Hall of Fame's A. Bartlett Giamatti Research Library in Cooperstown, New York; Vanderbilt University's Jean and Alexander Heard Library, Special Collections, in Nashville; and Columbia University's Rare Book and Manuscript Library in New York.

Ultimately, though, I owe my utmost thanks to my family for their unwavering support and boundless love, especially to the most important women in my life—my mother Gina, my grandmother Laura

Jean, and my dear great-grandmother Nellie, who taught me that perseverance and hard work make success tangible. I also am grateful to my husband David, who provided unconditional love and encouragement and was an able assistant during my time at the National Baseball Hall of Fame. Finally, thank you, Dad, for inspiring my passion for the national pastime.

Inventing Baseball Heroes

Prologue

BASEBALL BECKONS

As a young girl in the early 1980s, I spent hours playing catch with my father in our backyard. On those early summer evenings before lightning bugs came out to play, I liked to pretend that I was Ty Cobb, the "Georgia Peach." My goal was simple: to hit a line drive over the rickety shed near the forest. Doing so would not only earn the pride of victory but the spoils: a Dairy Queen ice-cream sundae. Connecting with the perfect pitch, however, was elusive. Even so, each evening, as dusk settled on the foothills of northeast Georgia, I begged for just one more pitch—one more chance to meet my destiny.

As divine providence would have it, my fate was not to trample the base paths of a Major League ballpark. It was not even to toil in the press box of a big league stadium or to sit in the grandstands all that often. My destiny, instead, consisted of long stretches in newspaper offices and library basements.

It was during one of those stints in a newsroom that I first reconnected with Cobb. In June 2004, I wrote a series about mill league baseball for the *Gainesville Times*. As I researched stories of blue-collar textile workers who fielded line drives alongside baseball royalty such as the "Georgia Peach" and "Shoeless" Joe Jackson on primitive baseball diamonds in rural communities in northeast Georgia and upstate South Carolina, I was intrigued by the local interest in heroes of the Dead Ball Era (1900–1919), a period in professional baseball known for its quality of pitching, relatively low batting averages, and innovative small-ball techniques.

Men such as Jake Miller of the New Holland squad recounted pitching against local legends such as Demorest's Johnny "Big Cat"

Mize.[1] As children, others claimed to have spotted Ty and Shoeless Joe playing in tiny towns throughout the region. These individuals shared stories of what the national pastime had meant to them and their communities. Each day after the original series was published, emails and letters poured in from men and women of all ages who wanted to share their memories, too. As I perused countless letters, I became certain that I had stumbled on a story that ran deeper than an enterprise piece. This yarn, I realized, was rooted in the hearts and minds of countless Americans, and newsprint would not do justice to the tale of America's love affair with baseball's first cast of sports heroes.

This thought returned to me a little more than two years later as I scanned microfilm of *Sporting Life* for a graduate seminar paper. In the basement of the University of Georgia's Richard B. Russell Library, I once again encountered the "Georgia Peach." I was struck by the reverence with which *Sporting Life* editor Francis C. Richter and his correspondents wrote about Cobb and another Dead Ball Era hero—New York Giants pitcher Christy Mathewson. In that moment, I resolved to embark on a larger examination of the practice of herocrafting in early twentieth-century sports journalism and its contribution to the national adulation of two of baseball's greatest paragons.[2]

Along the way, memories of the words of my father often rang in my ears. During the more trying times, I would remember an old saying he taught me: "For when the One Great Scorer comes to mark against your name, He writes—not that you won or lost—but how you played the Game."[3]

Legendary *Atlanta Journal-Constitution* sportswriter Furman Bisher was familiar with those words and plenty of others written by Grantland Rice and his pals in the sports pages at century's turn. They were guilty pleasures of his youth, the ninety-year-old columnist admitted, smiling as he leaned back in a swivel chair in my Athens, Georgia, office on a warm afternoon in October 2009. Bisher had encountered this "gee whiz" school of journalists, as they later became known for their rosy rhetoric, in his local post office in the early 1920s. There, he "devoured the Major Leagues" for breakfast.

"Each morning around nine o'clock," he recalled, "I would go down to the post office, open up the sports section, and spread it out over the post office floor, and all of these men coming in to get their mail would just kind of nudge me out of the way." Sprawled on the floor, he leafed through countless feature articles about Dead Ball and Golden Age (1920–60) heroes such as Cobb, Mathewson, and New York Yankees slugger Babe Ruth penned by some of the best-known sports journalists of the age. "You had to be off the planet if you didn't run into Ty Cobb" in the sports pages, he remembered. "I never got to see him play, though."

Like millions of other Americans, Bisher never had the opportunity to watch from the stands of Detroit's Navin Field as Cobb connected with a pitch for a hit and slid spikes-first into third. Instead, he and other baseball enthusiasts barred from the stands because of cost or proximity followed him from the pages of newspaper sports sections, specialty baseball journals, and general-interest magazines. They relished the tales of triumph and tragedy supplied en masse to millions of Americans by their favorite bards.

It was in part the words of Rice and his cronies that inspired Bisher to become a sportswriter upon his return from serving in World War II. When he began his career with the *Charlotte* (North Carolina) *News* in 1946, he arrived at the office of the afternoon newspaper by 7:00 a.m. to type up his column. After polishing it off, he served as the rewrite man, handling telephone call-ins from correspondents before overseeing the make-up of the sports page in the composing room.

Unlike present-day sportswriters who claim a level of detachment, he never left his love of sports heroes along with his hat and overcoat at the office door. Instead, his passion for the game and its cast of characters was always present as he pecked away at his latest column on his Royal typewriter. "Sportswriting was different in those days," he acknowledged. "The reason I was in it was because there was a purity about it, and there was a fascination with the athletes. You knew the athletes. You traveled with them, wrote of them, got to know them well.

"We had our favorites," he went on to admit. "Take Ty Cobb, for instance. . . . I did not choose to write about the skeletons in his closet. I don't think sportswriters today have that kind of respect for an athlete. If they get something on someone, they fire away. If I liked an athlete, if anything bad came up about him, I thought, 'Damned if I'm going to write that.' . . . I would say that I was an honest sportswriter, though. I wrote what I saw. I may have picked a fellow and overlooked his glitches but most [sportswriters] were that way."

Bisher's reminiscences sound eerily similar to those of another sports journalist who covered Cobb during his heyday. "Sporting writers have their particular idols—some whom they cherished from boyhood," wrote Grantland Rice in his posthumously published autobiography, *The Tumult and the Shouting: My Life in Baseball,* "others whom they helped create in the headlines."[4]

With the voices of Bisher and Rice echoing in my ears, I set out on a journey to gain a new understanding of the practice of "gee whiz" sports journalism. This book is the end result of my trek to baseball grandstands, press boxes, newspaper morgues, institutional archives, and library basements across the nation. As I unearthed historical artifacts in these disparate spaces, I came into contact with what cultural historian Raymond Williams referred to as the material traces of "a whole way of life."[5] Through the process of examining these relics, I gained a greater sense of how the sportswriting of the early twentieth century influenced the lives of a generation of Americans—from writers such as Furman Bisher to U.S. Senator Richard B. Russell. I discovered how these tales have contributed to the negotiation of constructs about gender, nationality, and success; and I have even come to grips with how stories about this "noble American game" have shaped my family and myself.[6]

Ultimately, this is the story of two of the Dead Ball Era's greatest heroes, the storytellers that helped make them, and the implications that their tales had for American culture. In part, it is also the chronicle of the rise and fall of the "gee whiz" school, and its resurrection in a different form after the stark days of the Great Depression. But most of all, this study sheds light on what heroes such as Mathewson and Cobb meant to America in the early twentieth century and by extension what they mean to us today. So now, in the words of Ring Lardner, one of the era's most famous sportswriters, "Sit down here a while, kid, and I'll give you the dope" on two of the biggest stars of the Dead Ball Era and the men who crafted them.[7]

–1–

Constructing Heroes

On February 18, 1912, Ina Russell of Winder, Georgia, wrote a last-minute scribble on the letter addressed to her teenaged son Dick, who was away at Gordon Institute in Barnesville. "Do you see [Atlanta] *Constitution*?" read the hastily written postscript above the greeting. "I have a nice piece about Ty Cobb." In the article, the star outfielder shared his thoughts on inside baseball.[1]

The future U.S. senator was undoubtedly grateful for his mother's note, for he often clipped articles about his favorite Major Leaguers and pasted them into scrapbooks. When he was not engaged in these endeavors, he was jotting notes about sandlot games, collegiate nines, and professional squads in his baseball diary. Like many youngsters, he also collected memorabilia associated with the national pastime. He carefully safeguarded ticket stubs and baseball cards in cigar boxes, which he hid in his bedroom closet.[2] His highly prized collection featured multiple likenesses of two of the Dead Ball Era's greatest icons—Detroit Tigers outfielder Ty Cobb and New York Giants hurler Christy Mathewson.

Russell was not alone. More Americans than not were consumed with the sport. *Saturday Evening Post* editor George Horace Lorimer had acknowledged baseball's near universal appeal four years earlier in October 1908: "It is important to remember, in an imperfect and fretful world, that we have an institution which is practically above reproach and above criticism. Nobody worth mentioning wants to change its constitution, or limit its powers. . . . No one claims that it is vulgar like the newspapers, or that it assassinates genius like the magazines. It rouses no class passions, and while it has magnates, they go unharmed with our approval. This once comparatively perfect flower of our sadly defective civilization, is of course, baseball. The only important institution, so far as we remember, which the United States regards with a practically universal, uncritical, unadulterated affection."[3] Baseball was a cultural craze. It so resonated with the American public by 1919 that it prompted noted American philosopher Morris Raphael Cohen to label the game the national religion. And if baseball was indeed the national religion, then sportswriters were its proselytizers, the sporting press was its bible, and the American public was its willing worshippers. Families such as the Russells communicated regularly about baseball icons. They sought news of their manly idols in the popular press. They collected artifacts related to them. They made hero-worship a regular part of their way of life.

Hero-worship was not a phenomenon unique to the early twentieth century. "Heroes, it would seem, exist always, and a certain worship of them," wrote nineteenth-century Scottish historian Thomas Carlyle.[4] Heroes, he contended, are a product of human nature, and hero-worship, the "life-breath of society." His friend Ralph Waldo Emerson agreed, writing that life is "tolerable only in our belief in great men."[5]

The study of heroes continued to inspire scholars after Carlyle. Mythologists, anthropologists, and even psychologists joined historians such as Dixon Wecter in the examination of cultural archetypes. Some, such as Wecter, chronicled hero-worship in specific times and places.[6] Others, such as Swiss psychologist Carl Jung and later mythologist Joseph Campbell, contended that heroes transcend cultural contexts and are rooted in the human psyche; with that psychoanalytic premise in mind, they set out to explore the similarities of archetypes across cultures.[7]

Campbell identified the standard monomythic formula. He noted that all heroes regardless of cultural origin encountered similar rites of passage, one marked by separation, initiation, and return. Stories of cultural heroes involved an uncommon birth, a call to adventure, special assistance from a loyal companion, a series of trials, a final battle, and a return home. Upon his return, the hero imparted wisdom gleaned from his adventure to others. A hero's journey home was the most difficult task of all. Nonetheless, he must return to teach his people the lessons he had learned.[8]

Scholars from Carlyle to Campbell acknowledged the cultural function of heroes. A society's great men served as exemplars to enlighten the world. They were more than men to be admired; they taught individuals how they should behave. Heroic tales were models for social behavior that contributed to the "maintenance of an established order."[9]

Heroes, however, are something more than static cultural archetypes. Cultures are regenerated through their stories of great men, and heroes are reborn in societies. The individual and society are mutually constituted through the practice of hero-worship. Individuals in societies attempt to emulate the behaviors and values celebrated in their great men, but societies also remake their heroes to fit their current needs. Although the basic elements of the hero's story remain unchanged, the behaviors and values that a society celebrates in its heroes are in a constant state of flux. America's greatest heroes, such as George Washington, Thomas Jefferson, and Abraham Lincoln, have been celebrated in different eras for different qualities—for their honesty, their bravery, and even their ingenuity. The gods of men, then, are malleable, and heroic tales "teach us lessons of the essential oneness of the individual and the group."[10]

Hero-worship is a "secular religion," acknowledged Dixon Wecter of the uneasy tension between the religious and pagan roots of hero-worship, but our great men are not always good at heart.[11] When the ancient Greeks coined the word *hero* to describe their society's great protectors possessing superhuman strength and courage, they did not deny that their heroes were, in the last instance, mere mortals with their share of character flaws. Throughout human history, we have celebrated pirates, warmongers, and scoundrels alongside altruistic saints and priests. In times of war, we have commemorated soldiers in battle, and in times of peace, we have venerated the man who comes closest to signifying the warrior—the adventurer, the frontiersman, or in modern times, the athlete. We have learned lessons from them all.

By the middle of the nineteenth century, commentators such as Carlyle were beginning to bemoan the absence of heroes in modern life.[12] Carlyle contended that America was a land that denied the existence and desirableness of great men. Heroes, great men of war and peace, were increasingly being replaced by celebrities, famous individuals who were known simply for being well known.[13] They were pseudo-heroes, acclaimed for their feats in the boardroom, on the stage, or on the field of play.[14] The worship of science, technology, and celebrity had replaced religion, Campbell observed, and in the process, killed the hero.

The study of heroes is at the heart of this story. I do not, however, endorse the idea that heroes are culture-bound, nor do I propose the wholehearted acceptance of Campbell's contention that heroes are universal figures that completely transcend time and place. Instead, I take a middle path, suggested by folklorists and literary critics, by examining the "cultural manifestations" of heroic tales in American culture.[15]

From 1900 to 1928, Americans were inundated by mass-mediated images of Cobb and Mathewson.[16] As veteran sportswriter Furman Bisher explained, someone would have been "off the planet" not to have encountered the "Georgia Peach" or "Big Six." For even if baseball enthusiasts were not among those who snagged seats in grandstands to cheer on the peerless Detroit Tigers outfielder or the beloved New York Giants pitcher, they undoubtedly encountered the pair in the media—in newspapers and magazines, on vaudeville show posters, on advertising billboards, even while playing their favorite board game. News of their performances on the diamond appeared in the headlines of sports pages, general-interest magazines, and baseball publications; by the late 1920s, live news about the standouts also could be heard on the radio.[17]

Both icons also appeared in national advertisements for a host of goods—from products such as Louisville Slugger baseball bats to little-known soda fountain drinks such as Coca-Cola.[18] For a time, Mathewson even served as one of the spokespersons for a popular board game, “Play Ball, Mathew’s Parlor Baseball Game,” but he eventually developed his own board game, “Big Six: Christy Mathewson Indoor Baseball Game,” and called on his chum Cobb to endorse it. “I have played ‘Big Six’ and find it so intensely interesting that I expect every fan will welcome it,” Cobb told children in a 1908 *Youth’s Companion* magazine ad.[19]

It was the sportswriters, however, who shared the icons’ exploits most often with the American people. They traveled by train with the Tigers and the Giants. They shared meals and drinks with Cobb and Mathewson. During the regular season, they palled around with them in clubhouse dugouts, hotel lobbies, and on golf courses; in the off-season, they visited the men en route to vacation destinations. They even went on hunting trips with the pair.[20] During these encounters, the nation’s cadre of elite sports journalists gathered heaps of information—some of which they passed on to their readers, some of which they kept in strict confidence. National sportswriters such as Hugh Fullerton, Grantland Rice, Ring Lardner, Damon Runyon, and John N. Wheeler delivered everyday baseball news along with tidbits from the personal lives of star ballplayers in news articles, feature stories, and columns.

Editors of specialty sports magazines such as F. C. Lane’s *Baseball Magazine* and general-interest publications such as Ray Long’s *Cosmopolitan* hired top reporters to furnish regular features about the best-known big leaguers. In these pieces, many baseball writers praised the likes of Cobb and Mathewson and endorsed baseball as the most worthy national pastime.

They penned fable-like odes to the diamond’s greatest stars. Sportswriter William F. Kirk, for instance, waxed poetic about Mathewson: “Of course, you kids love ‘Matty’ and the deeds that he can do; He’s just your big blond idol, and your father’s idol, too.”[21] Writers offered similar verses about Cobb.[22] They ultimately crafted the pair as embodiments of the American dream for boys such as Russell and Bisher. Mathewson and Cobb were household names in the first three decades of the twentieth century, and the media helped make them the talk of the nation.

Of course the focal point of the sportswriters' job was to chronicle Mathewson's (1900–1916) and Cobb's (1905–28) feats on the field. In his seventeen-year career in the National League, in all but one of which he wore a New York Giants uniform, Mathewson won 373 games.[23] He was known for his near-flawless control and impeccable motion. He perfected his famous fadeaway, a reverse curve that modern experts refer to as the screwball, en route to twelve consecutive twenty-win seasons and a career ERA of 2.13 that ranks fifth in professional baseball's current record books. His number of victories still stands in the top three in Major League history, and his winning percentage ranks sixth.

"Matty was the greatest pitcher who ever lived, in my opinion," noted Fred Snodgrass, his teammate from 1908 to 1915.[24] In 1955, Branch Rickey, one of baseball's greatest masterminds, contended that Mathewson was one of the greatest pitchers he had ever seen. "Matty," as he was lovingly called by a sizable segment of the American public, was celebrated for more than his prowess on the mound. He became a national idol for his clean-cut look, his unimpeachable moral standards, and his exemplary attitude. He came to be known as the "Christian Gentleman." He was the sports world's moral hero.

If Mathewson was the saint, Cobb was one of the game's unapologetic sinners. He did not hesitate to hold out for a higher salary, and he showed no remorse when he brawled with his teammates and fans or sharpened his cleats before sliding feet-first into anyone barring his way. "The base paths belonged to me, the runner," he once said. "The rules gave me the right. I always went into a bag full speed, feet first. I had sharp spikes on my shoes. If the baseman stood where he had no business to be and got hurt, that was his fault."[25] He claimed that baseball was a lot like war. "Baseball is a red-blooded sport for red-blooded men. It's no pink tea, and mollycoddles had better stay out. It's a struggle for supremacy, survival of the fittest." He lived by that logic and was determined to be the best player on the diamond. Many baseball experts have argued that he was, in fact, the greatest.[26]

In his twenty-four years as an outfielder for the Detroit Tigers and the Philadelphia Athletics, Cobb won twelve consecutive league batting titles, accumulated 4,191 hits, and snatched 892 bases. Although his colorful personality often overshadowed his feats on the diamond, more than fifty years after his death in 1961, the "Georgia Peach" retains the highest lifetime batting average (.367) of any Major League player.[27] In 1939, when the nation's sportswriters selected the first group of inductees to the National Baseball Hall of Fame, it was Cobb, not his successor, New York Yankees slugger Babe Ruth, who collected the highest percentage of votes. Mathewson also was elected, receiving the most votes of any pitcher in the inaugural class.

There were many other great players in the Dead Ball Era, but none achieved the level of adulation that Mathewson and Cobb received in their own time or in subsequent eras.[28] Not until the 1920s did other sports idols—men such as Ruth, boxing's Jack Dempsey, football's Red Grange, and golf's Bobby Jones—temporarily displace their images in the hearts and minds of the American public. From 1900 to 1919, they reigned as the nation's chief sports heroes, and their images lingered in the American imagination.

The tale of Mathewson and Cobb has been told on many other occasions. But how and why did society's storytellers tell these tales, and what was the impact of these stories on American culture? Their legacies exemplify the production of heroes in the early twentieth century. The term "hero-crafting" suggests both a skill-based practice and an art or a trade. Others have dubbed the process "mythmaking," and while that term does have a certain alliterative ring, it does not connote the nuance of the activity. Likewise, "mythmaking" might mislead readers. "Myth," like its sister term "legend," implies that a story is somehow untrue. But these heroic tales were based in fact. The details were sometimes exaggerated by sportswriters for the sake of the narrative but often provided insight into greater cultural truths.

In an earlier age, it was the bard or the sculptor that practiced the art of hero construction. Later, it would be the filmmaker. In an age before electronic media, however, it was the literary journalist, the playwright, and the sportswriter who crafted fable-like odes to the nation's heroes.

Other sports historians have argued that mythmakers of the Golden Age of Sports Writing (1920–30) manufactured heroes; they have suggested that these sports heroes were somehow unique to the Roaring Twenties.[29] But sports hero-worship goes back to an earlier era. It emerged along with the promotional practices of sportswriters, who were in cahoots with club owners to establish baseball as the national pastime with a unique cast of characters.

The story of hero-crafting involves relationships among a handful of men at the pinnacle of their careers, close friendships and business partnerships that emerged among men who wanted what most individuals desire—career advancement and job security. It chronicles their respective rise to the top of their games. But what is needed is more than a historical account of the relationships among prominent men. The story of good-old-boy clubs has been told before. These systems always seem to operate by excluding women and minorities in an attempt to maintain power, and we might have guessed that these structures were driving two of the era's biggest industries.

Instead, I trace the growth of two parallel culture industries, professional baseball and sports journalism—what would later become known as the sports-media complex.[30] They had a symbiotic relationship, and the system of sports promotion was at the crux of their alliance. This "gee whiz" school of sports journalism helped produce the likes of Cobb and Mathewson and contributed to the hero-worship so pervasive in early twentieth-century American culture.

Top sports journalists formed close associations with baseball's elite stars and then crafted them into heroes for the masses, using creative literary techniques. Their stories served as public morality tales about success and American manhood. A number of cultural constructions in early twentieth-century America—notions of hero and celebrity; public and private lives; sinner and saint; objective facts and moral truths; and success and failure in the man's world of business—collided to produce a story of loss, the disappearance of a simpler way of life, the temporary decline of a literary brand of sports journalism, the degeneration of religious life, and the death and rebirth of the American hero.

–2–

The Sporting Press

BASEBALL'S BIGGEST BACKSCRATCHER

On Monday, August 2, 1858, *Brooklyn Eagle* sportswriter Henry Chadwick wrote about baseball's increasing popularity with the American public: "Base ball is epidemic just now and particularly catching."[1] He told of six upcoming games and two start-up clubs in the Brooklyn area.[2] Over the next half-century, the prominent sportswriter became one of baseball's biggest boosters. He promoted the sport as a wholesome pastime, an American game, which would help cure the nation of its urban ills and vices.

His efforts were largely successful. By 1901, more than 3.6 million individuals attended professional baseball games, and countless others followed every inning in their daily encounter with the sports page.[3] Baseball magnates owed much to Chadwick and his colleagues in the press box. They objected to only one small detail of Chadwick's narrative. He insisted that the national pastime evolved from the English game of rounders. Baseball's national leadership, in contrast, insisted upon the game's unique American origin. They endorsed a competing narrative, which contended that General Abner Doubleday, a Civil War hero, had drawn up the rules of the game on a rugged field in the sleepy burg of Cooperstown, New York.[4] Chadwick's longstanding debate over the game's origins marked one instance when a sportswriter and a league magnate stood in direct opposition; more often than not, they were guided by a common set of interests.

In the last instance, they were all determined to promote the wholesome national character of the game. As baseball developed into a commercial endeavor, it was in their best financial interests to do so. It meant that both parties could continue to make a living by pursuing their love of the children's game. It meant job security. By 1904, when sporting goods tycoon Albert Goodwill Spalding enlisted Chadwick and six other baseball barons to determine the genesis of the game, professional baseball moguls and sportswriters were firmly engaged in this symbiotic alliance.

By the mid-1840s, as puritanical restraints over leisure activities eroded, the sporting culture was gaining popularity, and news of athletic endeavors was becoming a regular feature in the pages of the penny press. Journalists such as Chadwick were profiting from the trend. In the early 1850s, he landed a job as the cricket beat writer for the *New York Times.* He was on assignment in fall 1856 when he witnessed a spirited baseball game between the Gothams and the Eagles, two rival New York nines. On the grassy meadows of the Elysian Fields, he decided that the fast-paced, rugged game was "suited to the American temperament," and he determined to do all in his power to make baseball the "national game in word and in truth."[5]

Over the next five decades, Chadwick became baseball's chief proponent. He was its de facto organizer, innovator, adviser, and visionary. He was above all the game's preeminent promoter, regularly publishing pieces in the sporting press.[6] His message was consistent: baseball, the manly pursuit, had the potential to teach young boys how to be virtuous American men.

A young man, like a ball player, Chadwick contended, should be, first and foremost, a gentleman "who abstains from profanity, always has his temper under control, and takes matters good humouredly."[7] American boys, he wrote, should model themselves after men such as Excelsior pitcher James Creighton. From 1859 to 1862, the game's first superstar dazzled sportswriters and fans alike with his feats on the field.

"As a base ball player, Creighton had no equal," Chadwick wrote in the *New York Clipper*'s October 25 edition after the player's untimely death from internal injuries acquired in a game against the Union Club on October 18. "As a pitcher, he stood alone. . . . He was remarkably unassuming in his manners, and obliging and courteous in his demeanor, and was a favorite with all who knew him well."[8] He had only one fault, it seemed. "In the melancholy death of James Creighton there is warning to others," Chadwick wrote in the October 20 issue of the *Brooklyn Eagle.* "Exercise is a good thing; but like other good things, one may take too much of it."[9]

One could also take too much of baseball in other ways. Chadwick often warned about the culture of rowdyism—the hard drinking, cursing, brawling, and gambling that sometimes accompanied the game. He believed that the culture of rowdyism went hand-in-hand with the creeping commercialism that had infected baseball in the 1860s. Early in the decade, he had hoped that the "gentlemanly youth of America" would "play the game in its purity; not for gate money, not for empty honors of championship, but for the honor, the reputation and manliness of the players themselves."[10]

It quickly became evident, however, that "the spirit of faction" had contaminated the game.[11] Soon, the clubs and their fans became consumed with winning at all costs. Club presidents began charging admission for ball games so that they could pay exceptional players, and baseball's superstars began jumping from club to club for more money—a practice known as "revolving." Chadwick vilified players who engaged in the habit, but even his favorites, National Association of Base Ball Players (NABBP) stars such as Creighton, utility player Al Reach, and shortstop George Wright, began accepting money for their services.[12]

Baseball's evolution into a commercial spectacle came with other unforeseen consequences for the sportswriter. When club presidents began charging spectators for admission, they became concerned about eroding their fan base by giving away their product to newspapers and telegraph companies. Amateur clubs had been enjoying free publicity from newspapers and magazines for years, but some club presidents failed to see the potential of these platforms to whet the appetite of fans. Instead, they saw telegraph companies such as Western Union, who wired inning-by-inning scores and game results to newspaper offices, saloons, and pool halls around the Northeast, as a threat. As a result, they began to charge reporters for admission and attempted to bar telegraph operators from the stands. In retaliation, some sports publications began charging club presidents standard advertising rates to list notices of upcoming contests. Others quit covering baseball altogether.[13]

Most publications, however, continued to include listings of the day's biggest games as a service to their readers, but sportswriters were increasingly disgruntled about their treatment. In 1860, for instance, Chadwick admonished club owners and recommended that "every facility should be granted to the authorized representatives of the press to whose assistance the various clubs are greatly indebted for the publicity given to their doings on the field."[14] Later that season, he repeated his rebuke, reminding club presidents that they should be indebted to sportswriters for the publicity.

Club presidents did not see it that way. During this era, an adversarial relationship had emerged between segments of the sporting press and the baseball community. Individual clubs, players, and fans became frustrated when sports journals published errors in their game accounts. Individual clubs also were angered by stories of their defeats. Baseball leadership wanted only coverage of their triumphs, but sportswriters were obliged to provide more than free promotion. Their readers had come to demand regular coverage of all the games on a club's schedule, even the matches that they lost.[15]

Criticisms of the era's sporting press were not entirely unjustified. The sports pages were filled with errors and spiteful attacks on individual players, clubs, and their peers in the press. Sports publications such as the *New York Clipper* and the *Spirit of the Times* condemned their print competitors for their errors and accused them of stealing content—a common practice in the age of the penny press. Sometimes they lambasted them in an attempt to discredit and eliminate them.

Even with its flaws, however, some club presidents did realize the value of the sporting press. In 1867, Chadwick observed that three clubs had erected press boxes for "legitimate members of the press."[16] His only critique was that the press box at Brooklyn's Union Grounds did not have more seats. Reporters continued to snipe about the conditions of press boxes in years to come, but those in baseball's highest ranks had finally acknowledged the professional virtues of the sportswriter.[17]

Still, in October 1875, professional baseball's future was anything but certain. It may have been America's chief national pastime, but it was receiving bad press about pervasive evils in the professional game. Chicago White Stockings president William Hulbert believed that the only way to alleviate those ills and to restore prosperity to the commercial enterprise was to create a new league. In fall 1875, he recruited *Chicago Tribune* sports editor Lewis Meacham to condemn the evils of the National Association of Professional Base Ball Players (NAPBBP) and to promote the idea of establishing another, stronger league. Meacham agreed and on October 24, 1875, published an article chronicling what professional baseball "must do to be saved."[18] With rumors of a new league circulating in the press, Hulbert leapt into action. First, he strengthened his own club with star talent. Then, he approached other club owners about forming a new league to replace the National Association.

On February 4, in the *Chicago Tribune,* Meacham predicted a new era of lively but wholesome play and told his readers just how National League leaders planned to give players and fans a "square deal."[19] He reported that Hulbert and his associates sought to stabilize business operations by limiting the number of clubs allowed to join the league, giving each club a territorial monopoly, and engaging in a gentleman's agreement not to raid another club's roster during the course of a season.[20] League magnates planned to restore middle-class respectability by banning Sunday games; prohibiting gambling, drinking, and brawling from the grandstands; and charging a fifty-cent admission price that would effectively weed out the riffraff.

Understanding that "the National Game need[ed] the support of the press," Hulbert attempted to establish open channels with sportswriters. He did so by encouraging individual club secretaries, who kept official records of all baseball business, to act as publicity agents and provide information to reporters. They did when it served their interest. They allowed sportswriters to check their records with those of official scorekeepers. After road games, they also wired game results back to friendly hometown reporters.[21]

They increasingly supplied this information to a new cadre of reporters at daily and weekly newspapers—men such as Will Rankin of the *New York Herald,* Carl Joy of the *New York Tribune,* Al Wright of the *Philadelphia Sunday Mercury,* and O. P. Caylor of the *Cincinnati Enquirer.*[22] By decade's end, baseball writers such as Francis Richter would establish sports pages at newspapers such as the *Philadelphia Public Ledger.*

These men incorporated box scores and statistics gleaned from scorecards with a new lexicon of baseball jargon. Outfielders did not drop balls; they "muffed them." Pitchers were plagued by "wild arms." Hitters "lined balls to left field" and sometimes "popped them up." The best teams "blanked" their opponents.[23]

This new breed of sportswriters became professional baseball's biggest cheerleaders. They endorsed the social virtues of the sport and its stars. In addition to basic game recaps, local baseball reporters began focusing more attention than ever on the exploits of their club's star players. They were taking part in antecedent forms of herocrafting; sportswriters at the turn of the century would come to perfect these techniques. Although these reporters were generally loyal to their hometown clubs, they sometimes second-guessed a manager's decisions and could be downright critical of a player's mistakes.

The league, however, was not content to rely solely on the goodwill of sports reporters. Hulbert and other league organizers also resorted to other promotional strategies. To supplement newspaper coverage, they relied on promotional baseball guides. The league began publishing *Spalding's Base Ball Guide* in 1878. The annual guide offered readers the official playing rules, a basic history of the sport's founding fathers, biographies on all of the league's leading players, and recaps of all major and minor league teams across the nation.[24]

During this era, individual club owners began incorporating other publicity tactics and marketing strategies.[25] At the beginning of each season, they published and distributed free copies of pocket schedules. They also incorporated streetcar billings, handbills, and banners to promote individual games. The players got in on the act as well. They served as "moving billboards" as they paraded down the streets in their uniforms.[26] Once at the games, fans enjoyed a wide variety of promotional souvenirs, from scorecards to programs.

Despite competition from rival leagues, professional baseball thrived.[27] It prospered, in part, because of its publicity efforts, but its success was also due to several alliances that had developed among like-minded entrepreneurs. Baseball magnates forged mutually beneficial relationships with city promoters, railroad tycoons, hotel and restaurant owners, and beer and tobacco manufacturers.[28] Their interests were often one and the same—to sell products geared to adult men.

City promoters understood that professional baseball was becoming a popular commercial amusement. They helped club owners purchase land for baseball parks at discounted prices, used their political influence to sway trolley car companies to extend lines to distant ballparks, and touted these spaces as popular tourist destinations. Railroad tycoons, likewise, extended discounts to baseball clubs. Reduced fares contributed to additional business as fans from outlying rural communities flocked to nearby cities to watch their favorite stars. Once in the city, baseball clubs and their fans needed places to eat and to lay their heads. Restaurant and hotel owners were only too happy to accommodate these needs.[29]

Baseball aficionados represented a valuable market to many manufacturers. Brewery owners sponsored baseball clubs to better tempt middle- and working-class men with their wares. Tobacco companies looked to expand their customer base by appealing to young boys with baseball cards neatly tucked into packs of cigarettes.[30] Whole economies crept up around professional baseball. Business-savvy men began selling bratwursts, peanuts, and popcorn at ballpark refreshment stands. Others such as Spalding realized that the game could not survive without the basics—baseballs, bats, and mitts. Perhaps the most important of these essentials was the sporting press.

Magazine publishers such as Frank Queen, Thomas Dando, and Al Spink had been the first to recognize the baseball reading public. Their coverage of professional baseball not only attracted male readers from all social classes, it also appealed to advertisers looking to sell their products to the masses. In the 1880s, newspaper and magazine owners across the nation joined these men. They believed that the public craved constant baseball coverage, and they delivered. They provided basic baseball news—pre-season previews, series promos, daily game coverage, box scores, basic statistics, and news of trades and rival leagues.[31]

In the era before professional public relations firms, baseball club owners and magnates relied on promotional tactics supplied by the sporting press. In exchange for providing free travel, lodging, and press box seats, clubs received a relatively unlimited supply of good publicity. The sporting press, however, did more than provide basic baseball news.

They also supplied readers with news of their favorite players—regional stars such as Chicago White Stockings slugger Mike Joseph "King" Kelly, who arguably became the nation's first sports hero in the 1880s. Behind Kelly's bat and bold base running, Chicago captured five consecutive league pennants. The hard-drinking player's daring feats on the base paths prompted his fan's rallying cries and the nation's ragtime hit "Slide, Kelly, Slide."

Although some reporters critiqued individual players and managers for their peccadilloes, they had a vested interest in the game and promoted baseball as a wholesome national pastime. They provided their readers with "a steady diet of information" about the "American" game and its cast of stars.[32] To better deliver this diet, newspaper managing editors hired full-time sports reporters, developed sports departments, and incorporated sports sections.[33]

Under the beat system, baseball reporters gathered news about upcoming sporting events, covered local squads, and attended to other duties such as overseeing the make-up of the sports section. They covered games in crowded press boxes, in grandstands, or in the grass behind home plate.[34] Like their colleagues in other departments, most sportswriters worked long hours, toiling more than fourteen hours daily.[35] They also spent a large amount of time in transit, traveling by train for days at a time with local clubs during road stints. Baseball reporting was a year-round commitment, comprised of nine months of regular season coverage and three months of off-season coverage.[36]

Like other newsworkers, baseball reporters did their jobs for as little as twenty dollars per week, meager pay when compared with salaries of other working professionals.[37] The lack of monetary reward can be attributed to the shift in labor conditions that resulted from the emergence of the commercialized press. With profits threatened by increases in annual overhead costs associated with equipment and resources, publishers kept wages low. Under an increasingly complex organizational system, low-ranking reporters failed to demand higher salaries, fearing they would be replaced.[38] Instead, sportswriters often took second jobs as umpires, official statisticians, ghostwriters, and magazine freelance writers.[39] Like other journalists, they also were offered extra pay from advertisers and sports promoters to write promotional puff pieces.[40] Low salaries and grueling working conditions led to widespread alcoholism and burnout within the profession.[41]

Sports journalism was primarily a male profession. By the last decade of the nineteenth century, only a handful of women had gained entry.[42] The brave souls who did encountered a powerful backlash. When Ella Black, one of the first female sports reporters, began contributing to *Sporting Life* in 1890, she faced persecution from the sporting world. Despite these affronts, by the turn of the century, Black was joined by other female correspondents. National publications sought baseball-savvy female fans to write about the sport as a peculiar feature of daily coverage.[43]

Specialized sports journalists transformed the style of baseball coverage.[44] Prior game recaps had been brief, written in a tone partial to the hometown club.[45] Like other news colleagues, sportswriters began implementing a detached approach in daily coverage. They incorporated summary leads followed by descriptive game accounts.[46] They included interspersed quotations gleaned from interviews with players, managers, and club owners. Their game accounts were characterized by an "informational" news model.[47]

Although it became less common to find accounts slanted in favor of the home team, in the age of yellow journalism, newspapers and magazines were professional baseball's biggest advocates. Early sports journalists engaged in mutually beneficial relationships with sport promoters, league and event organizers, and club owners.[48] Baseball writers provided club owners with much-needed promotion, and professional baseball supplied the press with engaging copy that sold newspapers and magazines.

The publishers of the sporting press were not the only ones who reaped the rewards. By the early twentieth century, talented sportswriters were well compensated, earning salaries as great as one hundred dollars per week. The cozy relationship prompted media historian Charles Ponce de Leon to note: "Sportswriters recognized that heightened public interest in sports was good for them too, creating a huge audience of people who had no choice but to turn to the daily press for coverage of events that they were unable to attend in person. Accordingly, many journalists joined forces with athletes and promoters, producing articles that were vital to the fortunes of the industry."[49]

Sportswriters contributed to the establishment of "the business as a commercialized entertainment," converting it "into an integral part of the American social scene."[50] At the turn of the century, promotional storytelling was pervasive in sports journalism. The nation's arsenal of sportswriters churned out a heavy supply of feature articles, columns, and books about baseball's most prominent icons. To engage readers, they incorporated literary techniques in their human-interest stories. In his advice manual for aspiring reporters, journalist Edwin Shuman in 1894 encouraged writers to avoid "the unpardonable sin" of dry prose with "imaginative writing."[51] This "gee whiz" school, as the strand of literary journalists later became known, was distinguished by sentimental, optimistic tones and narrative structure.[52]

"Gee whiz" sportswriters gave Americans a new kind of hero. They "regularly produced heroes for a society that seemed unable to produce many heroes in other areas of public life," contended sports historian Robert Mandell.[53] Sports stars enjoyed traditional heroic portrayals mixed with celebrity-style coverage.[54] Sports reporters touted their brute strength and speed as comparable to that of Greek warriors. They crafted heroic journeys complete with a story of separation, initiation, and return.[55] They celebrated the physical prowess of athletes, along with their mental and moral attributes. They applauded scientific play, comparing managers and team leaders to military tacticians and praised icons that played "clean" ball and practiced good sportsmanship.[56] In a culture obsessed with statistics, however, they ultimately emphasized the "primacy of deeds over virtues."[57]

After surviving a global economic depression in 1893 and another round of league wars with former Cincinnati sportswriter and Western League president Ban Johnson from 1901 to 1903, professional baseball flourished.[58] After National and American League leaders introduced the World Series in 1903, it became the indisputable national pastime.[59] More than seven million fans watched professional baseball games in the first decade of the century. Of course, these figures do not include the countless millions who participated in the sport as a leisure pursuit. Baseball was endorsed as a respectable middle-class amusement, and early twentieth-century crowds reflected its status.

Although middle-class men composed the vast majority of fans, the attendance of women was commonplace, especially on Ladies Days. With ample leisure time and financial means, the professional-managerial class was uniquely suited to take part in the commercial amusement. Though working-class attendance was less frequent, blue-collar workers still handed over their hard-earned dollars for Sunday games and read about their favorite stars in the sports pages.[60]

Baseball had a firm grasp on the American imagination. Endorsed as a pastoral escape from the urban jungle, the sport enjoyed "a myth of cultural and geographical uniqueness," which worked hand-in-hand with ideas of American exceptionalism and the American dream.[61] Baseball appealed to the nation's newfound fascination with scientific order and precision. Consequently, it became the preeminent middle-class leisure activity. Social reformers promoted it. Industrial leaders sponsored it. Millions of men, women, and children participated as competitors and spectators.[62] With the sport firmly entrenched in American culture at the turn of the century, journalists turned their full attention to the promotion of its cast of stars.

–3–

Enter Christy Mathewson and Tyrus Cobb

Although baseball had achieved a level of middle-class respectability, to retain mass appeal it continued to distance itself from the rowdyism associated with earlier leagues such as the NAPBBP. Sports scribes such as Henry Chadwick were doing their part to promote baseball as a clean sport, free from gambling, alcoholism, and riffraff.[1] Their attempts to brand baseball as a wholesome game, however, were jeopardized by the working-class players, who comprised most Major League rosters.

Despite reports to the contrary, baseball was still a rough sport played, to a large extent, by uneducated men who engaged in cursing, gambling, brawling, smoking, drinking, and other undesirable behavior. Its stars, men such as Philadelphia southpaw Rube Waddell and New York Giants manager John "Mugsy" McGraw, were seen as a crude and disreputable sort not far removed from confinement at a local penitentiary. The Detroit Tigers outfield of the mid-1910s later attested to the violent nature of the sport. Sam "Wahoo" Crawford, Cobb's teammate from 1905 to 1917, reminded sports historian Lawrence Ritter: "Baseball players weren't too much accepted in those days, either, you know. We were considered pretty crude."[2] Davy Jones, their teammate from 1906 to 1912, agreed: "A lot of people looked upon ballplayers as bums. . . . They were thought to be too lazy to work for a living."[3] Perhaps Cobb summed it up the best. "When I began playing the game," he remembered, "baseball was about as gentlemanly as a kick in the crotch."[4]

To shore up baseball's clean image, sportswriters needed a symbol of morality. When at first they could not find one, they made one up in the pulp magazines. In 1896, Gilbert Patten, under the pen name Burt L. Standish, created a heroic athlete of great renown and flawless character for *Tip Top Weekly,* the era's most widely read nickel novel. Over the next sixteen years, Frank Merriwell of Fardale Academy, and eventually Yale, dazzled fans with his "unmatchable feats of derring-do."[5] The all-around athletic superstar excelled at every sport from boxing to baseball, and in the pursuit of excellence, he was above all an honorable sportsman, who led his life above repute. His adventures would go on to be told in dime novels and comic books, on radio and television, and in film. Millions of American boys idolized Merriwell; among his admirers was a teenaged boy from Factoryville, Pennsylvania. In time, as one sports historian aptly noted, that youngster would become just what the image-conscious National League needed—a moral hero, and it was the sportswriter that would craft the sportsman into the national pastime's saint. America was a few years removed from that fate in 1880—the year that Christopher Mathewson was born in a tiny hamlet about fifteen miles north of Scranton.

Factoryville, so named for the textile mill that it briefly housed in the mid-1810s, was a pastoral village located along the south branch of Tunkhannock Creek in the scenic Endless Mountains region of northeastern Pennsylvania. The first European settlers arrived in the early 1800s. They were part of the initial wave of massive westward migration that followed the end of hostilities with Great Britain. During the War of 1812, Mathewson's ancestors built a hydro-powered textile mill with the intention of supplying materials to the troops, but the site proved too remote, too isolated from the Northeast's major hubs. The mill was soon bankrupt, but the settlers remained. They established a post office, churches, and schools and became farmers and coal miners.[6]

By the time that Minerva Mathewson gave birth to her first son on August 12, 1880, Factoryville was a booming railroad town with a college, a tannery, a gristmill, two hotels, three doctors' offices, and countless multistory houses lining its thriving Main Street. Christopher was born in the second-floor bedroom of one of these white-trimmed, Victorian-style homes. He was named after an uncle, who vowed to bestow a thousand dollars upon his namesake.

Gilbert Mathewson soon moved his young family a few hundred yards down the street, to a slightly larger Victorian home on the original site of his ancestors' log cabin. Although the family was not wealthy, Minerva's background as the daughter of a prominent physician and hotel owner meant that they did not lack material necessities. "I've never had anything in my home too good to be used," she recalled years later. "I have always wanted my children to enjoy everything in it."[7] Minerva, however, did not want her children to over-amuse themselves. A church-going Baptist, she was sometimes stern. She was adamantly opposed to smoking and drinking and could be a rigid disciplinarian.

Despite his mother's authoritative parenting style, Mathewson enjoyed a rather idyllic childhood. When not in classes at the Factoryville grammar school, he helped out on the family farm, fished and hunted, and played children's games such as "hailey over," which involved tossing a ball over the barn to friends.[8] Of all his pastimes, he most loved playing ball. He fielded grounders at second or in the outfield of country pastures with older boys in the area, and when no one was around, he would pick up stones and practice pitching on his own. "I got to be a great stone thrower," he recalled years later. "When I was nine years old, I could throw a stone farther than any of the boys who were my chums."[9]

Long after Mathewson made his Major League debut, Minerva reminisced to the press about his childhood. Sportswriters used these accounts as proof of Mathewson's wholesome background. She told reporters that, in addition to teaching him how to throw, she had trained all of her children in Christian values such as honesty, kindness, and fairness. As evidence of her son's virtuous upbringing, she recounted his integrity in the face of misfortune. One day, when he was playing a rousing game of "hailey over" with some older neighborhood boys, he shattered a neighbor's window. "He was scared," Minerva recalled. "Well, I told him, you'll just have to pay Mrs. Reynolds. Go over and ask her how much it is and then take the money out of your little bank. It took Christy a long time to save up the dollar that the broken window cost. But it taught him a sense of responsibility."[10] After the incident, she had fervently hoped that her eldest son might become a preacher, but he had a different career path in mind.

Baseball resonated with Mathewson. He later wrote that he "would rather play baseball than eat."[11] He gained his early baseball experience pitching and playing second base for Keystone Academy, a local college preparatory school founded by his great-grandmother; for the Scranton YMCA; and for his hometown team, the amateur Factoryville nine. As a ten-year-old boy, he tried out to be the squad's "second catcher," a position that amounted to being a glorified ball boy. He fetched foul balls and water for the adult men on the team's roster.

His first chance to play for Factoryville did not come until he was fourteen.[12] When illness plagued the team's pitcher, they sent for Mathewson to try out. He impressed the team enough to earn a spot on the roster against their Mill City rivals. It was not his arm, however, that intrigued his teammates later that day—though he did manage to strike out every man and boy on the opponent's roster in a nineteen-to-seventeen victory over Mill City. It was his bat. With the bases loaded in the bottom of the ninth inning, he drove in the winning run. "Husk," as the folks around Factoryville called him, became the hometown hero that afternoon. He had earned a dollar in the process.

His performance that day also left an impression on the Mill City squad. They offered him a position on their team and matched the pay of his hometown club. Mathewson accepted their offer and played for both squads when he was not busy at Keystone Academy, where the studious, athletic youngster played football, basketball, and baseball.

After graduating from Keystone in 1898, he stumbled onto another pitching assignment. One early summer day, with a five-cent bag of peanuts in his hand, he awaited a Scranton YMCA baseball match. Shortly before the game was to begin, a member of the Scranton YMCA nine scrambled up into the bleachers and asked Mathewson, whom he had seen play before, if he would not mind pitching that day. They were in a pinch, it seemed. Their hurler had not shown up. He agreed, and delivered a doozy. He was rewarded for his fifteen strikeouts with a standing offer to pitch for the squad. He took them up on it, but he also continued to play for Factoryville.[13]

Mathewson's stellar pitching for local clubs led to higher-paying assignments. After being soundly defeated by Mathewson in July 1898, the Honesdale Eagles offered him twenty dollars a month and board to be their twirler.[14] Throughout the summer of 1898, he notched eight wins for the Eagles, pitching two impressive shutouts and a five-to-one victory over Port Jervis for the league championship in July.

Mathewson had become something of a local celebrity. Minerva Mathewson, however, was not pleased with her son's career as a semi-professional baseball star and clung to the hope that he might still end up in a pulpit one day. She and her husband were undoubtedly relieved when he entered Bucknell College, some ninety miles away in Lewisberg, on scholarship that fall.

At Bucknell, Mathewson, like his fictitious boyhood hero Frank Merriwell,[15] was a well-rounded student-athlete. The Phi Gamma Delta fraternity member and class president excelled in the classroom, participated in a number of literary societies and fraternities, sang in the glee club, and played football, baseball, and basketball, as well as checkers and chess. Here, he began attracting the attention of the sporting press not for his prowess on the mound, but for his performance on the gridiron.[16] He earned national media attention as a fullback and punter. His abilities as a kicker prompted "Father of Football" Walter Camp to brand him the greatest drop kicker in college football and to honor him on the All-American Team in 1900.

In spite of his busy lifestyle, Mathewson even found time for love at Bucknell. He courted several women during his time on campus, including his future bride, Jane Stoughton. Stoughton, like many women, was likely attracted to his strapping six-foot-one, 196-pound frame; his stunning blue eyes; his chiseled jaw; his jostled blond hair; and his pleasant sense of humor. After an extended correspondence and engagement, the "big blond idol" would go on to marry Stoughton in winter 1903.

It was his first love, however, that occupied most of his time. When not pitching for the college team, he continued to compete on the semiprofessional circuit. In summer 1899, he returned to the Honesdale Eagles roster, but after pitching a three-hitter on July 18, he once again found that he could earn more money elsewhere.[17]

After watching Mathewson pitch in Honesdale's fourteen-to-six victory over rival Port Jervis, Taunton manager Nathaniel Kellog offered him ninety dollars a month to play in the New England League. Pitching in seventeen games, he posted a dismal two-and-thirteen record with Taunton.[18] Even so, it was with this squad that Christy was rumored to have picked up his famous fadeaway. He likely learned the pitch from right-hander Virgil Lee Garvin or from a southpaw named Williams.

He also learned another hard lesson that many professional players had discovered over the years. Many leagues and clubs struggled financially. Leagues often collapsed. Clubs disbanded. Taunton was no different, and by season's end, Mathewson was struggling to collect his salary amidst rumors that the New England League was on the verge of collapse. Nevertheless, the last game of the season brought a glimmer of hope for the Bucknell star. After defeating the Portland Sea Gulls, he was approached by Manager John "Phenomenal" Smith, who offered him a chance to play the following season. That fall, he returned to Bucknell with a simple promise and no guarantees.

When Bucknell's football team faced Penn State in Philadelphia later that autumn, Smith approached Mathewson again; this time, in his hotel before the game, he was made an offer of eighty dollars per month to play with the Norfolk nine in the Virginia League. After witnessing his athletic feats on the gridiron, Smith matched his previous year's salary of ninety dollars a month.[19]

When summer arrived, he joined the Norfolk Club, and he did not disappoint Smith or area fans. He delivered dominant performances on the mound and from the batter's box. He was so good, in fact, that ole "Phenomenal" decided to play him in the outfield when he was not pitching. On June 26, 1900, William M. Hannan, the owner of the

Norfolk club, wrote a letter to New York Giants owner Andrew Freedman. The young pitcher, he wrote, had the potential for greatness, and "it would be worth the trip to look Mathewson over."[20]

While with Norfolk, he delivered an impressive twenty-and-two record and gained the attention of Freedman and Philadelphia Athletics owner-manager Connie Mack. In mid-July, Freedman offered the remarkable right-hander fifteen hundred dollars to come aboard the struggling last-place Giants roster. It is a wonder that Mathewson agreed to the move. Manhattan was a rough place in 1900, and Freedman, a real estate speculator and bondsman, was rumored to be part of the Tammany Hall political machine. He was particularly hated within the baseball community. Some club owners disliked his ideas about syndicate baseball, or joint ownership in multiple clubs. Individuals within the New York Giants organization also disdained his violent temper, his strong-arm tactics, and his tightfisted approach. Even sportswriters despised him. Top reporters such as *New York Journal* baseball writer and humorist Charles Dryden found that they might be banned from the Polo Grounds' press stands if they portrayed Freedman or his club in an unfavorable light. Even so, Mathewson realized that the Giants were lacking strong pitchers, and the opportunity to pitch in a major big-league market appealed to him.

Giants manager George Davis was looking for a savior, but Mathewson would not deliver any miracles in his first partial season in the majors. The rookie struggled. In his first four games as a reliever, he gave up twenty-eight hits and twenty-two runs. He complained to friends of a "lame shoulder," and by season's end, he had tallied a zero-and-three record with an ERA of 5.08.[21] Unimpressed with his uninspiring performance, Davis sent Mathewson packing.

Back in Norfolk, Cincinnati owner John T. Brush drafted Mathewson for $100. Soon after, Mack offered the college-educated player $1,550 to sign with the fledgling American League Athletics, but it was too late. Brush had already traded him back to the Giants in exchange for aging veteran Amos Rusie.[22] His tactics may seem odd, but Brush had his eye on purchasing the New York Giants. His move to trade Mathewson for Rusie proved savvy. Rusie pitched twenty-two innings the following season before retiring from baseball. Mathewson, meanwhile, would go on to a seventeen-year career in Major League baseball. When Mathewson rejoined the Giants in April 1901, he was completely focused on the game. His first outing with the club was proof of his renewed interest. He impressed fans and sportswriters alike with a four-hit, five-to-three victory over Brooklyn in the home opener. His performance prompted a *New York Times* sportswriter to label his style of pitching as "splendid."[23] He went on to win eight consecutive games.

In his first full season with the Giants, Mathewson tallied a twenty-and-seventeen record with 221 strikeouts and a 2.41 ERA. His most impressive performance was a no-hitter against St. Louis on July 15. Despite his success, a nagging sore arm worried him. He dropped fifteen games after June 1. Although his record might not suggest it, his 2.41 ERA and thirty-six complete games were among the best in the National League. The seventh-place Giants considered Mathewson to be a "young pitcher of promise" and offered him a thirty-five-hundred-dollar salary for the following season.[24]

His concerns about his sore arm were confirmed in 1902. He lost seventeen of thirty-two games and was moved to first base. Although his 1902 win-loss record looked downright dismal, newly hired manager John "Mugsy" McGraw realized his potential.[25] Under McGraw's helm, Mathewson won thirty games for the Giants in 1903; he became just the second Major League pitcher behind legendary Red Sox pitcher Cy Young in 1901 to accomplish the feat. Even so, he was not even the best player to grace the mound for the Giants.

That honor went to Joseph "Iron Man" McGinnity. He was McGraw's ace over the next two seasons. Ever the astute ballplayer, Mathewson took note of his style and strategies. From the "Iron Man," he learned that he should not hurl each ball as hard as he could. He needed to conserve energy throughout the game so that he could be masterful in a pinch.

Under McGraw and McGinnity's tutelage, he won thirty-three games in 1904, and the Giants captured the National League title. They had risen from the league's cellar to the top of the national pastime in two years, and Mathewson had earned a new nickname—"Big

Six." The name stuck, but it is not completely clear how he got it. His biographers have suggested that the most likely rationale behind the moniker was a firefighting image. Historian Ray Robinson noted that sportswriter Sam Crane had previously dubbed Mathewson the "great flame-thrower," and may have extended the metaphor comparing him to an antique horse-drawn engine used by a volunteer fire department in New York. Others have contended that the label came from a reference to his height, a comparison to a "peerless car" manufactured by the Matheson Motor Company, or an allusion to a famous fighter.[26] Whatever its origins, Mathewson had achieved a level of acclaim worthy of a nickname.

By 1905, Mathewson was so dominant on the mound that some sportswriters were coining additional nicknames for him. *Sporting Life* correspondent Ren Mulford Jr., for instance, called him, "Christy the Great."[27] In 1905, Mathewson was superb, at the peak of his game, delivering his third consecutive thirty-plus-win season. On June 3, in one of his classic duels with Chicago Cubs ace Mordecai "Three-Finger" Brown, Mathewson turned in a performance for the record books. He became the first hurler to pitch two no-hitters in the modern era. The one-to-nothing performance was all the more impressive against the celebrated infield trio of Tinker, Evers, and Chance on the grounds of Wrigley Field. "He did wonders with the ball," a *New York Times* reporter praised.[28] It would have been a perfect game, he acknowledged, if it were not for two costly errors on the field.

Under Mathewson's helm, the Giants dominated the competition in the National League, finishing the 1905 season with a record of 105–48. He won 31 games, and his 1.27 ERA was the best of his career. It was during the 1905 World Series that he first gained national acclaim. In the series opener against the Philadelphia Athletics, Mathewson entered into a bitter battle with ace Eddie Plank. The game remained scoreless through the fifth inning when he singled to ignite a two-to-nothing Giants' lead. On the mound, his pitching was almost flawless. He allowed only four hits in the three-to-nothing shutout, and he was called on again to pitch two days later in Game 3 of the World Series. This time, he held the Athletics to four hits and a walk in a dominant nine-to-nothing victory. The Giants went back to their workhorse in Game 5, and pitching on just one day of rest, he allowed six hits in the two-to-nothing win. Over the space of six days, Mathewson had pitched twenty-seven scoreless innings, allowing only thirteen hits.

The national press did not fail to notice. On October 15, 1905, the *Los Angeles Times* reported that "Mathewson was the cause" of the Giants' World Series victory. "All hail to the conquerors. The Giants. . . . Who won? Mathewson won. . . . Great are the Giants, but greater is Christy."[29] He was becoming known not only for his prowess on the mound, but also as a "Christian Gentleman," who displayed good sportsmanship at all times and never played baseball on Sundays. Some sportswriters crafted Mathewson as baseball's saint, others as its savior. If baseball had a national saint in Mathewson by 1905, it was about to get something quite different in a young rookie from Royston, Georgia.

It was some nineteen years earlier, on December 18, 1886, that the man who would one day be referred to as a "demon in spikes" was born to William Hershel and Amanda Cobb in his grandfather's log cabin in Narrows, Georgia. There, in the tiny hamlet tucked away in the northern corner of Banks County, W. H. Cobb, a teacher known around northeastern Georgia as the "Professor," settled on a name for his firstborn son. "Tyrus Raymond" was meant to evoke images of Alexander the Great's siege of Tyre and the dogged resistance of the locals.[30] Stubborn would eventually become one of the kinder ways to describe Cobb's unruly nature on and off the diamond.

The family would not stay in the log cabin for long. Over the next few years, the itinerant schoolmaster and his growing family, including Cobb's two new siblings, Paul and Florence, moved to several spots in northeast Georgia, including Commerce, Lavonia, and Carnesville, before settling into a two-story home and eventually a hundred-acre farm in Royston. Along the foothills of the Appalachian Mountains, his family thrived in the small town of about five hundred residents over the next decade. When Professor Cobb was not teaching, he was plowing his cotton fields, serving as the town's mayor, or publishing the *Royston Record,* the small weekly newspaper that he established in the 1890s. The rigid disciplinarian made sure that his children earned high marks in their studies at the local primary school. Cobb's father had high hopes that his firstborn might become a doctor, a lawyer, or even an officer at West Point.[31]

Tyrus wanted to please his father, but he—like Mathewson—was often distracted by a certain children's pastime. One of his first memories, he noted in his 1961 autobiography, *My Life in Baseball,* was of winding yarn around a small-core ball in the back of a buggy headed down a red, clay road somewhere between Commerce and Carnesville.[32] His mother Amanda later recalled to an Atlanta reporter that, when he was just five years old, he earned twenty-five cents for tending his neighbor's cows; with his earnings, he bought a baseball mitt.[33] When not in school, he worked on his family's farm, fished and hunted, and played baseball.

Even at this early age, Cobb demonstrated many of the characteristics that would come to define him. Childhood friends such as Bud Bryant reminisced that Cobb had a quick temper; he once beat up one of his peers for losing a spelling bee to a bunch of girls. Cobb later admitted that he was obsessed with winning from the start. "I saw no point in losing, if I could win," he wrote in his memoir.[34]

The ten-year-old farm boy often forsook his chores to play town ball in the cow pastures around Royston. It was about this time that he joined the Royston Rompers, a feeder team for the town's local nine—the Royston Reds. The fourteen-year-old was called up from the Rompers when the Reds found themselves shy of a shortstop one Saturday before a game with their Commerce rivals. The slender, ninety-pound country boy connected on three hits that day.

Soon thereafter, Royston Reds manager Bob McCreary told W.H. that he believed Cobb had a great deal of potential and encouraged him to let the boy play for Elberton's nine. In his first game with the squad, Cobb slugged three hits, driving in the winning run. On another occasion, his diving outfield catch guaranteed victory over rival Harmony Grove. Fans, who had flocked to see the match-up in their buggies, cheered his daring feat and tossed coins to him to show their praise. That day, Cobb, like Mathewson before him, became a hometown hero.[35]

A few days later, Cobb decided that it was time for a glove befitting a champion, so he traded several of his father's books for a new baseball glove. His father rebuked him. He did not always approve of his son's "unsuitable acts," nor did he understand his newfound passion for baseball.[36] At the time, the sport was thought to be a game played by ruffians, and William wanted his son to have nothing to do with it. "Be good and dutiful," his father wrote him on January 5, 1902, while he was away visiting his grandparents in North Carolina; "conquer your anger and passions that would degrade your dignity and belittle your manhood."[37] Although he longed for his father's approval, he could not set aside his passion for the sport. By the following winter, Cobb had decided that he wanted to give semiprofessional baseball a try.

At the encouragement of Van Bagwell, a local baseball star who tried out for the Southern League, he secretly wrote to all of the teams in the South Atlantic ("Sally") League for a tryout. Only one response came back. Augusta Tourists manager Con Strothers offered him a tryout and a potential fifty-dollar contract.[38] After a heated argument, Cobb convinced his father to fund his trip a hundred miles east to Augusta.

The youngster made his debut with the Tourists on April 26, 1904. "Sleuth," as a local reporter for the *Augusta Chronicle* had taken to calling Cobb, was not in the original lineup of the Memorial Day season opener against the Columbia Skyscrapers, but a last-minute adjustment occurred.[39] Hitting seventh in the batting order, the young center fielder went two-for-four in his first appearance with the Tourists. He followed his double in the eighth with an impressive home run to give the Tourists the lead in the top of the ninth.

His story was not to be a hero's tale that day. Columbia's pitcher George Engel responded with a four-bagger of his own in the bottom of the inning, giving Columbia the eight-to-seven victory. Nevertheless, local reporters praised his late-inning heroics. Sleuth "slammed the ball over the ridge in left field for a clean home run," the *Chronicle* reported the following day.[40] For a moment, it appeared as if Cobb might be heading to the Major Leagues as a home-run slugger; instead, his manager planned to send him back home several days later. Like Cobb, Strothers had a temper. He had asked his rookie to bunt in the ninth, and when Cobb didn't, he took revenge by showing him the door. After his second outing, the Tourists' manager told the youngster from Royston that he just did not have room on the roster for him.

Cobb had failed. But he was determined not to give up. He heard from Thad Hayes, a pitcher from Alabama, that there might be a spot for another outfielder with the Anniston squad. After consulting his father by phone, he was encouraged to take the job, but was admonished not to "come home a failure."[41]

In Anniston, Cobb dominated the base paths, hitting .370 and often stealing bases.[42] He played so well that by early August the Tourists, now under the management of Harlan Wingard, wanted Cobb back. Understanding that the Southeastern League of which Anniston was a part was on the verge of collapse and that Augusta was under new management, he did not hesitate to return. He reappeared on the Tourists' lineup on August 9.

In Augusta, inconsistent hitting and poor fielding plagued Cobb. He finished the season with a lackluster .237 batting average. The team did not fare much better, and Wingard struggled to pay his players. At the end of the season, Cobb traveled by train to Royston with two hundred dollars in his pocket, wondering if his career in professional baseball was over.

In the off-season, the deflated farm boy contemplated enrolling at the University of Georgia and becoming a surgeon. These considerations were put on hold when he received a feeler from the Tourists' newest manager-owner, catcher Andy Roth, inquiring whether he would be willing to rejoin the semiprofessional squad in the spring. In the first of many salary holdouts throughout his career, Cobb demanded $125 per month. Augusta agreed, and the former Royston Romper joined the Tourists for spring training.

In March 1905, Cobb impressed his fans and the local press alike in his three-game spring-training series against the American League's Detroit Tigers. Manager Bill Armour noticed his "star work" at this time, but soon Cobb was struggling from the plate and making costly errors in the outfield and on the base paths.[43] He also had developed a reputation as an arrogant firebrand. Roth was so tired of

Cobb's antics that he considered selling him to the Charleston Sea Gulls, league cellar dwellers, for a measly twenty-five dollars. Roth decided otherwise.

In mid-July, despite a lineup that featured four future Major Leaguers in Cobb, pitchers Eddie Cicotte and Nap Rucker, and infielder Clyde Engle, the Tourists were in a slump, dropping fifteen of their last twenty games. Roth decided to hand over managing duties to outfielder George Leidy. Like Roth, Leidy was particularly unimpressed with Cobb's behavior. One day, after witnessing him muff a catch because he was idly eating a bag of popcorn in the outfield, Leidy laid into him. His fatherly admonishment, along with early morning bunting sessions that he oversaw, seemed to help Cobb turn his season around. By early August, he was leading the league with one hundred hits and forty steals, and he had improved his batting average to .320.[44] His progress did not go unnoticed. Major League scouts were looking at the young Sally League star. Cobb's dreams were on the verge of coming true, and there was only one person in the world with whom he wanted to share this success—his father.

On the morning of Wednesday, August 9, Cobb received news by telegram that his father had been shot and killed in Royston the previous night. His "blackest of days" was further complicated when, after an agonizingly slow train trip back to his hometown, he discovered that his mother was rumored to have pulled the trigger of the double-barreled shotgun that delivered the fatal wound.[45] Cobb's mother was arrested for voluntary manslaughter the following day. Two weeks later, she was indicted by a grand jury. During this difficult time, Cobb stayed by his mother's side, making plans for his father's funeral and supporting his family.

Ten days later, after stints with semiprofessional minor league clubs in Augusta (1904, 1905) and Anniston (1904), the Sally League's 1905 leader in hits and stolen bases was purchased by Detroit Tigers manager Bill Armour for seven hundred dollars.[46] After hearing his fate, the only thought that crossed the youngster's mind was that his father would never know it. "The father I'd loved and respected so much never knew that his six $15 checks set me on the road to a whole new life," he wrote in his autobiography.[47]

A "whole new life" it was. Cobb, who had never traveled above the Mason-Dixon line, was in for an unpleasant adjustment in Detroit, one of the nation's major metropolitan hubs. Not only would he encounter a wide array of accents, confusing trolley lines, and teammates prone to hazing bush leaguers, he would also have to master the game at the next level, played by the roughest sort of men.

With his father's words about the unacceptability of failure likely echoing in his ears, Cobb made his Major League debut on August 30, 1905. He smashed a double off New York Highlander twirler Jack Chesbro, a two-time National League shutout leader, in his first time at the plate.[48] That was his only hit of the afternoon, but the Tigers defeated New York five-to-three before a crowd of twelve hundred at Navin Field that day.

The following morning, a sportswriter from the *Detroit Free Press* conceded that "Tyrus was well-received and may consider a two-base pry-up a much better career opener than usually comes a young fellow's way."[49] In his second outing, Cobb got a taste of just how brutal the game could be. After sliding face-first into second, Highlanders second baseman Kid Elberfeld ground his face into the dirt with his knee. The scar on his nose taught the youngster a valuable lesson: always slide spikes-first.

Despite his solid performance in his debut, he ended the partial season with a lackluster .240 batting average. It would be the only season that Cobb hit less than .300 in his twenty-four seasons in professional baseball.[50] Over the next few seasons, he would become known in the national media for his "scientific" style of hitting and base running.

In the first decade of the twentieth century, Mathewson and Cobb gained acclaim in professional baseball for their daring feats on the diamond. In the ensuing years, they would become national celebrities for their prowess on the field and for their colorful personalities in their private lives. Millions of Americans would clamor for news of these two baseball giants, and the nation's elite sportswriters would oblige their requests.

Sports journalists provided their readers with stories of the players' antics on and off the field. While on the job, they formed close relationships with the two. In both icons, they discovered intriguing personas. In Mathewson, sportswriters found a respectable middle-class hero; in Cobb, they saw a complex character that defied definition. They featured the stars prominently in the headlines of sports pages, on the covers of specialty sports magazines, and in the pages of general-interest magazines.

– 4 –

The Making of a Gentleman, a Peach, and a Sportswriter

In 1902, a decade before Grantland Rice landed a lucrative position as a New York–based syndicated newspaper columnist and freelance magazine writer with *Collier's, McClure's,* and *American Magazine,* he accepted a job as the sports editor at the *Atlanta Journal.*[1] For a salary of $12.50 per week, less than the average pay of most working professionals, he not only edited and composed the entire sports section but also served as the paper's theater critic.[2]

One mid-March afternoon in 1904, after filing stories, editing copy, and designing the sports page, he settled in for a regular round of poker with his colleagues while waiting for the presses to roll. At around 2 p.m., a Western Union messenger interrupted his hand. "Tyrus Raymond Cobb, the dashing young star from Royston, has just started spring training with Anniston [of the Southeastern League]," read the anonymous wire. "He is a terrific hitter and faster than a deer. At the age of 18 he is undoubtedly a phenom."[3] Rice tossed the message promoting the unknown semiprofessional player in a nearby wastebasket. After sharing a laugh with his colleagues, he replied that in the future regular mail would suffice to deliver news of Anniston's rookie.

Throughout the spring, he received a flood of mail signed by Joneses, Smiths, Browns, and Kellys postmarked from cities across the Southeast. "Ty Cobb is a sure-fire big league prospect," Mr. Brown confided in Rice, encouraging him to be the first to file the scoop.[4] As the "meaty" letters and postcards from his "correspondents" continued to pour in, his interest was piqued.

Before watching him in person, Rice wrote a brief column about "the darling of the fans . . . a young fellow named Cobb who seems to be showing an unusual lot of talent."[5] A few days later, he made the 130-plus-mile trek to Augusta, where the eighteen-year-old bush leaguer was now playing, to see whether "this hotshot Cobb was as good as my correspondents claimed."[6] Before the game, he strode into the dugout. "I've been hearing about you," he told Cobb. "My name is Rice. I write baseball for the *Journal*." Cobb replied, "Is that so? I've heard of you, too."[7] In the Augusta Tourists' dugout, the well-known southern sports editor broke his "first big story," and initiated a fifty-year working relationship with someone who was to become one of baseball's most prominent players.

The following season, Rice caught his first glimpse of Christy Mathewson while covering the 1905 World Series. Before the series began that October, many national fans yearned to see a match-up between Mathewson and Philadelphia Athletics ace Rube Waddell, but it was not to be. Waddell was one of the best pitchers in the American League, but he also was an eccentric drunk, and in the waning days of the 1905 season, he developed a sore shoulder. The injury persisted, and he was forced to sit out the series amidst rumors that he had been paid by New York gamblers to lay out of the event.

With this news in hand, the twenty-five-year-old Atlanta editor predicted that, behind Mathewson's "potent" arm, the Giants would defeat Connie Mack's Philadelphia Athletics. After watching the tall youngster with the "cheerful smile" in Game 1, he amended his previous prophesy.[8] The Giants would win, he wrote, and their top pitcher would blank the competition in his three outings.

He watched from the press stands of New York's Polo Grounds as Mathewson did just that. The Giants' big blond idol pitched three shutouts, giving up only fourteen hits in six days, to steal the second Fall Classic from the Athletics. Rice "marveled at the handsome right-hander and wrote as much," but he only briefly met him during the series.[9] It was not until he joined the *New York Evening Mail*'s staff in December 1910 and covered the New York Giants on a regular basis that he developed a close working relationship with Mathewson.

Even so, he crafted the champion as a hero for his Atlanta-area readers. "There is a new champion ball team on this globe tonight and its name is Christy Mathewson, sometimes called the New York Giants," he marveled on October 15 in the Sunday morning edition of the *Atlanta Journal.* "The incomparable Christy achieved the greatest feat ever accomplished in the annals of the game."[10] Based on reports like this, Mathewson's national fame soared after the series. He became an American hero.

After accurately predicting the outcome of the series, Rice became something of a legend himself. When he arrived home from covering the 1905 World Series, a letter from newspaper-chain owner Edward W. Scripps greeted him. He was offered fifty dollars per week to edit the sports page of the *Cleveland News* and to cover the American League's Cleveland Naps. He accepted the position.

Since landing his first paid position with the *Nashville Daily News* in 1901 for a meager five dollars per week, his salary had risen to more than four times that of most sports reporters.[11] His fame would follow. Over the next decade, he would distinguish himself as a leading national sports journalist. He shared the experience of many of his contemporaries, who built lucrative careers at big-city dailies after years of gathering scoops at smaller newspapers.[12]

It may have been the love of the game that attracted Rice, a former semiprofessional baseball player, to his position at the *Nashville Daily News* in 1901, but it was a desire for more money that sent him packing for Cleveland in 1905. Rice was not a particularly materialistic guy, but he was in love and "for a fellow with marriage on his mind—money never hurt."[13] The young suitor hoped to bankroll enough cash to win over his love, Katherine Hollis, and to set a sufficient amount aside for their future life together. It was for that reason that he left his well-known world of Atlanta and its friendly baseball writing fraternity for an unfamiliar midwestern city in autumn 1905.

When Rice departed the capital of the New South, he had been the toast of the town; in Cleveland, he was a virtual unknown, and upon his arrival, the jovial southern gentleman stumbled upon an unnerving situation. When Grant, as his friends called him, entered the offices of the *World-News,* he encountered some unfriendly faces. It seems that half of the newsroom had voted against hiring Rice; instead, they had hoped to offer the position to a popular midwestern sportswriter by the name of William Phelon. As a result, some of his colleagues were cold and even hostile to the newcomer.

Rice may have found an inhospitable atmosphere in the office, but he soon became close friends with the Naps' namesake—Cleveland second baseman and player-manager Napoleon Lajoie. The Naps' star player and fearless leader awed fans with his hitting ability. From 1900 to 1905, he excelled at the plate, earning four consecutive league batting titles; he appeared poised to repeat the feat in April 1906 when Rice began covering the club's spring training tour through Georgia.

Shortly after taking an uncharacteristic day off on April 11 to marry Hollis in Americus, Georgia, Rice caught up with Lajoie and the Naps for their season opener in St. Louis on April 17. After winning their opening series three-to-one, Cleveland dropped two games to the Chicago White Sox before heading to Detroit by Pullman car. In Henry Ford's Motor City, the Naps wandered over to Bennett Park on the corner of Michigan and Trumbull shortly after noon Wednesday. There, as rain threatened the afternoon sky, Rice watched from behind home plate as one of baseball's most intense offensive rivalries developed.

Early in his first full season in the majors, the young Georgian had earned his fourth consecutive start in place of injured star right fielder Sam "Wahoo" Crawford, and he did not disappoint from the batter's box. As drizzle turned into a downpour, Cobb went two-for-four against Naps ace Addie Joss, who would go on to post four twenty-win seasons and six sub-2.00 ERAs by 1910.[14] Lajoie, the four-time American League batting champ, paled in comparison, batting one-for-three in the two-to-two tie called in the eighth because of darkness. Despite his offensive dexterity, Cobb struggled in the field, muffing a fly ball hit by Joss. Even so, the "Georgia Peach," as sportswriters such as Joe S. Jackson and Rice had begun to call him, showed a glimmer of what was to come in the competitive outing.[15]

Cobb's bat remained hot that spring, especially against right-handers, and the twenty-year-old's prowess at the plate began to attract the attention of national sportswriters. *Sporting Life*'s local correspondent, for instance, called him "the most timely hitter of the Detroit club."[16] By late June, the Georgia phenom had become one of the best hitters in the league with a batting average of around .350.

Less than a month later, everything changed. Cobb suffered a nervous breakdown in mid-July. In addition to harboring profound grief over his father's death the previous year and the embarrassment of his mother's impending trial for his father's murder, he had encountered severe hazing from his teammates that spring. His resentment toward the ringleader, veteran outfielder Matty McIntyre, had boiled over, and Tigers manager Bill Armour ordered Cobb to return home to Detroit to rest. Local sportswriters reported that once there, he had checked into a sanitarium, where he had a stomach ulcer removed.

Cobb rejoined the team in late August, but the Tigers had suffered without him. They ended the season in a distant sixth place in the American League standings. He concisely summed up the season later as "the most miserable and humiliating experience I've ever been through."[17] Still, he finished with a batting average of .320, which ranked fifth among American League players.

By the end of the 1906 season, both Rice and Cobb had risen through the ranks in their respective fields. Over the next three seasons, they moved to the forefront of the national stage. They would be joined there by an unlikely character—a reclusive writer from an upper-class background in Niles, Michigan. In October 1906, he too was breaking into the big leagues as a professional sportswriter.

Like Rice, Ring Lardner considered other career opportunities before succumbing to his passion for baseball. After the unexpected loss of his family fortune, Lardner's father encouraged his son to find a suitable career. In 1901, he set out for Chicago. He worked briefly as an office boy and an employee of the Michigan Central Railroad. He even enrolled as an engineering student at Armour Institute in Chicago in 1902, but he could not extinguish his love of the national game. Shortly after his return home to Niles in autumn 1905, the editor of the *South Bend Times* knocked at his door looking to offer his brother Rex, a reporter with the newspaper's local rival, a position as "society reporter, courthouse man, drama critic, and sports editor."[18] Lardner liked the ring of "sports editor" and managed to secure the twelve-dollar-per-week job for himself. In his new position, he had a chance to see Cobb firsthand when Detroit played the Chicago White Sox at the Thirty-ninth Street Grounds. “He ran the bases like a fool,” Lardner later wrote of Cobb’s performance in his inaugural season in the big leagues.[19]

By 1907, Cobb was becoming known for his feats on the base paths. As one observer noted, “he was daring to the point of dementia.”[20] On June 11, he even managed to hoodwink New York Highlanders first baseman Hal Chase when after a basic bunt he dashed past third base on his way home. In desperation, a stunned Chase flung the ball over the head of third baseman George Moriarty, committing a costly error. Later that season, he would steal home for the first time in his career. By June, the Georgia phenom also was sizzling at the plate with a batting average well over .300.

Behind Cobb’s skillful play, the Tigers were in the thick of a pennant battle with the prior year’s league champions, the Athletics. His contributions were duly noted in the national press. Even the widely admired New York sportswriter Joe Vila grudgingly admitted that he was one of the “best all-around ball-players in the country today.”[21]

At the end of September, the pennant race was in a dead heat, but after defeating the Athletics in the opener of a decisive three-game series, Cobb knocked a two-run homer over the right-field fence off Waddell to tie the game in the ninth inning, forcing extra innings in what he later remembered as the most thrilling game of his career. The umpires called the seventeen-inning stalemate on account of darkness. The tie ultimately proved most costly for the Athletics. It effectively eliminated them from pennant contention. A few days later, Cobb became the youngest ballplayer ever to win a Major League batting title. In the process, he had earned 212 hits and 49 steals en route to a .350 batting average.

Meanwhile, Mathewson’s Giants were not faring well, as fledgling *New York Herald* reporter John N. Wheeler could attest.[22] After suffering from a case of diphtheria and a disappointing season in 1906, Mathewson was back to his old form in 1907.[23] With a 2.00 ERA, he led the National League with twenty-four wins and 178 strikeouts. He also posted eight shutouts, but it was not good enough to lift the

Giants out of fourth place behind the league-leading Chicago Cubs. The Cubs finished sixteen games ahead of their nearest competitors, the Pittsburgh Pirates, and were primed to avenge their loss in the world's championship the previous season.

At the invitation of *Chicago Tribune* sportswriter Hugh Fullerton, Lardner watched from the press box of Chicago's West Side Ball Park, as Cobb was honored for winning the league batting title. After accepting his prize, an ornate, diamond-studded medal, Cobb proceeded to be held hitless by Chicago pitcher Bill Donovan in the three-to-three, twelve-inning tie.[24] He would fare better in Game 4, but his team—now down by two games—would not.

On the evening of October 10, Lardner traveled with Fullerton by train to Detroit's Bennett Park to take in the spectacle. In the following day's game, the Tigers claimed an early one-to-nothing lead when Cobb scored teammate Claude Rossman on his triple, but that would prove all the offense that Detroit could muster. At the end of the following day's rout of the Tigers, Lardner was offered a raise of $3.50 and a position with the *Chicago Inter-Ocean*. He was climbing up the ranks in Chicago's journalistic world.

In 1908, he would have the opportunity to cover the squad's attempt to repeat as world champions. "There's only one thing for the world's champs to do this year, and that's repeat," Chicago Cubs manager Frank Chance bragged to reporters covering the National League's annual meeting at New York's Waldorf Astoria in February. "We've taken two pennants in a row and there's nothing to indicate we will not make it three in a row."[25]

In the interim, Lardner's new readers at William Randolph Hearst's *Chicago Examiner* showed unbridled enthusiasm over their world champions.[26] Early in the season, Cubs fans were not merely content to read updates in Chicago's daily newspapers. More than forty thousand people also gathered at downtown bulletin boards to watch the Cubs "live" progress. It soon, however, became readily apparent to Lardner and every other reporter covering the National League that McGraw's Giants might stand in the way of the hometown favorites.

By early May, behind the near flawless pitching of Mathewson, who had not yet dropped a game, New York was in a virtual dead heat with four other clubs for the National League pennant. His early work had impressed New York's sportswriting community, who called him the "greatest pitcher in the land."[27] Wheeler, too, was in awe. He was especially amazed by the performance that the injured star turned in on "one foot" against the Brooklyn Superbas on April 18. After Mathewson twisted his ankle while covering first early in the game, McGraw "was ready to take him out, but Mathewson decided he would fight the game to the finish," Wheeler reported.[28]

Mathewson continued his masterful ways in May. "Mighty Mathewson appeared in the box for the home talent, bright-eyed and rosy as a flower of June," Wheeler wrote of his pitching expertise in his outing against the Philadelphia Phillies two weeks later. "He toyed with the sphere as a cat would with a ball of yarn, putting it where he pleased."[29] Wheeler, like Rice and Lardner, was beginning to experiment with literary journalism. He was freely using rhetorical techniques such as similes and metaphors in his game recaps.

On May 9, Mathewson's winning streak appeared on the verge of collapse when he gave up two runs in the first inning to the Boston Doves, but as Wheeler told his *New York Herald* readers, he refused to lose that day.[30] Three days later, on May 13, Mathewson lost his first game of the season five-to-one to the Pirates before a packed house at Exposition Park. After his loss in Pittsburgh, he dropped two more games in Cincinnati in the span of three days. The Reds rocked Mathewson from the mound, and New York sportswriters speculated that he had lost his edge; the problem, they suggested, was not his throwing arm, but distractions such as his penchant for checkers. The losses, however, proved uncharacteristic in the 1908 season. Mathewson returned to his early season form in June, and by late August, behind his arm, the Giants had climbed from fourth place back to the top of the National League.

On September 1, they found themselves one game ahead of the Cubs. Some New York sportswriters contended that the Giants would have been even further ahead if Mathewson had not insisted on sitting out Sunday games because of his faith. Wheeler had watched from the press stands of the Polo Grounds as the Giants staged their comeback; Lardner, by contrast, did not have to watch his Cubs falter.[31]

In March, he had been pulled from his sports desk position at the *Examiner* to cover the Chicago White Sox full-time. He relished the opportunity to "associate with big league ball players" and partake in what for years was his "real and only ambition." "The season opened with Detroit at Sox park, the park at Thirty-ninth street, where every day was a thriller to reporters," he wrote. While traveling around the country with the likes of pitchers Doc White and Ed Walsh, he collected material that would later serve as inspiration for his famous fictional character Jack Gibbs. He also had an opportunity to watch the "Georgia Peach," an individual he was beginning to take a liking to.[32]

In 1908, Cobb was evolving from a solid everyday contributor into a truly great player, and he knew it. To begin the season, he entered into bitter salary negotiations with Detroit owner Frank Navin. Cobb was portrayed as a villain in the national media for his holdout, but despite this bit of bad press, both men eventually compromised, and Cobb signed a one-year contract for four thousand dollars on March 20. Soon he was attempting to claim his eight-hundred-dollar bonus for hitting .300, and he was succeeding. By mid-May, he was hitting .365.[33]

His prowess in the batter's box and on the base paths prompted the national sporting press to feature the twenty-two-year-old more prominently in their sports pages. Reporters wrote about Cobb in game recaps, full-length feature articles, and personality profiles. In April 1908, one *Sporting Life* correspondent reported that the "Georgia Wonder" enjoyed dancing when not in the "swatting business."[34]

Along with this portrait of a lighthearted "nifty kid" that liked to dance a "jig," another picture of Cobb was beginning to emerge in the national media. He also made headlines that season for sharpening his spikes, scuffling with teammates and fans, and engaging in off-the-field antics. Some reporters painted him as a hero, but an increasing number crafted him as a sinister villain. They did so even when their reports were not based in fact. One day in 1908, for instance, two Tiger benchwarmers attempted to intimidate the New York

Highlanders by filing their spikes in the dugout. New York's press would later claim that the "demon on the base paths" filed his spikes, too.[35]

In early October, Lardner had another chance to see Cobb in action. He told his *Examiner* readers of the Sox's remarkable battle for the pennant against the Tigers behind the late-season heroics of Walsh and White. On Monday, October 4, Walsh defeated the Tigers six-to-one before an overflowing crowd in South Side Park. Chicago's victory left Detroit with just a half-game lead over the Sox and the Naps. The following day, Cobb sealed his team's pennant hopes with a triple, two singles, and three runners batted in. He appeared poised to take on New York's peerless pitcher in the World Series.

After defeating Pittsburgh with Mathewson on the mound on September 18, the Giants lost four of their next five games, including a doubleheader to the Cubs on September 22. They desperately needed a victory at the Polo Grounds to preserve their chance at the National League pennant.[36] Throngs of their fans turned out to root on their hometown team. By the time the Giants' workhorse sauntered out for the opening pitch, more than thirty thousand of New York's faithful followers had settled into their seats. Through four innings, Mathewson only allowed two hits, both from the bat of Cubs second baseman Johnny Evers. In the fifth, he got into some trouble from the mound when shortstop Joe Tinker connected on one of his famous fadeaways. Thanks to center fielder Cy Seymour's muffed catch, Tinker stretched the double into a home run. In the sixth, the Giants responded, capitalizing on an uncharacteristic error from Cubs third baseman Harry Steinfeldt. The score remained tied for the next three innings, but a misty darkness had settled onto the field. It was so dense, as Wheeler told his *New York Herald* readers, that Mathewson had to walk up to the plate to see his catcher's signals. He managed to find the plate and was untouched by the Cubs in the ninth.[37]

With two outs and a runner on first, New York fans were hopeful as eighteen-year-old rookie Fred Merkle strode to the plate. With regular Giants first baseman Fred Tenney out with an injury, Merkle was starting in his first game of the season. Down to his last strike, he connected on a pitch and drove the ball over first baseman Frank

Chance's glove down the right-field line. For moments, as Moose McCormick rounded third for home, it appeared as if the Giants would defeat their National League rivals two-to-one, and young Merkle would become the latest storied hero of the 1908 season.[38]

In their adulation, New York's rooters had surged forward. Many had stormed the field. After running a few steps toward second, Merkle, concerned over the rushing onslaught of fans, made his way toward the clubhouse. He made one mistake, however. He never touched second. Evers saw this, and hollered at home plate umpire Hank O'Day to enforce the new force-out rule. Mass chaos ensued. Mathewson called for Merkle to return to second, as Evers yelled for outfielder Art "Solly" Hofman to throw him the ball so that he could claim the force out and nullify the game-winning run.

No one is quite sure what happened next. One version of the story is that a New York Giants fan caught Hofman's throw and heaved the ball back into the stands. Another version contends that Evers touched second after the ball was wrested away from a Giants fan.

Whatever the case may be, in the midst of the masses, a heated argument broke out among Chance, McGraw, and the umpires down near the dugouts. Eventually, O'Day ruled that the contest be called because of darkness, and all parties fled from the field. "A flying squadron of police, reinforced by special men rushed O'Day under the grandstand and Chance was escorted off the field," Wheeler reported.[39] They attempted to regain control of the crowd and to stop the impending riot.

In the meantime, Wheeler had "hurried down from the press box to get an interview with the umpires." He would not get his interview that day. Later that night, the umpires met with National League president Harry Pulliam. They announced the following day that, because Merkle had not touched second, the game had been ruled a tie and would be replayed if necessary at season's end. The press made Merkle the scapegoat of the affair, and the incident became known as the Merkle boner. He would never live it down.

Most people believed that a make-up game would not be necessary, but when the Cubs and Giants ended the season in a tie, the National League Board of Directors ordered that the rematch would be held on October 8 at the Polo Grounds. New York's World Series hopes, as Wheeler reported, would come down to this one game. He told his readers as much: "Never before have two teams been tied at the end of a season. Never before has the race been so close. Never has it been necessary to play off the tie of a six months' baseball season in a single gigantic battle. That the game will be a struggle to the death is certain. The town is in the grip of the greatest excitement. . . . Whether the city will be gay with a rejoicing crowd or plunged in sadness depends entirely on the outcome of the game."[40]

His readers took his description of the significance of the day's game to heart; by one o'clock, the Polo Grounds had quit selling tickets. Droves of fans were making their way over to Harlem. Police and firemen had to beat back those who could not find tickets. Both clubs and the umpires struggled to make their way onto the field amidst more than thirty-thousand fans rushing into the Polo Grounds. The conditions in the press box were no better; reporters struggled to take their seats among unofficial outsiders.

By the time that Mathewson marched onto the field, a thousand more fans had crowded onto Coogan's Bluff to catch a glimpse of the game. Their roars rattled Cubs pitcher Jack Pfiester in the first inning. He gave up one run and was replaced by Chicago's stalwart veteran Mordecai "Three Finger" Brown. Sparked by Tinker's triple, the Cubs rallied to a four-to-one lead in the fourth inning. Mathewson had pitched more than four hundred innings during the 1908 season, and now it appeared that he did not have another one left in him. Nonetheless, he persevered, holding the Cubs from scoring again. The Giants, however, could only muster one more run, and lost four-to-two.

Tinker, Evers, and Chance headed to Detroit's Bennett Park looking to repeat as world champions; the Tigers, meanwhile, sought revenge. In his first two outings, Cobb played solid baseball, delivering four hits, scoring twice, and driving in two runs of his own. His best performance came in Chicago in Game 3. There, Lardner watched as Cobb went four-for-five, and the Tigers handed the Cubs their first loss of the series. In Game 4, however, their bats turned anemic at the hands of "Three Finger" Brown, and they went down without too much of a fight in the series finale. Despite being held hitless in his last two outings, Cobb managed an impressive .368 batting average in the series.[41] Nevertheless, the 1908 World Series proved to be anticlimatic in comparison to the game played weeks earlier at New York's Polo Grounds.

The most important development from the series from a journalistic standpoint was the formation of the Baseball Writers' Association of America.[42] Philadelphia sportswriter Joseph McCready resurrected the idea in 1908, and after the most recent overcrowding incident at the Polo Grounds, the *New York Times* reported that a group of baseball writers had met in Detroit to discuss the formation of the Baseball Writers' Association of America in order to "promote a uniformity in scoring methods, to act in conjunction with the leagues in rules revisions suggestions, and to gain control of baseball press boxes, the conduct of which is a sore spot with working newspapermen all over the country."[43]

Although both of their clubs had suffered defeat at the hands of the Cubs in 1908, Mathewson and Cobb were at the peak of their careers. The season proved to be Mathewson's best single year. He finished with thirty-seven wins, twelve shutouts, 259 strikeouts, and a 1.42 ERA.[44] Cobb, on the other hand, led his club to its second consecutive World Series. In the process, he had knocked in 101 runs and earned his second consecutive batting title with a batting average of .324.[45]

Boston-based sportswriter Jacob Morse's new upstart monthly, *Baseball Magazine*, had much to say about the impressive season of both stars. *Baseball Magazine* freelancer and *New York Globe* sportswriter Harry Niemeyer called Mathewson "almost invincible" in the publication's November issue, and Morse himself lauded the "famous" Cobb's athletic virtues the next month.[46] "Any talk of the batting honors of the American League going to anyone except 'Ty' Cobb of the champion Detroits is pure tommyrot," he wrote.[47]

Over the next two seasons, Lardner also caught sight of the icons as he covered the Chicago Cubs and their crosstown rivals from his new post at the *Chicago Tribune*. The offer had been extended in January 1909 when retiring sportswriter and humorist Charlie Dryden recommended that Lardner replace him. Lardner jumped at the chance to cover baseball for Chicago's best morning newspaper, which would soon proclaim itself the "World's Greatest Newspaper."[48] He likely did not mind the ten-dollar weekly raise all that much either. After working desk for several months, he joined the Cubs at spring training in March, but he did not stay with them for long. His sports editor Harvey Woodruff believed in the emerging notion of detached journalism, so he often switched Lardner and his colleague Sy Sanborn back and forth between the Cubs and the Sox in their daily beat writing duties, which included penning a fifteen-hundred-word game story and often a column, too.

When Lardner encountered Cobb or Mathewson in 1909 and 1910, he often caught glimpses of greatness. *New York Herald* sportswriter John N. Wheeler also could attest that Mathewson was in top form. Although the Giants struggled in 1909, Matty allowed fewer hits than at any other time in his career. His 1.14 ERA still ranks among the greatest in National League history, and his twenty-five wins were commendable. The following season, he added twenty-seven more.[49] He was becoming regarded in the sporting press as a national hero not just for his prowess on the mound, but also for his gentlemanly demeanor regardless of a game's outcome.

In 1909, Cobb was on his way to his third consecutive league batting title with a .377 batting average.[50] Even so, it was his feats on the base paths, not his slugging average, that were getting the most attention from the sporting press. By early August, some sportswriters had already begun taking shots at him for injuring players with his base-running tactics. Others joined in later that month, painting him as a "demon in spikes," after his infamous run-in with Philadelphia Athletics star Frank "Home Run" Baker. His antics had even rattled the unflappable Mack, who told newspaper reporters that Cobb was the "dirtiest player" in the league.[51] A few players and journalists came to his defense, but a villainous picture of the Cobb was beginning to emerge in the national press. It gained further credence less than a week later when, on September 3, Cobb slapped an African American elevator operator at Cleveland's Hotel Euclid for his perceived insolence and then knifed the interceding night manager, George Stansfield. Stansfield filed both criminal and civil suits against Cobb.

Cleveland police issued a warrant for Cobb's arrest for attempted murder, and the national sporting press branded him as a "ruffian" of the worst sort. Stansfield eventually dropped the criminal suit, and the civil suit was settled for one hundred dollars, plus court costs. Even so, the damage had been done to Cobb's reputation in the press.

Despite Cobb's behavior, the Tigers excelled in 1909, earning their third consecutive trip to the world championship. The series pitted Cobb against Honus Wagner, the National League's batting champ for the past four consecutive years. Before the game, sportswriters begged the nation's two greatest hitters to pose together, and a primitive motion-picture camera captured the moment. Soon after, the niceties between the two players drew to a close, and Lardner reported on the outcome of the first game from the confines of Pittsburgh's crowded press box.

"In the presence of the biggest crowd that ever saw a world's championship ball game," he wrote, "the Pittsburgh National League Champions this afternoon took first blood in their series with the Detroit Tigers. The score was 4 to 1."[52] Cobb had scored Detroit's only run, but Wagner would outmatch him in most offensive categories for the series. Although the Tigers took the series to seven games for the first time in its brief history, Cobb experienced World Series woes for the second consecutive year, batting only .231 over seven games. He may have left Detroit's Bennett Park on the evening of October 16 believing that the Tigers would claim the title next season. What he did not know, however, was that there would not be a next year in the World Series for Detroit until 1934, six years after he last hung up his cleats.

For the first few months of the following season, *Baseball Magazine*'s newest contributor, F. C. Lane, witnessed the Tigers battle with Mack's Philadelphia Athletics and the New York Yankees for first place in the American League standings, but by mid-July, they were out of contention for the league pennant.[53] They may have finished a distant third, but Cobb was determined not to lose his title as the league batting champ. Cobb had a penchant for automobiles, and this time, a new Chalmers roadster was at stake. After going four-for-five in Chicago, an overconfident Cobb decided to sit out the final two games of the season with the calm assurance that his fourth consecutive batting title was secure.

Lajoie, however, had another idea in mind. So, too, did the St. Louis Browns, who shared a mutual dislike of Cobb. They decided to help Lajoie in his quest by playing the slugger shallow in the outfield on the final day of the 1910 season. Behind their efforts, the Naps' star recorded eight hits in the day's doubleheader, just what Lajoie needed to capture the title from Cobb.

The batting title, however, was still too close to call. American League president Ban Johnson held a special meeting to determine the league's leading slugger. On October 15, he declared that it was Cobb by .000860 of a percentage point. Because of the close nature of the contest, however, Hugh Chalmers, president of the Chalmers Motor Car Company, announced that both stars would receive a Chalmers "30" at the opening game of the World Series between the Cubs and Athletics.

After accepting the prize before a crowd of more than twenty-six thousand fans at Philadelphia's Shibe Park on October 17, Cobb headed up to the press box to cover the game as a correspondent for the *Detroit Free Press*.[54] He was joined by correspondents for the nation's leading newspapers and specialty baseball magazines. He did not, however, run into Rice or Lardner that day. They were absent from the press box at the 1910 World Series, but they would join Cobb and their other colleagues the following year.

In the meantime, the two reporters were in the process of transitions that would put them atop the baseball-writing world. In November, Lardner accepted a position as the editor of the *Sporting News*; the following month, Rice, who had returned home to Nashville as the sports editor of the *Tennessean* in 1907, was lured back to the big city by an offer he could not turn down from *New York Evening Mail* owner Henry L. Stoddard.[55] Instead of working twelve- to eighteen-hour days to pen a daily column, cover Nashville's theater scene, and edit a two- to four-page sports section, he would earn fifty dollars per week to cover New York's sports scene.

By December 1910, both Rice and Lardner had accepted lucrative positions at the nation's top-circulating dailies. They had gained experience at small-town newspapers in the South and Midwest. They had jumpstarted their careers by reporting on emerging baseball stars. From their posts at mid-sized dailies, they had had an opportunity to witness the rise of two American idols in the nation's sports pages. Now, from their new positions in the country's biggest sports-media markets, they would find a community of friends who would help further their careers. They would get to know Cobb and Mathewson intimately as they traveled with them by train across the country, and they would have a chance to contribute to the legends and lore surrounding the pair.

Future U.S. senator Richard B. Russell of Winder was one of millions of children who collected T-206 baseball cards. Icons such as New York Giants pitcher Christy Mathewson and Detroit Tigers outfielder Ty Cobb were crafted as kings of the diamond in every possible media platform, from baseball cards to general-interest magazines.

Library of Congress, Benjamin K. Edwards Collection.

Mathewson became known as the Christian Gentleman for his positive attitude and exemplary demeanor on and off the field.

Library of Congress, Prints and Photographs Division, photo by Paul Thompson.

After his dramatic performance in the 1905 World Series, Mathewson became a national hero. In spring 1912, shortly after this photograph was published, Mathewson—with the assistance of his ghostwriter, *New York Herald* reporter John N. Wheeler—published his autobiography, *Pitching in a Pinch.*

Library of Congress, Harris and Ewing Collection.

Cobb, working as a player-correspondent for the *Philadelphia Public Ledger,* greets Mathewson before the 1911 World Series.

Library of Congress, George Grantham Bain Collection.

Cobb, known to millions of Americans as the "Georgia Peach," snagged 4,191 hits and twelve consecutive batting titles during his twenty-four-year playing career. More than fifty years after his death in 1961, he retains the highest lifetime batting average (.367) of any Major League player.

Library of Congress, George Grantham Bain Collection.

Cobb was safe at third after lining a triple in the fifth inning against Washington Senators pitcher Firpo Marberry on August 16, 1924. "Tyrus the Terrible," as some sportswriters called him, became known as a "demon in spikes" for snatching 892 bases over the course of his career.

Library of Congress, National Photo Company Collection.

A decade before Grantland Rice landed a lucrative position as a New York–based syndicated newspaper columnist and freelance writer with *Collier's*, *McClure's*, and *American Magazine*, he encountered a young Sally League star by the name of Ty Cobb from his post at the *Atlanta Journal* in March 1904. He caught his first glimpse of the New York Giants star hurler Christy Mathewson while covering the World Series the following year. He would get to know both stars well in the years to come.

Library of Congress, *New York World-Telegram* and the *Sun* Newspaper Photo Collection, photo by Paul Thompson.

First as a New York–based beat writer and then as a ghostwriter and syndicate owner, John N. Wheeler (*standing, left*) crafted his chums Mathewson and Cobb into heroes of the diamond in feature articles and autobiographies such as *Pitching in a Pinch* (1912) and *Busting 'Em and Other Big League Stories* (1914). Wheeler posed here with other beat writers at the Polo Grounds in 1911—John B. Foster (*standing, right*), and (*seated in chairs, left to right*) Sam Crane, Fred Lieb, Damon Runyon, Bozeman Bulger, Sid Mercer, Grantland Rice, and Walter Trumbull. Concessionaire Harry Stevens and his nephew (name unknown) are seated on the ground.

National Baseball Hall of Fame Library, Cooperstown, NY.

In 1911, the press box at the Polo Grounds was filled to capacity as beat writers such as Grantland Rice and John N. Wheeler battled with Ty Cobb and other player-authors to file their stories. They watched as the Philadelphia Athletics defeated Mathewson's Giants four games to two.

National Baseball Hall of Fame Library, Cooperstown, NY.

First as a newspaper beat reporter and then as a freelance magazine writer, Ring Lardner experimented with the techniques of literary journalism. His hero-crafting tools were in fine form in his odes to baseball greats Cobb and Mathewson published in *American Magazine* in 1915. Lardner [*second from right*] is pictured here with President Warren G. Harding, pal Grantland Rice, and Undersecretary of State Henry P. Fletcher in April 1921. The foursome headed out for a friendly round of golf after posing for the camera.

Library of Congress, National Photo Company Collection.

From his post as editor of *Baseball Magazine*, F. C. Lane "maintained an extensive correspondence" with all the game's stars. "He has talked with these players at their hotels, in the club houses before and after the game, on the player's bench, in the bull pen, everywhere," the introduction of his 1925 how-to book acknowledged.

National Baseball Hall of Fame Library, Cooperstown, NY.

In March 1912, *Baseball Magazine* featured one of its first player-themed issues. To produce the Ty Cobb Number, F. C. Lane doled out assignments to several player-writers, including Detroit Tigers manager Hugh Jennings, and enlisted the talented young illustrator Gerrit A. Beneker to sketch the cover. The issue, which promised readers the "greatest Ty Cobb stories ever written," portrayed Cobb as "the uncrowned king of baseball."

LA Foundation.

In December 1914, Lane released the Christy Mathewson Number of *Baseball Magazine.* The end result was a mythmaking masterpiece. Illustrator J. F. Kernan produced an iconic image of the broad-shouldered, blond-haired, blue-eyed Mathewson. Within the magazine, Lane and his staff painted Mathewson as "the brainiest pitcher the diamond ever knew"—a heroic sportsman who came from "blooded stock, imported from England."

LA Foundation.

– 5 –

Gathering the "Inside Dope"

Grantland Rice had planned to head over to Takeiteasy Tavern, Somewhere, USA, for his vacation in December 1910, but at the behest of *New York Evening Mail* owner Henry L. Stoddard, he rerouted his trip. He instead traveled to Nashville's Union Station and hopped aboard an L&N train bound for the Northeast. Once in lower Manhattan, he arrived at the *Mail*'s headquarters, located in the heart of New York's publishing district on Park Row. There, from behind his office desk, Stoddard warmly greeted Rice. "I've been reading your verse," he told the anxious journalist. "I never knew a sports writer worth fifty bucks, but in your case I'll risk it."[1]

The offer was twenty dollars less than he had been bankrolling at the *Tennessean* for the last 180 or so weeks, but he knew that it was rare for a small-town reporter to land a position in New York. It was even more unusual for a publisher to invite a reporter to the nation's biggest media market to offer him a job in person. After consulting his young wife, Kate, he accepted the offer. With her encouragement, he entered the New York sports scene.

After his meeting with Stoddard, Rice bumped into a friendly face. It was that of Rube Goldberg, the morning paper's well-known cartoonist and sports columnist. He, in turn, introduced Rice to the paper's resident humorist, columnist Franklin P. Adams. Upon learning that Rice had not yet found a place to stay, Adams recommended a spot in his own building at 616 West 116th Street.

In the nation's biggest media market, Rice socialized with sportswriters such as Heywood Broun of the *New York Tribune,* John N. Wheeler of the *New York Herald,* Damon Runyon of the *New York American,* and Ring Lardner of the *Chicago Tribune.* He joined a community of mostly male sports journalists.[2] In his autobiography, Rice noted a close sense of camaraderie among New York–based sportswriters.[3] His observations support the contentions of others. New York sportswriters such as John N. Wheeler, Dan Daniel, and Marshall Hunt later described congenial relationships among their colleagues.[4] The reporters quickly learned that the key to landing newsworthy information was the establishment of "friendly" working associations among professional colleagues and sports stars.

By the time Kate and their four-year-old daughter Floncy arrived in Manhattan in February 1911, Rice was feeling more settled. He had made a few new pals and secured an apartment at 450 Riverside Drive.[5] From this venue, the Rices entertained some of the most notable faces in the New York sporting and literary scenes over the next two decades. They visited often with Adams and other journalists such as Walter Trumbull, Max Foster, Irvin S. Cobb, and Damon Runyon. Runyon, a fellow sportswriter and New York newcomer, for instance, often wandered by for a nightcap around midnight at the end of his shift at the *New York American.*

On April 12, 1911, Rice entered the press box at the Polo Grounds for his first time as a New York Giants beat writer. Seated beside Runyon, he was introduced to Fred Lieb, another rookie in New York's press row. Rice was a veteran sportswriter, but Lieb was still a neophyte in every way. After getting his start at Morse's *Baseball Magazine* two years earlier, Lieb had recently replaced Ernest J. Lanigan at the *New York Press.* Also in the press box that day was another newcomer—*New York Morning Telegraph* baseball reporter Heywood Broun.

The freshman baseball writing class of 1911 was surrounded by New York press veterans such as George Tidden of the *New York Morning World,* Bill Hanna and Joe Vila of the *New York Morning Sun,* John Foster of the *New York Evening Telegram,* and Wheeler, who was wrapped up in a bearskin coat and sitting in the corner.[6]

Legendary sportswriter Sam Crane, the longtime baseball reporter for Hearst's *New York Journal,* was also there. Like several other notable sportswriters of the day, Crane had gotten his start as a professional baseball player and manager before entering the field of sports journalism. By 1911, the well-respected writer had more than twenty-four years of experience covering New York's sports scene and was a close friend and consummate advocate of New York Giants manager John "Mugsy" McGraw.[7] The men working that day in the Polo Grounds' press box would get to know each other well while covering McGraw's Giants over the next three seasons during professional baseball's prewar golden age.

After introducing him to the fellows, Lanigan encouraged his replacement to settle into his seat for the season. He and the others watched as the Giants fell to the Phillies two-to-nothing. On the following day, before a sizable crowd in the much-adored, horseshoe-shaped ballpark, the New York Giants beat writers thought for sure that the nation's most beloved pitcher would even the score.[8] But Mathewson did not look like his old self, and the Giants lost five-to-one. It should have served as an omen of the trials to come in the 1911 season for the New York Giants and the men who covered them.

The sportswriters did not have a chance to get too comfortable in the New York Giants' press box. Around midnight on April 14, Harlem residents were awakened by shouts of fire. New York firemen attempted to take control of the stunning blaze, which was visible for miles, but in the end it consumed the Polo Grounds in its entirety, as well as the terminal of the nearby Interborough Railway Company.[9] The entire press box went up in flames. New York fire officials were never able to determine how the fire started, but it left the Giants and their press corps temporarily without a home.

The Giants would not be homeless for long. The New York Highlanders, soon to be renamed the Yankees, allowed their rivals to play at Hilltop Park for the remainder of the season. Rice and his peers settled into the press facilities a few blocks away from the Polo Grounds. Nevertheless, it looked as if it might be a long season from the press box when the Giants dropped two more games in Philadelphia's Baker Bowl later that month.[10]

Baseball beat writers then, like today, put in twelve-plus-hour days at the office—the press facilities of Major League baseball parks and the bullpens of pressrooms in New York's publishers row. They did so in overcrowded spaces, which were often open to the bare elements—the cold drizzle and frost of early spring and fall and the hard-driving rain and steamy humidity of mid-summer.[11] They covered the clubs to which they were assigned year-round—for nine months during the Major League baseball season and for three months during the off-season. They reported on home games from the confines of intimate spaces such as the press boxes at the Polo Grounds or Hilltop Park, and they ventured out to America's East Coast and midwestern urban hubs during weeklong road stands. "Back in the olden days," *Atlanta Journal-Constitution* reporter Furman Bisher (1918–2012) recalled in a 2009 interview, "sportswriters would travel with the team. The newspapers didn't pay their expenses. The team did, and they would put them up in hotels and feed them. It was a matter of them coddling the journalists to get publicity through the newspapers." During these daunting treks, sportswriters palled around with their colleagues and rubbed elbows with baseball royalty. Despite the often brutal working conditions, most baseball beat writers loved their chosen careers.

After long days of covering home games and filing their stories at Park Row, some of the New York writers would join their newsroom colleagues for a drink or two at Lipton's.[12] In addition to sharing laughs over a couple of beers, America's cadre of baseball writers forged close working alliances. While covering the New York Giants and other Major League clubs, writers from competing dailies often worked together to report on game stories. Lieb, for instance, shared the stats that he had collected for the day's box score with the men around him in the press box.[13] Packed into press boxes, train cars, hotels, and restaurant bars, others sometimes worked together to break stories.[14] For instance, when McGraw was being particularly closed-lipped, reporters from competing newspapers ganged up on him at informal pre- and post-game press conferences.[15]

Early twentieth-century baseball journalists relied on each other to gather newsworthy information. This practice was not unusual within the profession. "Combination reporting," as journalism historian Ted Curtis Smythe called it, had existed in newsrooms since the late 1800s.[16] In his 1927 book *Ballyhoo,* former newspaperman Silas Bent provided anecdotal evidence that group newsgathering techniques were commonplace across all newsroom departments. He argued that reporters worked "in squads. . . . They interview celebrities in groups, and apportion among themselves the labor on a big story, sharing their gleanings later."[17]

Not only did baseball writers develop close working associations with one another, they also established relationships with local sports stars. This was made possible by virtue of their daily proximity. They interacted with players "almost on a daily basis."[18] They traveled, lodged, and dined with players on road trips. Following afternoon games, Daniel recalled, sportswriters often mingled with players and managers in hotel lobbies.[19] On their days off, they enjoyed leisure activities together. The best-known reporters at prominent national dailies gained a level of access to national celebrities unavailable to lesser-known journalists. Major market sports reporters thus formed more intimate relationships with baseball stars. In addition to casual mingling, these journalists developed rapport over "friendly" dinners, golf rounds, and hunting trips.

Rice, for instance, had initiated cordial relationships with Cobb and Mathewson as the sports editor for the *Atlanta Journal* around 1905. In his position as a beat reporter with the *Evening Mail* in 1911, he looked to rekindle his association with the pair.[20] Lardner would do the same in his short-lived post as editor of *Sporting News* and later that year as sports editor of the *Boston American.*[21] On those seemingly never-ending road trips, they played friendly games of poker, chess, and checkers with Mathewson and his teammates.

In addition to being a nationally renowned pitcher, Mathewson was a first-rate checkers player. As the Giants made their way across America, he often played anyone he encountered, even sportswriters. He sometimes engaged in competitive battles with the college boys such as Runyon, Broun, and *New York Evening World* reporter Bozeman Bulger.[22] McGraw had introduced Broun to Mathewson earlier that season. After a few rounds of checkers, Mathewson told Broun that he was a "sound player."[23] They became consummate checkers foes, but they also paired up in a variety of other card and board games.

Rice may have played the occasional game of checkers, chess, or poker against Mathewson, but mostly he just observed the master at work. On one occasion that season, he watched from a nearby table at the Philadelphia Athletic Club as Mathewson took on and defeated twelve checkers opponents at one time. Mathewson was "just a little bit better at all games than anyone else," Rice wrote. "He played chess and checkers and poker better, for example, and usually drew in most of the pots."[24] On their rare days off, Rice played golf with Mathewson and his buddies. "I played a lot of golf with [Mathewson]—from New York to St. Louis," he recalled in *The Tumult and the Shouting*.[25] These friendly outings and gatherings contributed to the sense of camaraderie between Rice, Mathewson, and his teammates.

They also often resulted in colorful tidbits for Rice's new "Sportlight" column or juicy details for his personality sketches, but sometimes the excursions backfired. On one off-day in mid-June 1911, Rice played a round of golf with Mathewson and two of his teammates—first baseman Fred Merkle and outfielder Mike Donlin. Like longtime cronies, they made wagers and sparred over impolite chatter during backswings. The day also brought a first for Rice's favorite Giant. "Matty broke 80 for the first time in his life and knew a joy that meant more to him that morning than a pitching victory," he later recalled.[26] After the grueling round of thirty-six holes with Mathewson, Merkle, and Donlin that Saturday afternoon at Pittsburgh's Schenley Hotel, Rice landed in McGraw's doghouse, when the Pirates shellacked a still-exhausted Mathewson in the next day's game. "I hid out from McGraw for four days," he later wrote of the incident.[27]

Wheeler also had befriended Mathewson several years prior when he landed his position with the *New York Herald* in 1907. He palled around with Mathewson during road trips and on hunting trips in the off-season. Soon, Rice would join them on these outdoor excursions. After August 1914, they spent time hunting wild game with Cobb and other baseball notables at Dover Hall, a twenty-four-hundred-acre estate near Brunswick, Georgia, which had been purchased by some fifty individuals associated with professional baseball in 1914 to serve as the future site of a spring training facility and retreat center.[28]

After Mathewson's death in October 1925, Wheeler reminisced about these intimate times. "He was a great companion on a hunting trip, always giving the others the best of it, and usually getting the bird after I had missed," he wrote.[29] All of the New York–based beat writers shared a mutual affection for the perennial champion on the mound. Wheeler and Rice, however, enjoyed a special relationship with Mathewson. Rice later recalled that he was "as fine a companion as I ever knew."[30] Even so, in an age of heightened anxiety over men's relationships, Wheeler made sure to clarify his relationship with the Giants pitcher by confirming that Mathewson was no pansy in several of his articles for national magazines.[31]

Rice and Wheeler were not the only sports journalists who socialized with the stars while covering baseball clubs. In the introduction to his 1925 book *Batting*, F. C. Lane admitted to being on "friendly terms" with all the day's baseball legends.[32] His networking had served him well, and after being hired as a correspondent in 1910, he quickly rose through the ranks to associate editor in July 1911 and sole editor in December of that same year. Such relationships between journalists and the individuals they covered were typical in this era. As legendary *New York Daily News* sports editor Paul Gallico noted in his 1965 memoir *The Golden People*, "one hobnobbed with famous athletes, played golf with them, looked in upon their private lives."[33] They formed companionable relationships not only to pass the time and have a few laughs on long road trips, but, as Gallico admitted, to gather material "for the sake of inside stories."[34] Their publishers had come to demand celebrity-style journalism. They knew that these personal stories sold papers. In the last instance, then, sportswriters befriended star athletes, as Gallico readily acknowledged, to "earn a living." By forming close friendships with baseball stars, journalists gained access to insider material for their human-interest features.

Rice learned this strategy shortly after landing his position with the *New York Evening Mail* in December 1910. He immediately went to work establishing rapport with the New York Giants. On his first road trip with the club in late April 1911, he recalled "pecking away" on his typewriter. McGraw sidled up. Taking a seat next to him on the Pullman car, he asked what Rice was writing about. When he replied that he had not yet "stumbled on anything worth wiring the paper," McGraw said, "I've got a story for you," and "together they worked out a good yarn," Rice recalled.[35] The incident taught him that gallivanting with the Giants had its advantages. It was a good cure for writer's block.

After forming relationships with the stars, Rice gathered material for his columns on Pullman cars, at hotels, in restaurants and bars, and on the golf course. He later noted that he often gained better scoops on the golf course than in the dugout. In his memoir, *I've Got News for You,* Wheeler recalled that sportswriters were encouraged to collect "inside dope" in all places at all times of the day. "Those of us who stayed in the newspaper business generally took to heart [Chicago-based journalist] George Ade's comment: 'Early to bed and early to rise and you meet very few prominent people,'" he wrote.[36]

Sportswriters mimicked the strategies of entertainment reporters who culled inside information about celebrities for the national print media. In the early twentieth century, reporters used informal newsgathering techniques. Even the interview, a journalistic convention that gained prevalence in the last half of the nineteenth century, was a relaxed practice. Reporting handbooks encouraged journalists to avoid taking notes since "real reporters on real newspapers do not use notebooks."[37] Therefore, it was common for reporters across departments to gather interviews through casual daily interactions with their sources. Sports journalists incorporated the comments made by sports stars in interspersed quotations throughout human-interest features.

After his first start of the 1911 season, Mathewson settled down. His pitching was almost automatic as he held his ERA under 2.00 and won twenty-six games over 307 innings. His impressive stats prompted New York–based sportswriter Edward Lyell Fox to tell *Outing Magazine* readers in May 1911 that he was the "greatest pitcher that the world has ever seen."[38] Runyon agreed. After Mathewson defeated Cincinnati in July, he wrote for *American Magazine* readers:

"Mathewson pitched against Cincinnati yesterday. Another way of putting it is that Cincinnati lost a game of baseball. The first statement means the same as the second."[39]

In his first season covering the Giants, Rice also was struck by Mathewson's brilliance on the mound. Yet, even more than his feats on the field, it was Mathewson's attitude that stood out. As a result, Rice branded him the "knightliest of all the game's paladins."[40]

In 1911, the fearless and faithful leader was assisted by something of a late bloomer in pitcher Rube Marquard, who had landed a spot in the Giants' starting rotation in 1908 but, thus far, had not lived up to his buildup. During the regular season, he had become the league's strikeout leader.[41] Thanks to the arms of Mathewson and Marquard, the Giants overtook the Cubs and the Pirates for first place in the National League in early August. They never faltered, earning the league pennant by seven games over Chicago, their nearest competitor. On the last day of the season, it appeared they would face Mack's Athletics in the World Series once more.[42]

By October 1911, sportswriters had developed chummy relationships with Mathewson and Cobb, and they were beginning to pay off. They did more than provide colorful material for human-interest features. They afforded a unique opportunity to pad the pockets of newspaper publishers, prominent sportswriters, and star athletes alike and to supply the behind-the-scenes flavor that the masses were said to crave.

In the late 1880s, sportswriters had begun ghostwriting autobiographies and writing specialty books for baseball stars such as Mike "King" Kelly, but in the early twentieth century, the demand for such work was great.[43] In 1907, Naps pitcher Addie Joss had provided *Cleveland Press* readers with an insider's glimpse of the World Series. Joss was a talented writer and ball player, who had begun supplementing his meager minor-league salary from the Toledo Mud Hens with money that he earned during the off-season as a sportswriter for the *Toledo Bee*. As a World Series correspondent with the *Cleveland Press* from 1907 to 1909, he provided intimate first-person accounts of the championship series and its cast of stars.[44]

His World Series and off-season coverage proved so popular that newspaper sales increased. Other newspaper publishers also looked to profit from this trend, but not all Major League players possessed Joss's skill with the pen. To eliminate the problem of potentially dry prose, sports editors began pairing talented baseball beat writers with elite baseball players. Together, they would collaborate on colorful first-person game accounts and capitalize on the public's desire for this brand of insider celebrity journalism.

The *Detroit Free Press*'s Joe S. Jackson and Ty Cobb did just that at the 1910 World Series. After accepting his batting title, Cobb, with the help of Jackson, covered two games between the Cubs and the Athletics from Shibe Park's press box before heading back to Augusta. His accounts were quite popular, and as the World Series once again approached, Jackson, Cobb, and other elite writers and athletes looked to cash in on the phenomenon.

That October, Cobb teamed up with *Philadelphia Public Ledger* sportswriter "Stoney" McLinn to write daily World Series pieces, which were syndicated in a dozen or so newspapers, including the *New York Herald* and the *Washington Post*. McLinn later recalled Cobb's meticulous note-taking practices in the press box during the series. "Every story that [he] wrote, when I was his associate was his very own—it was dictated by Cobb, read and corrected by Cobb," he contended.[45] Although it is likely that Cobb, ever the micromanager, had his fingers on the pieces, it is unclear to what extent his "ghost" contributed to his handiwork.

They would be joined in the press box by the likes of Detroit manager Hugh Jennings, former New York Giants manager Adrian "Cap" Anson, New York Yankees first baseman Hal Chase, and Boston Red Sox center fielder Tris Speaker.[46] Mathewson and Marquard, the Giants' top two aces, also would find a way to claim their place alongside other player-authors. Players of this era—even those of Cobb's and Mathewson's caliber—were always searching for a way to capitalize on their star status and supplement their salaries with projects such as these. Most opportunities for extra money came from speaking engagements and appearances in theatrical performances in the off-season, but now Mathewson and his elite peers had an opportunity to profit from their fame while they played ball.

Shortly before the series began, the *New York Herald*'s eccentric publisher James Gordon Bennett Jr., offered Mathewson five hundred dollars per bylined story to "cover" the World Series.[47] He agreed. Over the next three weeks, he collaborated with Wheeler to turn out daily columns about the rematch of the 1905 World Series. For these pieces, Wheeler chatted with Mathewson briefly before and after the game; then, he pieced together the material into an entertaining column. The process was much the same as his daily routine, except for one detail—he wrote each article from Mathewson's perspective, not his own.

Before Mathewson stepped onto the mound at the newly rebuilt Polo Grounds for the first pitch of the 1911 World Series, Wheeler and his cronies in the press box had helped work the American public into a frenzy over the historic rematch. "No World's Series to date has aroused so much excitement, speculation, and debate," wrote *Sporting Life* editor Francis Richter. "Every base ball writer in the Major League circuit has given his view of the personnel and chances of the two contesting teams."[48]

The World Series was the toughest ticket in town. Many of those who could not acquire tickets gathered at street corners near newspaper offices around New York and Philadelphia to watch the game on electronic boards or at theaters to see it recreated before their eyes. More than fifty telegraph operators sent constant game updates to these venues.[49] After Mathewson easily retired the first three batters that he faced in the first inning of the opening game of the World Series, it must have appeared to New York's rooters and its cadre of sportswriters that the Giants were on their way to repeating their dominant 1905 performance. After all, Mathewson had just pitched his twenty-eighth scoreless inning over the A's in World Series play, and he showed no signs of faltering.[50]

In the second inning, the Athletics would put an end to their scoring drought against the Giants' hurler when first baseman Harry Davis singled to drive in third baseman Frank Baker, but the Giants would not trail for long. In the seventh, they took a two-to-one lead on a Josh Devore double. They stayed ahead due to Mathewson's near-flawless arm, which gave up only six hits on the day.[51]

With the assistance of McLinn, Cobb explained to *New York Herald* readers the magnitude of Mathewson's performance the following day. In "Mathewson's Headwork Superior in Pitchers' Battle, Says 'Ty' Cobb," published in the October 15 *New York Herald,* he wrote, "the opening contest was a battle pure and simple between two masters of the art of pitching. . . . Mathewson's work was ideal."[52]

The Giants looked invincible going into Game 2 with their other ace, Rube Marquard, on the mound at Philadelphia's Shibe Park on October 16, but "Home Run" Baker would prove that they were anything but. With the score tied at one in the bottom of the sixth, Baker connected on his twelfth home run of the season. The Athletics won three-to-one.[53]

On the following day, Marquard found criticism from an unlikely source. Under the headline, "Marquard Made the Wrong Pitch," Wheeler, under Mathewson's byline, soundly condemned Rube for his lack of judgment in pitch selection. "One ball pitched to Frank Baker in the sixth inning here to-day cost the Giants the game," Wheeler wrote. "The sixth inning was the critical inning of the game—victory hung on that one ball, and Marquard served Baker with the wrong prescription."[54] The column noted that McGraw and Mathewson had instructed him not to pitch fastballs to Baker, but Marquard had not heeded their warnings. "Rube pitched just what Baker likes," Mathewson carped to *New York Herald* readers.[55]

Although Wheeler always claimed that Mathewson played a major role in writing these player-author columns, it is unclear how much of a say he had in crafting this particular piece. As sports historian Richard Orodenker acknowledged, "Long before the invention of the tape recorder, ghostwriters either wrote the player's words entirely," enhanced their comments, or made up stories altogether.[56] Some historians have claimed that Mathewson had no previous knowledge of the piece; whatever the case, his column provided an uncharacteristic display of an unsportsmanlike attitude from the man who was becoming known to the American public as the Christian Gentleman.

His critique shocked the baseball world. Richter told the readers of *Sporting Life* that Mathewson had "roasted Marquard for trying to sneak a fast one" past Baker.[57] Still, Mathewson stood by the piece and refused to publicly criticize Wheeler for the miscue; after all, his column had left readers with one final, hopeful, if critical, thought: "The teams are now even and to-morrow we get a new start. The mistakes of to-day will be forgotten, but that one straight ball was what cost us the game."[58]

Looking for a clean start, Mathewson would be on the mound before a home crowd in Game 3. The man known for his moral fortitude was likely familiar with the biblical principle of "reaping what you sow." His critical column had sown discord among the Giants, and later that day after his piece appeared, he too would face Baker's bat and endure a similar fate to the one his teammate had encountered the day before. Before a crowd of nearly forty thousand fans at the Polo Grounds with a one-to-nothing advantage in the middle of the ninth inning, Mathewson gave up a solo home run to Baker. Two innings later, the Athletics claimed victory after unlikely miscues from Giants infielders Art Fletcher and Buck Herzog.

Mathewson reaped the wrath of the sports world. First, Marquard sought revenge in the sports pages when Frank Menke, a writer for Hearst's International News Service, under his byline, lambasted Mathewson for committing the fatal error by tossing the wrong pitch. "Will the great Mathewson tell us what he pitched to Baker?" he taunted. "He was present at the same clubhouse meeting at which Mr. McGraw discussed Baker's weakness. Could it be that Matty, too, let go of a careless pitch when it meant the ball game?"[59] Even Richter, who had heaped praise on the big blond idol in the past, failed to show remorse for his malady. "Mathewson received a dose of the very same medicine that Baker had handed to Marquard," he told his readers.[60]

After the game, Mathewson turned to one of his closest friends in the press box to set the record straight. Rice later recalled that Mathewson told him that Baker was a "dangerous hitter." He discussed his pitching strategy, noting that he had taken a "chance, which cost us the game."[61] Although the interview did little to minimize the criticism in the national media in the immediate aftermath of the event, "friendly" writers such as Rice would eventually paint a more sympathetic portrait of his performance in the 1911 World

Series. They would remember him as a good sportsman for failing to condemn Fletcher or Herzog for their errors in the field.

This is all the more ironic since Mathewson heaped criticism on outfielder Fred Snodgrass for his costly base-running error in the tenth inning of Game 3 in his 1912 autobiography, *Pitching in a Pinch.* "It was bad baseball, but he was nervous with the intense strain and over-eager to score." Still, Mathewson wrote, "It cost us the game."[62] His comments may strike modern readers as uncharacteristically unsportsmanlike, but Mathewson believed that an athlete should "always have an alibi." He told Rice and other reporters that it was necessary to keep one's confidence. "If you lose . . . there must be a reason—a bad break," he said.[63]

Regardless of Mathewson's rationale for the critical comments, after Game 3, the Giants were indignant. It seemed that they, not the Athletics, were their own worst enemies. A week's worth of torrential downpours postponed post-season play and did little to lift their spirits. When play resumed at Shibe Park on October 24, McGraw put the ball in the hands of his perennial ace despite his recent war of words in the press. Mathewson, however, showed signs of folding under the pressure of the unusually critical glare of the media spotlight. He again showed an atypical side of his personality, yelling at a number of photographers who were taking pictures of him during pregame warm-ups.[64]

Nevertheless, he showed glimmers of his normal form in the first three innings of Game 4, but in the fourth inning, he again struggled to put out Baker, who doubled to spark a three-run rally. In the seventh inning, with the Giants down four-to-two, McGraw sent Marquard out to the bullpen but, likely still annoyed with both hurlers, he replaced Mathewson with Hooks Wiltse the following inning. McGraw would not turn to Mathewson again until the following season; instead, he would have to watch from the dugout as the A's bested the Giants' bullpen in Games 5 and 6 and claimed the nation's seventh World Series.

Mathewson and Marquard may not have won the World Series pennant, but they did reap some of its spoils. Each Giants player earned $2,346 in gate receipts, about one thousand dollars less than their counterparts in the A's organization. They also had found a relatively easy way of making some fast cash by ghostwriting articles with sportswriters such as McLinn and Wheeler. The player-author practice, as it had become known, was fast becoming controversial. An October 28, 1911, *Sporting Life* column decried the "petulant and disgraceful" practice as an attempt to "start a new lead for three editions of every afternoon" newspaper, noting that it would "detract from the dignity of the sport . . . with its partisan bias."[65]

Even so, a little controversy did not stop Cobb and Mathewson from taking advantage of the lucrative opportunity. After making an off-season trip to Cuba with his teammates, Mathewson sat down with Wheeler to collaborate on a weekly series of first-person "Inside Baseball" columns for the McClure Newspaper Syndicate. "Big Six," Wheeler later recalled, "supplied all the material, and I ran it through the typewriter, and it made a hit."[66] While touring as a stage actor in the play *A College Widow,* Cobb also continued to cash in on the practice. He served as guest sports editor at the *Knoxville Sentinel,* the *Atlanta Journal,* and the *Birmingham News.* The *Knoxville Sentinel* boasted of having Cobb, "the world's greatest ball player," as sports editor to provide some "live 'dope' as to his views of baseball and other sports."[67]

In spring 1912, G. P. Putnam's Sons published Wheeler's and Mathewson's "Inside Baseball" columns as *Pitching in a Pinch.* His memoir featured autobiographical tidbits about his rise in the big leagues woven together with a behind-the-scenes account of how to master inside baseball. The book featured chapters on the most dangerous hitters in professional baseball; the peculiarities of big-league pitchers; the superstitions of Major League ballplayers; the influence of fans, coaches, and umpires; and the ins and outs of pitching, hitting, and base stealing.

Intertwined throughout the book were "breezy" accounts from Mathewson's own career. In chapter 3, for instance, he told readers about one of the most poignant lessons that he had learned in the big leagues. The best pitchers, he contended, saved a little something for the pinch, "the time when each team is straining every nerve either to win or to prevent defeat."[68] "It is in the pinch that the pitcher shows whether or not he is a Big Leaguer," he wrote. "It is the acid test," and some men "cannot stand the fire."[69] "A man should always hold something in reserve, a surprise to spring when things get tight."[70]

He had learned to reserve something for the pinch during his first season with the Giants, he told readers. "Like all youngsters, I was eager to make a record during my first year in the big leagues," he remembered. "In one of the first games I pitched against Cincinnati, I made the mistake of putting all that I had on every ball."[71] He recalled once carrying a two-to-nothing lead into the ninth inning, but he had nothing left on the ball, and Cincinnati came back to defeat the Giants four-to-two. After the game, New York manager George Davis told him that the game should teach him "not to pitch your head off when you don't need to." "I have never forgotten that lesson," he wrote.[72] This strategy had served him well, he reminded readers; he had put the lesson to use in one of his classic pitcher's duels against Chicago Cubs hurler Mordecai "Three Finger" Brown in 1908.

Wheeler did his part to ensure the book's success. First, in March 1912, he penned a gushing introduction. Mathewson needed no introduction, he contended. The nation's schoolboys were more familiar with his name than that of George Washington because "George didn't play in the same league." "Besides being a national hero," Wheeler wrote, "Matty is one of the closest students of baseball that ever came into the Big League."[73] After putting his accomplishments from the mound in the proper context, he told his readers that the "college man" was "something of a writer, having done some newspaper work from time to time during the big series."[74] It was because of these accolades, he contended, that he had approached Mathewson to tell the "true tale of Big Leaguers, their habits, and their methods of playing the game . . . and he has done it."

Wheeler did not stop there. In addition to this fine piece of promotional bravado fit for a king, or at least baseball's greatest giant, he attempted to ensure the book's success with an endorsement in one of the best-read newspapers in the nation. In his memoir, Wheeler recalled that *New York Herald* book editor James Ford, unaware of his collaboration on the project, asked him to write the review. He jumped at the chance. "I could practically recite the book," he recalled. "I very much doubt whether any book ever got a more favorable review."[75] The publicity was effective.

Although exact sales figures for the book do not exist, the insider's look into baseball was a success. As baseball historian Frank Deford suggests, *Pitching in a Pinch* became a "fairly good seller" for Putnam.[76] Shortly after its release, it appeared on the *Boston Daily Globe*'s bestseller list. Librarians immediately endorsed the volume, celebrating it as an "inspiration to clean living."[77] Libraries from Chicago and Pittsburgh to Japan purchased copies of the memoir. In late 1912, Putnam would release two additional editions of the book under two subsidiary organizations—its Grosset & Dunlap children's division and the Boy Scouts of America's Every Boy's Library. The original book sold for one dollar, but the Boy Scouts edition, bound in cloth with the official Boy Scouts seal stamped on the front cover, was made available for fifty cents. G. P. Putnam's Sons were not the only ones to reap the rewards of the book's success. Wheeler and Mathewson would receive a half-interest in book royalties for the unforeseeable future.[78]

Over the next decade, the tight-knit relationships among Cobb, Mathewson, Rice, Wheeler, Lardner, and Lane would continue. In his memoir, Wheeler described sharing adjoining hotel rooms at Boston's Copley Plaza Hotel with fellow sportswriters C. E. Van Loan and Hugh Fullerton, cartoonist Clare Briggs, and baseball "experts" Christy Mathewson and Ty Cobb for the 1916 World Series.[79] Within these close confines, the two icons and reporters roughhoused with one another. They even pitched in when one of their chums got into a bit of trouble in the aftermath of a prolonged cocktail hour. When a still-inebriated Van Loan stumbled in during the early hours of the morning, complaining of a vicious hangover, Wheeler recalled that Cobb and Chicago-based sports journalist Hugh Fullerton were the first to step in. They supplied hangover remedies to their colleague.

The cronies, however, did more than share laughs over drinks; they profited from their cozy relationships. Sports journalists gained story material that, in the last instance, helped them earn a living. Cobb and Mathewson, on the other hand, earned a couple of extra dollars for doing little more than lending their names to sports stories. They also gained powerful advocates in their sports scribe pals. These men helped craft them into larger-than-life heroes, and through these friendships, they would have a hand in shaping their own images.

A little more than a year later, the companions—joined in their mutual admiration for each other, the national pastime, and its spoils—would head overseas together. This time, their foes would not consist of the mythological variety that coexisted in baseball dugouts and diamonds; instead, they would face a common enemy—the German Kaiser and his allies. The battle scars would entail more than a few bumps and bruises earned from sliding headfirst into third. These men would risk death fighting to extend American democracy. Some of the heroes of the sporting world almost did not make it back.

In the first three decades of the twentieth century, prominent sports journalists forged close working relationships with baseball icons. This, however, was not unusual. Human-interest reporters often formed personal relationships to gain insider information from celebrities. They gleaned material from a variety of interpersonal sources such as regular correspondence; personal conversations over dinner, on the golf course, or on hunting trips; or in interviews after games. They crafted these personal tidbits into dramatic myth-narratives and cast stars as cultural idols. Examining these interactions provides new insights into James Carey's ritual view of communication.[80] As cultural storytellers, sportswriters culled information from communal word-of-mouth interviews. Like Greek bards of another age, they wove these personal anecdotes into cultural myths that they retold to their readers.

As Sam "Wahoo" Crawford put it in his 1964 oral history with Ritter, Cobb was "palsy walsy" with top-notch beat reporters.[81] Entering into symbiotic alliances with baseball stars, these writers received rich interview material for human-interest features, and the icons, in turn, were granted some autonomy in their portrayal. By the mid-1910s, Cobb had begun suggesting story ideas to sympathetic sports journalists. In the 1920s, for instance, at his behest, Lane's *Baseball*

Magazine ran several articles about the plight of the retired ballplayer. Cobb also felt comfortable enough with his friends in the press to seek their counsel in times of crisis. For instance, feeling that he had been misquoted about an incident that occurred late in the 1920 regular season, Cobb sought Rice's help. When the Detroit Tigers arrived in New York, he called Rice at his Riverside Drive apartment, summoning him to his Commodore Hotel room immediately. He told Rice, "I've got to be at that game tomorrow and face the wolves. Your New York papers are sure steaming things up. But this, Grant, I want you to know! I never gave out any interview! I knew nothing of what happened until long after that game."[82] At times, these mutually beneficial working relationships evolved into something more. Journalists such as Wheeler moved into roles as collaborators and advisers that mirrored those of the era's public relations practitioners.

Sports journalists, like other entertainment reporters, engaged in celebrity promotion. In an attempt to remain in inside circles, however, they often only reported the positive information that they gleaned from working associations with increasingly publicity-savvy celebrities. Gallico noted that reporters who broke bread with icons found it difficult to maintain a level of detachment. The result was to become what *Detroit News* managing editor Malcolm Bingay called an "ungodly union" between sports stars and journalists.[83]

– 6 –

Crafting Kings of the Diamond

Baseball Magazine editor F. C. Lane gathered information about baseball stars everywhere. "He has talked with these players at their hotels, in the club houses before and after the game, on the player's bench, in the bull pen, everywhere," noted the introduction of his 1925 how-to batting book. "He has visited them in their winter homes and maintained an extensive correspondence."[1] By late 1911, he had stepped into the role of editor after the retirement of magazine founder Jacob Morse.[2] He soon, however, realized that in-person interviews and newsgathering strategies were not always feasible, and he learned to supplement on-site information gathered by freelance reporters with material gleaned directly from correspondence with players.

By the time Lane left the publication to pursue other interests in 1937, he had established an extensive correspondence with many well-known baseball stars. Most of his letters requested first-person accounts of off-season experiences. His letter to Max Bishop in October 1930 is typical of such correspondence. In a typewritten form letter, he wrote, "Public interest follows a popular Baseball player through the winter months. So our next few issues will carry a section devoted to personal letters and snapshots from my friends among the players of the Major Leagues." His letter continued, "As soon as you receive this letter won't you please sit down and write me a newsy account of what you have done since World's Series time, what you are doing now and what you plan to do before spring training?"[3] He also asked for several snapshots to be enclosed in a stamped addressed envelope. Over the years many players, including Mathewson and Cobb, complied with Lane's requests.

One of Lane's first actions in his position as *Baseball Magazine*'s editor was to write Cobb at his Augusta address. He told Cobb of his plans to dedicate the entire March 1912 issue to the star and asked for his assistance in assembling material. Cobb's response from Chicago on January 2, 1912, may have disheartened the fledgling editor. He replied offering his gratitude for the high honor: "I can only say I have never had such a compliment offered me in my life, and of course from my side of it I can't see where I deserve such notice." His touch of modesty was tempered by a noncommittal attitude about the whole affair. He explained that at present his busy schedule would not allow his assistance with the issue. "Whatever you suggest, I will try to carry out, but at this time I can't do anything as I have no time," he conceded.[4]

Cobb was being truthful when he said that his calendar was full. In winter 1912, he was touring the nation, appearing nightly as the football hero Billy Bolton in George Ade's comedy *The College Widow* for Vaughan Glaser's southern-based stock company. He was scheduled to appear in fourteen performances in the first week of January alone.

His lifestyle may have been taxing, but he was engaged in a lucrative off-season commitment. Newspapers reported that the budding thespian was earning ten thousand dollars.[5] While he was not as accomplished an actor as David Warfield, John Drew, or John Barrymore, he had a strong stage presence. As one critic aptly put it, he was "a better ball player than any actor and a better actor than any ball player."[6] When he was not on stage, he was filling his time with other commitments—attending post-performance receptions, visiting with prominent individuals in each community such as future president Woodrow Wilson, and serving as guest sports editor at newspapers across the Southeast.

Despite the generally warm reception he had received, by the time he wrote Lane he had decided to get out of show business as quickly as he could. "It is undesirable to me," he wrote, adding that he might have some time to help with the issue after the show closed in Cleveland on January 14. "After that date, I shall be glad to do anything I can toward making your magazine a success," he promised.[7]

Cobb was by now familiar with the power of publicity, and he soon changed his mind about the lengths he was willing to go to help with the special issue. He put Lane in touch with key sources, and he agreed to supply the new editor with answers to a few personal questions about his early life and career. His hectic schedule may not have allowed him to meet Lane in person, but he provided interesting tidbits about his personal life by mail. In doing so, he began a correspondence with Lane that would last until the end of his professional baseball career in 1928 and a friendship that would continue for decades.[8] In the end, he consented to participate, but his initial reply was not prompt.

Lane did not have time to worry about Cobb's tardy response. After taking the helm as editor of *Baseball Magazine* in late 1911, he had helped his associates move into their new office at 65 Fifth Avenue, in the heart of midtown Manhattan just a few blocks away from Central Park and Broadway. Lane might have even wandered over to the nearby Irish saloon, McSorley's Old Time Ale House, which was by that time a midtown institution entering its fifty-eighth year in operation.[9] He may have needed a beer to calm his nerves; he was, after all, putting together one of his first issues as editor, and at deadline, the magazine presses would not wait to roll for anyone, not even baseball's greatest hitter.

After making his initial inquiry, Lane set about constructing the issue. He assigned stories to a variety of individuals in the baseball community, from *Atlanta Constitution* sportswriter Howell Foreman to two well-known contributors—Chicago Cubs second baseman Johnny Evers and Detroit Tigers manager Hugh Jennings. Foreman would craft a feature article about Cobb's early background in Georgia while Evers and Jennings would write opinion columns about the Detroit star. The remaining articles would be handled in-house. Lane contributed much of the copy for the seven additional articles and briefs that ran without bylines.

He had only one more assignment to parse out. He needed to find someone to produce a striking cover. When Morse founded the monthly publication in 1908, he had made it his mission to provide readers with "first-class illustrations," and as the new editor, Lane retained this commitment.[10] It was one of the features for which the magazine was best known, and an intriguing cover helped move the product off newsstand shelves. For the formidable task, Lane turned to Gerrit A. Beneker, one of the promising young illustrators the magazine had on contract.

Beneker had begun his career as an artist when he moved to Brooklyn in 1905. Over the preceding seven years, he had found steady work as a freelance artist, composing ads for Ivory Soap and drawing illustrations for more than fifty magazine articles.[11] By 1912, he had gained acclaim for his early work, which reflected the industrial energy of America, and had become one of the magazine's featured cover artists the year prior. Cobb's visage was in good hands.

Now, only one piece was missing from Lane's hero-crafting work of art. After the initial inquiry, Cobb had volunteered to contribute some intriguing information to his very own number. Like his response to Lane's first letter, Cobb's story was late. He apologized for the belated reply, offering an alibi. Lane by now knew that Cobb had been trekking across the country as a stage actor, but this time his tardy response was because of a more practical matter. It seemed that Cobb was slow to adopt a new technological gadget. I "don't own a typewriter," he admitted. "I had to dictate it to a fellow who delayed somewhat by mailing it to me." After offering his excuses, he wrote that he hoped that his story would be "satisfactory," assuring Lane that he had free editorial control over the piece. "You can cut down as much as you like and make it appear as modest as you like," he wrote.[12] He ended the letter with one more apology and a guarantee, "Several points in this is [*sic*] new and never been in print."

Cobb's letter referred to his first bylined article for *Baseball Magazine*. In "Reminiscences of a Big League Player," he provided answers to a "list of questions" supplied by Lane that "the great American public would like to have answered."[13] Although he admitted in his sarcastic introduction that *Baseball Magazine* and its reading public had him up for "cross-examination" with a line of personal queries that he "would prefer to let someone else answer or dodge altogether," as a responsible "public servant" he had submitted to the interview. Contrary to Cobb's lead, the Q&A column was anything but hard-hitting journalism; in the piece, Lane lobbed him easy slow balls. Cobb told readers about his greatest plays, his favorite cities, his off-season hobbies, the toughest pitchers to hit, and the most difficult position to play on the diamond.

In the Cobb issue, Lane crafted the "Georgia Peach" as a hero in a "championship class" above the rest. Beneker's cover featured a smiling "Ty Cobb arriving at Training Camp." He was dressed comfortably in a regal three-piece suit with a white starched high-collar. He was surrounded by a cigarette-smoking sports reporter taking meticulous notes and a handful of African American children gazing up in awe of the star. Nearby sat his bat case and traveling trunk. Beneker's cover, like the magazine itself, paid homage to baseball's greatest hitter. Below the cover art, the magazine boasted of assembling the "greatest Ty Cobb stories ever written."[14]

Within the magazine, Lane, Foreman, Evers, and Jennings celebrated Cobb's virtues and accomplishments. Lane called him a "gentleman at all times, and under all conditions." He extolled his spectacular hitting and base-running feats, which drew thousands of spectators to games every season. The other professional sportswriter of the bunch crafted the famous southerner as "the hero of baseball . . . worshipped by every American boy . . . as well-known as President Taft—and more popular."[15] He wove a tale of a "chronic scrapper" with "an insatiable desire to play ball," who pulled himself up by the bootstraps to live the American dream as "the uncrowned king of baseball."

Baseball Magazine's player-correspondents also attested to his greatness. Manager Hugh Jennings wrote that he admired Cobb as a "player and as a man"; he decried the rumors that he was ever "inconsiderate of an opposing player," assuring readers from "personal knowledge that he would never be guilty of such an unsportsmanlike act."[16] Evers, too, crafted Cobb in heroic terms, writing that "the universal comparison of highest ability . . . is the model, the perfect stamp of the truly great ball player."[17]

Lane did not leave readers in doubt about the reason for his selection of Cobb for the issue. He was a national hero, worthy to be praised. In his editor's letter, he told his readers as much:

> This number of the BASEBALL MAGAZINE is dedicated to Tyrus Raymond Cobb. It seems like exaggerated praise to confer so much space on a single individual, but the man who has been for years the central figure of the National Game well deserves the title role in a magazine devoted to baseball and its interests. There are many popular favorites on the diamond, but only one Ty Cobb. Every city has its star; every section its particular shining light, but the wonderful outfielder of the Detroit Tigers is above and beyond them all. . . . It is fortunate, indeed, that the greatest player of the greatest game the world has ever known should be a man of so many admirable qualities. Barring an impulsive disposition, which shows itself to advantage in his lightning speed on the diamond, Cobb is an extremely likable person, fair-minded, generous, and altogether a typical American gentleman. We therefore cheerfully dedicate this number to the man whose brief, but meteoric career has made him the popular idol of American fans, the central figure of our National game, the king of ball players for all time.[18]

Lane always had a soft spot for Cobb and baseball's other great hitters. He would write a book about the art of hitting, but his admiration of Cobb was not the only thing that led to the magazine issue. In his editor's note, he offered another clue about his decision to construct a whole issue around "the greatest figure in our national game": "It seems popular nowadays to subpoena prominent men and make them disclose their opinions on various topics of general interest," he wrote. "Even John D. Rockefeller and Andrew Carnegie have been obliged to submit to the will of the people in this respect, as is eminently fitting." When he decided to dedicate a whole issue to Cobb in late 1911, Lane was responding to a new impulse in American journalism. The human-interest trend had given way to celebrity journalism, and the nation's publishers and editors now believed that their reading public had an insatiable desire to learn about the private lives of America's great men.[19]

Since the colonial era, magazine publishers had included biographies and later human-interest features and serials about American icons, but it was not until the early twentieth century that special issues centered on national celebrities were introduced. In 1905, *Collier's* and the *Saturday Evening Post* published special "Roosevelt" issues or numbers, as they called them.[20]

Lane's predecessor Jacob Morse had taken note of the remarkable popularity of these specialty publications. In summer 1908, he decided to create one for his fledgling journal. Just weeks after Boston Red Sox pitcher Cy Young recorded the third no-hitter of his career on June 30 and professional baseball honored him with Cy Young Day on August 13, Morse unveiled *Baseball Magazine*'s first player-themed issue—the Cy Young Number.[21] He followed the popular edition with another in June 1911. This one focused on the life and career of Cleveland Naps ace Addie Joss, who posted four twenty-win seasons, six sub-2.00 ERAs, forty-five shutouts, and one no-hitter before he retired in November 1910. Not long thereafter, he contracted tubercular meningitis and died suddenly in April 1911; Morse had chosen to honor him after his death.[22]

After Lane came on board as an associate editor in 1911, he and Morse began producing other special issues dedicated to the fans, the World Series, and even particular teams. After devoting two issues to pitching greats Cy Young and Addie Joss, in late 1911 Lane decided to publish an issue about baseball's greatest hitter. Although he did so under the auspices of giving the reading public something they were said to crave, he really had another motive in mind. He wanted to honor one of his favorite players and make a tidy profit in the process. He did just that.

In mid-May, shortly after the last of *Baseball Magazine*'s Cobb Numbers disappeared from newsstands across the country, the Georgia native made national news once again. This time, it was not for his batting average or even one of his notorious slides. Once more, Cobb stole national headlines for his off-the-field antics.

News of his fiery temper had begun to claim media attention back in September 1909 when he was charged with the attempted murder of an African American elevator operator. The following season, E. A. Batchelor of the *Detroit Press* reported that Cobb had nearly climbed into the grandstands of Tiger Stadium after being heckled by an African American New York Highlanders fan.[23] Police had defused the situation and thwarted what could have been an ugly brawl. At the time, Batchelor had defended Cobb: "Ty is a southerner born and bred, and naturally holds ideas of his own regarding the right of a colored man to abuse him in public."[24]

Although Cobb was rumored to be causing strife among his teammates, club president Frank Navin immediately came to his defense. "If [Cobb] were less impetuous, he would be less valuable to the club," he told reporters. "[He] comes from a section of the country where pride is strong."[25] Navin reminded the public of the South's culture of honor. Journalists would not be as understanding when Cobb's temper flared up against another Highlanders fan.

It all started when the Tigers, frustrated by their sixth-place league standing, stepped into New York's Hilltop Park for the first time of the season on May 11. The volatile crowd had applauded Cobb when he received an honor from popular entertainer George "Honey Boy" Evans. But soon enough their cheers turned to heckles when he almost came to blows with Highlanders third baseman Alvin Donlan. Their derision continued as the Tigers climbed out to a two-and-one series lead behind Cobb's sizzling bat. Despite the ceaseless taunts, Cobb posted a .416 batting average for the series.[26]

On May 15, the struggling club hoped to regain some momentum by winning the series finale. Throughout the series, Cobb had endured especially harsh scorn and ridicule from Highlanders fans down the left-field line. In the first inning, it continued. A man in an alpaca coat sitting near third base just behind Detroit's bench began insulting Cobb.

Cobb would later tell the reading public that the fan had heckled him in his previous appearances in New York. He had tried to keep his temper under control to avoid an incident. He even went so far as to return to the dugout from the first-base line in the middle of the first inning and to remain in the carriage park area located in deep centerfield when the Tigers went up to bat in the second inning. Nevertheless, by the second inning of the Wednesday afternoon game, Cobb and the man in the alpaca coat were trading insults back and forth.[27]

It became so vicious by the end of the third that Cobb asked New York manager Harry Wolverton and president Frank Farrell to remove the man. They refused, so he responded with another gibe of his own, yelling: "I was out with your sister last night."[28] The Highlanders heckler, Claude Lueker, responded in kind. Cobb later recalled: "He made a remark to me that no self-respecting man could fail to resent under any circumstances."[29] Tigers manager Hugh Jennings later told reporters that Lueker had called Cobb "a half-nigger" before making derogatory comments about his mother.[30]

Once in the dugout, his teammate Sam "Wahoo" Crawford asked if he was going to take the verbal lashing. Crawford's comment proved to be Cobb's undoing. The agitated outfielder hurdled over the grandstand railing, climbing twelve rows back before throwing himself at Lueker.[31] Even after being told by onlookers that the man in the alpaca coat had no hands, he continued to attack Lueker, who had lost one hand and several fingers in a printing-press accident. While kicking him, he reportedly yelled: "I don't care if he has no feet."[32] Cobb's teammates, who had an antagonistic relationship with the star, backed the southerner this time. Crawford and several Tigers stood near the railing, brandishing bats. After umpire Francis "Silk" O'Loughlin and park officers finally pulled Cobb off the badly beaten Lueker, "Tyrus the Terrible" returned to the bench with his teammates, where he remained until the middle of the seventh inning, when he trudged back to the clubhouse.

Sportswriters sitting in the press box behind home plate had a front-row view of the whole incident, and in the days following Cobb's brawl with Lueker, they wrote inch after column inch about it. Following the cue of Batchelor two years earlier, most baseball beat writers supported Cobb. The heckling by the Highlanders fan had gotten out of hand, they wrote, and all self-respecting southerners and, in fact, almost any white man would have reacted in a similar manner to such slurs.[33]

Sporting Life responded in kind. The journal's May 25 front-page news article presented Cobb's behavior as defensible but erratic. Richter acknowledged the heckler's inappropriate remarks, noting that Cobb was justified in his anger. Nonetheless, he had gone too far; his actions were, in the last instance, inappropriate. Richter still provided space for Cobb to defend himself. In a column-length statement, he explained: "The man who attacked me in New York is the same one who has made it unpleasant for me on other trips. . . . I lost my temper, jumped into the stand and let him have it. I am sorry for the effect which such an incident has on the game."[34] Charles Spink's *Sporting News,* however, was not so kind, calling Cobb a "natural insurrectionist" with a predisposition to "take the law into his own hands."[35]

After the Tigers' decisive eight-to-four victory, Johnson met with Cobb to listen to his version of the incident. On May 16, he wired Jennings that Cobb would be suspended indefinitely for the previous day's actions.[36] His decision would have far-reaching consequences. In an act of unity, Cobb's teammates refused to play until the southerner was reinstated. After defeating the Philadelphia Athletics six-to-three on May 17, fellow outfielder Davy Jones and his teammates issued a telegram to Johnson stating as much. The following day, Cobb and his teammates took the field, but the umpires told Cobb that he must leave. His teammates departed with him. Expecting the protest, Navin had arranged for a squad of strikebreakers, comprised of semiprofessional and college players, to take the field. They did. Nine innings later, they were soundly defeated by a score of twenty-four-to-two. Jennings canceled the series finale. On May 21, the players quietly ended their holdout when Cobb was reinstated.[37]

The incident and the subsequent players' strike—the first in professional baseball's history—was big news. National general-interest magazines even covered the affair. *The Independent,* a weekly journal of news and opinion, for instance, gave space to the episode.[38] In the end, most journalists were far more forgiving of Cobb than his striking teammates. Richter's *Sporting Life* called the players' strike "a woeful blunder . . . . [an] unprecedented, regrettable, and utterly useless revolt."[39] As one might imagine, Johnson found Cobb's actions to be less despicable than those of his teammates. He fined each of the striking players a hundred dollars. He only issued Cobb a fifty-dollar fine, and retroactively suspended him for ten days for the incident.[40]

Despite the costly fines, Detroit's strike was successful. Cobb was reinstated to professional baseball and by May 26 was back in a Tigers uniform. The incident created a new sense of solidarity among professional baseball players. After the episode, many players, disgruntled over low salaries and poor playing conditions, would lobby magnates for better treatment, and they would turn to professional baseball's royalty to serve as their spokesmen. Later that summer, Mathewson and Cobb agreed to serve as two of the co-vice-presidents of the fledgling Fraternity of Baseball Players of America.[41]

Cobb's name had been off the front pages of the nation's newspapers and magazines for only a few weeks when it returned to the headlines in August because of yet another violent episode. This time, he made news for his reaction to a would-be mugging. On August 11, he was traveling in New York with his wife, Charlie, in one of his prized Chalmers when three men jumped on the running board and began assaulting him. He thwarted the attempted robbery by beating one of his assailants with the end of his revolver and chasing the others away. He did not escape the incident without personal injury. He had sustained a knife wound but, after being treated, returned to Detroit's lineup in Syracuse the following afternoon.[42]

While Cobb's violent acts were claiming national headlines, Mathewson's name was not absent from the nation's sports pages. By mid-summer, while his new autobiography, *Pitching in a Pinch,* appeared on national bestseller lists, he was on his way to amassing another solid twenty-plus-win season, and his Giants looked primed to reclaim the National League pennant.[43] On the final day of the regular season, they led Pittsburgh, their nearest competitor, by ten games; by now, no one was left in suspense. They would take on the American League's dominant Boston Red Sox in the 1912 World Series.

A few days before the series opener, Rice, Wheeler, and three hundred of their peers attempted to cajole McGraw into announcing New York's starting pitcher. As they sat before McGraw in a pre-series press conference, he toyed with the nation's elite sportswriters. It might be Mathewson—or maybe it would be Marquard, or better yet, Tesreau. It might even be Hooks. "I'll see how the mood strikes me," he told them.[44]

Regardless of his antics, Rice reminded his *Evening Mail* readers on October 7 that the "advance fanfare [was] over. . . . And now, at the end of it, there is nothing left. Nothing left but the charge of the Night Brigade against the games at dawn to-morrow—and after that the first boding hush as Harry Hooper flies out from the Red Sox coop and stands face to face with Mathewson."[45] Like his colleagues, Rice believed that Mathewson would be the Giants' starter, but just as he had in the past, McGraw decided to reserve his veteran for Game 2; instead, he turned to the New York newcomer Jeff Tesreau, who had won seventeen games for the Giants during the regular season with a National League–low 1.96 ERA.

Unlike McGraw, Boston manager Jake Stahl had failed to surprise the cadre of sportswriters crowded in press row when he handed his ace hurler, "Smoky" Joe Wood, the ball in Game 1. Of course, some sportswriters might not have seen Wood saunter onto the field amidst the chaos of the press box. Although New York Giants owner John T. Brush had made significant improvements to the Polo Grounds when he rebuilt the facility a year prior, he had made only minor modifications to the press facilities. It was so cramped during World Series time, as Rice later recalled, that telegraph operators had to practically sit in the laps of the working press. It was virtually impossible to find space to type up their columns; even so, Rice had managed to elbow enough space to deliver more than fifteen hundred words about pregame warm-ups.[46]

Along with a sold-out crowd of more than thirty-five thousand fans, the sports scribes, among whom were Wheeler, Lardner, Lane, and player-author correspondents such as Ty Cobb, watched as Wood defeated Tesreau and the Giants four-to-three. Less than an hour later, Rice phoned in his twenty-five-hundred-word, inning-by-inning account of the match-up to his sports editor at the *Mail.* It appeared on the evening newspaper's front page a few hours later.[47]

After the game, Cobb, now collaborating with *New York American* baseball writer Damon Runyon, wrote a scathing critique of McGraw's late-game decisions to bring in a pinch hitter for Tesreau in the seventh and a pinch runner for catcher Chief Meyers in the ninth. McGraw was furious with Cobb, but after the first game he would do some carping of his own when his ghostwriter, *New York Times* reporter Harry Cross, condemned Meyers, not Tesreau, for losing the game.[48]

With all the finger-pointing going on in the national press, it looked as if the Giants might be fighting among themselves for the rest of the series. With the dissension of the prior year's World Series still fresh in his mind, Mathewson, once again collaborating with Wheeler, asked *New York Herald* readers if it was perhaps time "to put the pen and paper away and worry just about the bat and the ball."[49] His column appeared on Wednesday, October 9, the day he was slated to start in Game 2. He may have done well to take his own advice.

The Giants may have been critical of each other after the fact, but everyone on the roster felt very sure that their "old mainstay" would easily defeat the Sox in Boston. Alongside Mathewson's column, newspapers ran pieces with quotes from Marquard, Snodgrass, and even McGraw, who assured readers that the incomparable hero would tie the series at one. Mathewson, however, had more than thirty-eight hundred innings under his belt. Although the reliable right-hander had posted a stellar 2.12 ERA in his twenty-plus-win season, he was showing signs of fatigue.[50]

With his team down by one run in the fifth inning, he struggled from the mound. With one out, Hooper connected on his third single of the day; his teammate Steve Yerkes drove him home moments later after lining a triple over Snodgrass's head in centerfield. Mathewson's woes might have been worse if shortstop Art Fletcher had not masterfully handled a sharply hit line drive from Tris Speaker's bat on the next play.

In the top of the eighth, the Giants mounted a three-run comeback. After retiring Yerkes and Speaker, Mathewson was four outs away from tying the series; the New York faithful were confident that victory was near. Even after he allowed a ground-rule double to Duffy Lewis, the veteran appeared to have everything under control with the hitless Larry Gardner at the plate. Gardner hit what should have been a routine ground out toward Fletcher, but the ball scooted under his glove, and the Sox tied the game. Costly errors like these proved to be the hallmark for the Giants in the 1912 World Series. Even so, Mathewson managed to get out of the inning without giving up another run.

The score remained tied in the bottom of the ninth, and the game proceeded into extra innings. Both clubs managed a run in the tenth. The stalemate may have continued indefinitely, but umpire Silk O'Loughlin was forced to call the game. It was a heartbreaker, Rice told his *Mail* readers. "In a slashing, storming battle that tore the hearts out of 32,000 crazed fans and broke down even the players at work, New York and Boston fought eleven rounds into the edge of dusk today."[51]

Darkness had prevailed, but hope lingered for the Giants. The following day, amid national headlines that were already touting this year's world's championship as a "classic" for the ages, Marquard evened the series score.[52] The good fortune would not last for long.

Boston's ace "Smoky" Joe Wood easily outmatched Tesreau from the mound again in Game 4. He dealt a three-to-one defeat to a hostile crowd at the Polo Grounds. The two clubs were engaged in a bitter battle. "The opposing players do not talk to one another anymore except to snarl their remarks," New York's Christian Gentleman told the faithful readers of his column. "I suspect we haven't seen the last of the harsh words exchanged between us."[53]

Later that day, as Mathewson walked to the mound at Fenway Park, the Royal Rooters rattled the Giants with their incessant choruses of "Tessie." The Sox, likewise, gave Mathewson some trouble of his own early in the game. He managed to get out of pinches in the first and second innings; he even became the first Giant to connect for a hit on one of Boston's rookie ace Hugh Bedient's pitches, but he was left stranded in the third.

In the bottom half of the inning, he attempted to fool Boston slugger Harry Hooper with a change-up, but Snodgrass was the only one bamboozled during the at-bat. The New York center fielder had misjudged Hooper's high line drive. It soared over his head and became lodged in a tiny hole near the outfield bleachers. By the time Snodgrass retrieved the ball, Hooper was standing safe at third base. On the next play, Yerkes drove in Hooper. The Sox had claimed a one-run lead. Still, it appeared that Mathewson would clamber into the Giants' dugout with just one run on the board after tricking Speaker into getting on top of one of his famous fadeaways, but to the Royal Rooters' delight, the ball rolled under second baseman Larry Doyle's glove, and Yerkes headed home.

The Giants managed to drive in one run against Bedient in the seventh, but Doyle's miscue had cost them. After his error, Mathewson had walked off the field rubbing his arm; after the game, it was his heart that ached. He had gone on to retire the next fifteen batters after his troubles in the third inning, but it had not been enough. "It doesn't look like I'll ever win a world's series game again," he confided to friends later that evening.[54]

He would have another chance four days later. McGraw put the ball in the hands of the man who had proven to be his most reliable ace and his most trusted companion over the last decade for the deciding game of what would become the first true fall classic. The most hotly contested championship in the eight-year history of the World Series had left the sports scribes and their readers only to muse at the epic battle taking place. Rice may have summed it up best when he lamented two days earlier: "There is glory enough in a fight like this—and the only pity is that one must lose where another must win. Both have fought with too much heart and courage to miss the laurel which only one can wear."[55]

Crowds not only flocked to Boston's Fenway Park but also to electronic scoreboards located near newspaper offices across the nation, even as far away as Los Angeles. It appeared that the Giants had finally claimed the momentum in the series after handily defeating the Sox by a total of ten runs in Games 6 and 7. "The Red Sox had us on the ropes," McGraw told the New York press corps in the pre-game press conference, "but we survived, and now we're ready to take what is rightfully ours."[56] All of his players seemed just as convinced. A few games ago their public carping may have indicated that they were on the verge of in-fighting, but they were now the picture of solidarity. Everyone was certain that Mathewson would deliver the coveted title that had eluded the Giants the year prior—everyone except Christy, that is.

Earlier that day in his morning column, he had admitted to Wheeler and his reading public that he was "tired." "I think all of the fellows on both teams are tired," he conceded. "The baseball season is a long grind. . . . After today, we can relax. But we have a ballgame to play first."[57] Mathewson was no longer the sprightly champion of 1905 who had pitched twenty-seven scoreless innings and shutout the A's. His worn arm may have ached, but he appeared calm on the mound. He got into pinches in the first, second, and sixth innings, but he maneuvered his way out of them as quickly as they came. In the third inning, his teammates gave him all that it appeared he might need—one run, one piece of insurance.[58]

With two outs in the seventh and a runner on second, however, Mathewson faced a hitter he had never seen before. Olaf Henriksen would pinch hit, and "Smoky" Joe Wood would come in to relieve Bedient in the top of the eighth inning. Over the last twelve years, the Giants veteran had learned the peccadilloes of his opponents; he used this knowledge to fool his foes. He had never faced Henriksen, and the rookie knew it. He waited for Mathewson to toss a pitch he liked; with the count tied at two balls and two strikes, he bet that Mathewson might throw him one of his curves. He did, and Olaf drove the pitch down the third-base line.

The Sox had tied the game. In the tenth inning, it appeared that Merkle might forever redeem himself for the boneheaded base-running error that he had committed four years earlier. He lined Wood's fastball past Speaker in centerfield to drive in teammate Red Murray, the potential winning run, from second. After striking out Herzog on three consecutive pitches, Wood sacrificed his pitching hand to knock down what looked to be a hit from Meyers that would have scored Merkle and given the Giants a much-needed insurance run. His bloody hand may have stung, but it proved worthwhile as

"Smoky" Joe claimed the final out of the inning and made his exit from the field.

In the bottom of the inning, Mathewson faced pinch-hitter Clyde Engle, who had replaced the injured ace. One could almost hear the cheers from New York's Times Square as he got under one of Mathewson's fastballs and sent a lazy fly ball sailing into centerfield. If Snodgrass caught the routine fly, the Giants would be two outs from claiming their first series since 1905. Snodgrass, however, committed an unlikely error. He dropped the routine fly ball. Now, Engle, the tying run, was at second base with no outs.

"Snow," as his teammates called him, redeemed himself on the next play—making a diving catch in center to rob Hooper of a game-tying RBI. Even so, the close contest was beginning to rattle Mathewson's nerves, and he walked Yerkes, the next batter. The go-ahead run was on first base, and Speaker was striding to the plate. When Speaker popped up in foul territory on the next play, it appeared as if the Giants were one out away from their second world championship. Merkle was waiting to make the easy catch, but with his past boner likely in Mathewson's mind, the Christian Gentleman did something a bit unsportsmanlike. He called Merkle off, begging instead for Meyers to make the catch. In the chaos, the ball dropped between the trio.

Speaker crushed the next pitch. Engle scored. The game was tied. The momentum had once again shifted to the Sox. With the bases loaded, Gardner connected on a pitch that brought in the winning run. Lardner, now with the *Boston American,* wrote: "Just after Yerkes crossed the plate . . . there was seen one of the saddest sights in the history of a sport that is a strange and wonderful mixture of joy and gloom. It was the spectacle of a man, old as baseball players are reckoned, walking from the middle of the field to the New York players' bench with bowed head and drooping shoulders, with tears streaming from his eyes, a man on whom the team's fortunes had been staked and lost . . . the man was Christy Mathewson."[59] When the heartbroken hero trudged into the Giants' clubhouse, he attempted to soothe the inconsolable Snodgrass for what would become known in baseball lore as his "$30,000 muff."[60] It was his own fault, he claimed, for calling off Merkle. When he finally reemerged, a line of Sox fans were waiting to congratulate him on the hard-fought series.

The Giants' own blunders had cost them their second consecutive series, but New York's writers were looking for a fall guy, and they were not about to pin the loss on Mathewson. Instead, they found a scapegoat in Snodgrass. "Write in the pages of world's series baseball history the name of Snodgrass. Write it large and black. Not as a hero; truly not. Put him rather with Merkle, who was in such a hurry that he gave away a National League championship," Harry Cross told *New York Times* readers the next day. "Snodgrass was in such a hurry that he gave away a world championship."[61]

Even Rice could not avoid the temptation to place the blame at Snodgrass's feet. "By muffing an easy fly ball in the tenth round," he wrote, "Fred Snodgrass to-day cost New York the championship of the world and Christy Mathewson one of his gamest, greatest games."[62] Later, Rice had a change of heart. He admitted that Mathewson's own miscue had contributed to the club's defeat. Those two plays, he wrote, "which you or I, weary reader, who possibly haven't handled a ball in years, could make with one hand while lighting a pipe with the other," had cost the Giants their second title in a row.[63] Rice ended his fifty-thousand-word week with a rhyme to remind readers that in the end even baseball's kings were human:

> We hold no grief for what he's done;
> Nor classic "bone" he may have spun.
>
> . . . .
>
> But from the throng, with glaring grim,
> Who curse what happened there, let him
> Who's yet to make the first mistake
> Step up and pan him for the break.[64]

Still looking for a hero from the 1912 World Series, New York writers settled on their old faithful. Mathewson may have finished the series without a victory, but he was still the nation's peerless champion. He may not have been as reliable from the mound as he had been in 1905, but he was a remarkable man. He had given all of his effort, and even in defeat, he had proven that he was more valiant than ever. He was a fitting national idol, who was above all a Christian gentleman.[65]

In the November 16, 1912, issue of *Literary Digest,* editor Robert Joseph Cuddihy included an excerpt from *New York Evening World* sportswriter Bozeman Bulger. In the piece, Bulger had followed the cue of many of his colleagues. Mathewson, he told readers, was the "real hero" of the 1912 World Series.[66]

By 1912, on the shoulders of two giants, baseball had captured the attention of the masses. In 1913, writers would marvel over their fame in the nation's sports pages, its specialty baseball journals, and its general-interest magazines. Sportswriters continued to cast them as the two kings of the national pastime.

–7–

Ghosts and Ghouls

On December 26, 1912, a house editorial in *Life* magazine noted: "Americans are a natural race of hero-worshippers. From the days of Admiral [George] Dewey and [heavyweight champion] Jim Jeffries to the present era of Ty Cobb . . . we have steadily insisted upon exalting certain individuals into a limelighted sphere in which they are seemingly unhampered by any ordinary human attributes."[1] Americans, it seems, had a natural propensity for celebrating extraordinary men as superhuman. In the piece, the *Life* editor acknowledged the extent to which sports heroes such as Jeffries, Cobb, and Mathewson had risen to the level and even replaced heroes of war in American culture.

Four years later, America was on the brink of entering a great war, but the masses were still consumed by baseball heroes. Novelist Harold Kellock wrote in *The Bookman,* a literary journal established in 1895 by Dodd, Mead, and Company, that Cobb's fame and baseball's popularity were solely the creation of the sports column. "It is the Column that has made baseball. Before the appearance of the Column public interest in sport was sporadic merely," he wrote.[2] He contended that without the sportswriter professional baseball and its cast of characters would be penniless, virtual unknowns. Kellock was having a chicken-and-egg moment.

Regardless of which came first, Cobb's and Mathewson's fame or the coverage of it, one thing is certain: an American would have had to work hard to miss the mass-mediated coverage of them. They had reached the pinnacle of fame for their feats on the baseball field. In December 1912, general-interest magazines such as *Life* and children's magazines such as *Youth's Companion* continued to craft Cobb and Mathewson as national heroes. Their fates, however, were not altogether sealed. In 1913, both would be portrayed as greedy sinners by some segments of the national media. Still, they knew they would always have allies in Rice, Wheeler, Lardner, and Lane. The publicity-savvy icons attempted to use their relationships with these four sympathetic journalists to cement images of their own making in the American imagination.

No sooner had *Life* magazine cast Cobb as a national hero than did he once again make news for something other than his magnificent feats on the baseball diamond. In March 1913, he was back in the headlines for what amounted to treachery in some segments of the world of baseball. He was demanding a higher salary.

Cobb had first held out for more money in 1908. On that occasion, Detroit Tigers president Frank Navin had offered him a flat three-thousand-dollar annual contract, a standard amount for a quality player in those days. He had demanded much more—a three-year, five-thousand-dollar annual contract, which provided personal exemption from professional baseball's ten-day release and included a guarantee of pay even if he should become incapacitated. After extensive negotiations and a war of words in the press, the two parties had settled on a one-year, four-thousand-dollar contract with the promise of an eight-hundred-dollar bonus if Cobb could achieve another season with a .300 batting average. He did. He also delivered an American League pennant. Navin had been much more generous the following year, offering the star a three-year, nine-thousand-dollar annual agreement.[3]

By 1913, Cobb's contract was up for renegotiation. This time, the superstar demanded nearly twice his current pay—an annual salary of $15,000. After winning six consecutive batting titles and tallying a batting average of more than .400 for two straight seasons, he thought he was worth it. He believed that he was drawing fans to Detroit's Navin Field. He used the nation's sportswriters' own words to justify his demands. In August 1912, *Sporting Life* had estimated that he was responsible for contributing at least $30,000 to Navin's coffers during the course of the season.[4] He only wanted half of that, he reasoned; he was a bargain.

When Cobb held out in 1908, he found only one ally in the press, the *Augusta Chronicle,* his hometown newspaper. He did not fare much better in early 1913. The sports world, by and large, painted Cobb as a villain for his treasonous demands. On February 1, 1913, for instance, Francis Richter's *Sporting Life* chided the star for the "harm caused by his salary hold-out."[5] Even if Cobb had won a partial victory, Richter wrote, "it was dearly bought by appreciable loss in prestige, reputation, and public sympathy."

For the next two months, he and Navin traded words of venom in the press. Navin claimed that his antics were not only hurting the club's morale, they were also contributing to the Tigers' demise in the American League. "He has grown to believe that his greatness precludes his being subject to club discipline," Navin told reporters.[6] Cobb fought back. He told sympathetic sportswriters that Navin had not "seen fit to throw mud" and "blacken my name" during his undercompensated "pennant-winning years."[7]

In late April, after extensive contract negotiations, Cobb signed a one-year, twelve-thousand-dollar contract. Richter was right; the damage to his reputation had been done. Many sportswriters used the holdout as an excuse to craft Cobb as a villain in the national press. Charles Spink's *Sporting News,* for instance, wrote that his actions had been "detrimental to baseball." He predicted that his "most glorious years [were] behind him."[8]

Cobb did not mind the bad press all that much. He had always used his image of a "demon in spikes" to strike fear in the hearts of his opponents. He would use his villainous image now as motivation. It would be his personal inspiration. What he did not realize then was that he might one day come to regret his ruthless, cutthroat image that was emerging in the national press.

Despite the unfavorable publicity, Cobb still had a number of allies in the sportswriting community, among them Rice, Wheeler, Lardner, Lane, and former Detroit-based Tigers beat writer Harry Salsinger. Life, however, was changing for these writers in 1913. Salsinger had recently transitioned into his new position as sports editor for the *Detroit News;* meanwhile, Lardner had resigned from his position as editor of the *Boston American* to take one of the most coveted positions in the nation.[9] In the aftermath of legendary sportswriter Hugh E. Keogh's retirement, Lardner was to be the editor of the *Chicago Tribune*'s "In the Wake of the News" column. As Keogh's successor, he would pen the daily column, which consisted of a collection of humorous tidbits about the national sports scene and all the day's news. From this post, he also would freelance at some of the nation's most prestigious magazines—the *Saturday Evening Post, American Magazine, Collier's,* and *Redbook,* among others.[10]

He would be joined in this pursuit by Rice, who had begun writing for *Collier's* the year prior and would add many of these same magazines to his freelance list in 1913. By this time, he was making more than $100 per week at the *Mail,* and his "Sportlight" column was being syndicated to newspapers across the nation. In late 1914, he would accept an astounding offer from New York newspaper publisher Ogden Reid. For $280 per week, he would draft his daily "Sportlight" column. In accepting a position on the staff of the *New York Tribune,* he joined the ranks of New York sportswriting royalty with men such as editor W. O. McGeehan and columnist Heywood Broun.[11]

In the meantime, in 1913, his pal John N. Wheeler was in the midst of some transitions of his own. In 1911, Wheeler had begun collaborating on "Inside Baseball" columns with some of the game's biggest stars. He watched as the *New York Herald* sold these pieces to McClure Newspaper Syndicate for a tidy profit, earnings that he never saw. Over the next year, while he covered the New York Giants and attempted to polish Mathewson's columns into a best-selling autobiography, he had made a number of friends in the sportswriting and publishing world. It only stood to reckon in 1913, when his superiors at the *Herald* refused to give him a basic raise, that he would launch out on his own. He decided to establish Wheeler Syndicate. It would specialize as a sports news distribution agency.[12]

In the prior two decades, news clearinghouses had become profitable business ventures. They allowed smaller newspapers, which lacked the financial resources and interpersonal connections to obtain political exposés and celebrity human-interest stories, to purchase the material from the nation's elite journalists and news organizations. With sports celebrities now a popular cultural phenomenon, Wheeler hoped to capitalize on the new niche. His idea worked.

Ever the generous soul, he hoped to share his good fortune with his chums. In April 1914, he wrote Ring Lardner to inquire if he would be interested in penning a "series of humorous articles to be run once a week, for syndication purposes."[13] He had hoped to hire out one of the biggest names in the sporting world. To entice Lardner, he offered him 50 percent of the profits. It is unclear why, but Lardner declined this initial request. He would be quick to take him up on his next offer in 1919.

Despite Lardner's rebuff, over the next two years Wheeler's venture became quite profitable, so much so that he expanded the syndicate to include the collection and distribution of all news and entertainment content. In 1916, looking to eliminate their competition, McClure Newspaper Syndicate, the nation's oldest and largest news clearinghouse, purchased it. Not to be outdone, Wheeler immediately started another operation—Bell Syndicate—and set about to hire the nation's best writers, including Rice and Lardner.

In the hiatus, Wheeler continued to collaborate with Mathewson. By January 1913, Mathewson's *Pitching in a Pinch* was a success. It was so popular that *Sporting News* publisher Charles Spink approached Wheeler and Mathewson to serialize the story and republish it in his magazine. They agreed, and *Pitching in a Pinch* began appearing in the *Sporting News* the next month.[14]

Mathewson had been extra busy during the off-season. In the winter months, he and McGraw had appeared in the one-reel silent film *Breaking into the Big Leagues.*[15] After production ended, Matty sat down with playwright Rida Johnson Young to write the four-act baseball comedy *The Girl and the Pennant.* As always, he made headlines for his involvement in the two productions. In April 1913, the

New York Times reported on his part in the project. Mathewson likely read the piece. He read all the day's news, and he put his knowledge of current events to use in *The Girl and the Pennant.*[16]

The light comedy, which featured the story of a young girl who inherited her father's baseball club, was taken almost directly from newspaper headlines. Two years earlier, in March 1911, Helene Hathaway Britton had assumed control of the St. Louis Cardinals when her uncle, M. Stanley Robertson, died. Young's and Mathewson's main character, Mona Fitzgerald, was based in part on Britton. True to life, Fitzgerald refused to sell her club to the highest bidder. Over the next three acts, Fitzgerald and her friends faced overt sexism and subtle subterfuge from men who resented a woman's encroachment in the national pastime. In the end, Young and Mathewson portrayed Fitzgerald as a purifying element in professional baseball; however, she was ultimately dependent upon the trustworthy men in her life. It seems that the playwrights had taken a cue from journalists such as Chadwick in their fictionalized account.

The Broadway play debuted in the Lyric Theatre late that fall. Although Mathewson and McGraw starred in the comedy, it was not a successful production, running for only twenty performances. A *Life* theater critic considered the play's downfall in the November issue: "The baseball 'fan' is a wary bird, and perhaps not much of a theatergoer."[17] As for Mathewson's part in penning the play, it was the correspondent's conjecture that he probably had as much to do with it as the reputed authors of "most of the baseball stories printed in the yellow journals."

Wheeler's ears may have burned. The following year, he would pair with Cobb to craft his autobiography, *Busting 'Em and Other Big League Stories,* much as he had done for Mathewson. He also added other stars to the list of individuals with whom he collaborated. "In one World Series, I was turning out expert copy for about eight stars," he recalled.[18]

In the meantime, Cobb continued to write articles on everything from the element of luck in hitting to the value of a slide in 1913.[19] He still occasionally served as guest editor at local and regional newspapers. For instance, the *Atlanta Journal* gave readers notice that in three days Cobb would provide "plenty of good, live sporting gossip, as the 'Georgia Peach' is right there when it comes to handing out articles on the great national game."[20] The *Journal* assured readers that Cobb, who had covered the past few World Series for magazines and newspapers, "is a good writer and knows just what the baseball public wants making him a good sports editor."

The ghosts of Cobb, Mathewson, and other baseball stars kept them in the national spotlight year-round, but the player-author practice was becoming quite controversial. The players were painted as greedy ghouls for their part in the arrangement. On February 1, 1913, Frank Farrell, owner of the New York Yankees, derided ghosted material. "Everybody knows the majority of players do not write the articles which appear under their names," he told *Sporting Life.*[21] "Many arguments have resulted between players about articles which players are supposed to have written about other players, when in reality some newspaper man wrote the stories." He was likely referring to the infamous spat between Mathewson and Marquard in the 1911 World Series or McGraw's criticism of his own players throughout the 1912 season. He may have even had another incident on his mind, one that had hit closer to home. Whatever the case, by 1913 ghostwriting was prevalent in professional baseball; however, Farrell believed that the fad would soon die out. It did not.

By March 1913, American League president Ban Johnson publicly condemned the practice, issuing an edict forbidding American League managers and players from having pieces appear under their signature. "I would not mind so much if the players themselves wrote the stuff which appears in the newspapers throughout the land, but in the great majority of cases the players never see the stories to which their names are appended until after they have been printed," he told *Sporting Life* of the practice that he called "repugnant to the dignity of base ball."[22] The articles, he claimed, had injured the league. The "players have boasted of their 'soft money,' and asserted they never even saw the articles or the men who wrote them," he wrote. "This is unfair to the public and to the players who are criticized, not by a fellow player, but the writer of the article." The act tarnished the image of the game, Johnson and other league leaders contended, because it deceived the public and handicapped clubs by revealing insider information.

On March 15, *Sporting Life* followed Johnson's statement with an exposé. Correspondent William Peet revealed that more than a dozen player-authors had earned as much as a thousand dollars for articles appearing under their byline. Even the beloved Matty, for the sake of "soft money," allowed the "dear old public [to fall] for this stuff and [they] swallowed hook, bait and sinker," he contended.[23] Newspaper publishers, he wrote, "regarded these feature articles as good investments, for the reason that the stories were syndicated to twenty-five or more outside publications, and the revenue derived not only paid the amount guaranteed the baseball player for the use of his name, but left a handsome profit." Peet's investigative piece included an information box with the names of guilty player-authors and the journalists who actually penned the pieces. The list included John N. Wheeler of the *New York Herald;* "Stoney" McLinn of the *Philadelphia Public Ledger;* Ralph McMillan of the *Boston Herald;* Bill MacBeth of the *New York Tribune;* Walter Trumbull, the New York–based, Harvard-grad sports scribe; Tim Murnane, sports editor of the *Boston Globe;* George Tidden of the *New York Journal American;* Paul Shannon of the *Boston Post;* and Jack O'Leary of the *Boston Herald.*

By the final week of March, the New York and Brooklyn chapters of the Baseball Writers' Association of America had joined Johnson in condemning the practice. The resolution denounced player-scribes, who worked "to deceive the Base ball reading public; to lower the tone and dignity of the sport; to cause serious friction in the various teams; and to misrepresent the aims of the base ball writer."[24] It seems that the actions of Wheeler and some of his cronies were beginning to frustrate other baseball beat reporters. They were likely concerned that the players' expert accounts and behind-the-scenes glimpses might undermine their careers.

Although Wheeler claimed to have collaborated on articles for Cobb and Mathewson, writing copy based on detailed interviews, he later recalled why the practice was so widely scorned during the era. MacBeth, ghostwriter for Yankees pitcher "Wild Bill" Donovan, wrote under Donovan's byline that the National League Boston

Braves would sweep the American League Philadelphia Athletics in the April 1913 opening series. "Donovan, being an American Leaguer, was searching for MacBeth with murder on his mind," Wheeler recalled of the unauthorized statement. "He insisted MacBeth's prediction was ridiculous and made him look bad." After it came true, Donovan "stuck his chest out . . . [and] claimed MacBeth had had nothing to do with the prediction."[25]

Throughout the next two seasons, *Sporting Life* provided regular coverage of the "player-author evil." From March 1913 until September 1914, the publication ran twenty-three articles on the topic. Even Mathewson was not immune to criticism. On July 26, 1913, *Sporting Life* included an excerpt from the *Philadelphia Bulletin* belittling Mathewson, whose idea of collaborating consisted "of drawing royalties and watching your name on the programs, billboards, etc., while the party of the second part does the work."[26] Other columns reminded readers of the strife the practice caused among teammates or considered why National League president Thomas J. Lynch did not censure the practice.[27] Some player-authors such as Cobb argued that Johnson's edict curtailed player liberties, defending himself "on the ground that he really [wrote] the articles attributed to him."[28]

By September 20, 1913, Cobb made front-page headlines when he revealed his plan to syndicate articles about the upcoming World Series. "I have always written my own stories," he told *Sporting Life*, "and believe that any fellow who has been in the game any length of time and who has ordinary intelligence can write stories and write them so that the public can understand them."[29] He rebuked players who did not write the articles under which their bylines appeared but refused to have his freedom curtailed.

By September 27, 1913, Cobb, Mathewson, four of his teammates, and two Philadelphia Athletics stars had signed freelance newspaper contracts to cover the 1913 World Series. The defiant action prompted the National Commission to issue a rare bulletin forbidding any participant of the World Series from covering games. "This radical step," wrote *Sporting Life* editor Francis Richter, "was the result of the abuses that have been created and fostered by this fraudulent and mercenary player-author ship [*sic*]."[30] Under the legislation, World

Series participants who had signed contracts with news organizations prior to September 27, 1913, were permitted to honor their legal obligations, but future agreements were prohibited. The National Commission hoped to appease some members of the Baseball Writers' Association with the edict.[31]

During the 1913 season, Mathewson and Cobb had not only endured attacks from baseball moguls and sportswriters, who condemned ghostwriting; they also had encountered the grumbling of critics, who claimed that their best playing days were over. They had proven the naysayers wrong. Their best playing days were not over. Although neither posted numbers quite as good as they had at their peak, they still ranked among the leaders at their respective positions. Cobb once again delivered from behind the plate. His .390 batting average led the American League, but it did not help his team out that much. They finished in a dismal sixth place.[32] Mathewson, meanwhile, pitched four shutouts en route to twenty-four victories and a third consecutive World Series.[33]

The duo's unceasing national fame caused correspondents at national general-interest magazines to marvel. In July, one *Life* magazine contributor bemoaned the "awful ignorance" of not being able to say "what position does Ty Cobb play."[34] Any American man, woman, or child would reveal the "depth of [their] ignorance" not to know the names of Cobb or Mathewson. In late August, Wheeler, now also a freelance contributor for *Literary Digest,* pondered why "the fame of Christy Mathewson, of the New York Giants, seems to go on forever."[35] The two-page feature article contended that his love of the game was the key to his success and longevity.

Behind the arms of Mathewson and Marquard, the Giants headed to the World Series once more. Before a hostile crowd at Philadelphia's Shibe Park, Mathewson showed a glimpse of his 1905 self in Game 2. In a match-up with A's ace Eddie Plank, he pitched a flawless shutout into extra innings. In the top of the tenth, his teammates supplied three runs behind a crucial Art Fletcher single. The victory proved to be his fifth and final in world championship competition.[36]

Mathewson would not repeat his performance when he appeared on the mound again in Game 5. After some rough early inning play, he found himself down three-to-one in the fifth. His bat had been hot in the series. He had already logged three hits, but his arm was failing him. In the ninth inning, sensing that the peerless champion was done for, McGraw substituted a pinch runner for his champ. Mathewson was visibly shaken by what he saw as the ultimate betrayal. The Giants would go on to lose the series finale seven to five.[37]

After the series, Mathewson, with the assistance of his favorite collaborator, aired some of his complaints in an article in *Everybody's Magazine,* a literary publication founded in 1899 by Philadelphia department store tycoon John Wannamaker. He called McGraw the ultimate puppet master, who "manipulated" his "team of puppets" "from the bench on a string."[38]

Mathewson's comments may have cut McGraw, but they did not violate league rules. Although the National Commission had prohibited World Series participants from covering the event, it did not have the jurisdiction to forbid the act during the regular season, which was up to the discretion of individual clubs and newspaper publishers. Thus, the practice, though denounced in national magazines such as *Sporting Life,*[39] persisted.

Later that year, Lane's *Baseball Magazine* joined in the fight against baseball's ghosts. Instead of condemning the player-correspondents, Lane chose to ridicule them through parodies in a November 1913 column, "The Player Authors." This piece of literary journalism included fictional dialogue between the "poor gick" ghostwriter and the player-author. Lane included the "polished story" by "Hurler Jinxwell," along with what he had actually dictated to his ghost: "Huh? Aw, yuh know's well as I do. We got it in the neck. And we're goin' tuh get it there some more. To-day's game? Say, kid, take it from muh: we got as much chance to beat these guys out as a stewed monkey has tuh sing grand operaw. How'd we lose? We lost because that wart uv nature McIvoree stole third with the bases full."[40]

After the *Everybody's Magazine* piece was published, Mathewson would persevere as a pitcher and a player-author. Unlike the practice of ghostwriting, the American hero would no longer be condemned in the public eye. For Mathewson, Lane and his cronies only reserved praise. The following year, the *Baseball Magazine* editor would dedicate his latest player-themed issue to the Christian Gentleman.[41]

Cobb, too, remained in the headlines of the specialty magazine. Sportswriters continued to cast the pair as the kings of the diamond. In Mathewson, they found a respectable middle-class hero; in Cobb, they saw a complex icon that defied definition. Over the next four years, the duo was prominently featured in the headlines of newspaper sports pages, on the covers of specialty sports publications, and in the pages of general-interest magazines. It was within this space that sportswriters crafted baseball's preeminent sinner and its quintessential saint. Cobb, Mathewson, and the mythmakers that made them would continue to take advantage of their cozy relationships, and they would all reap rewards from the images they created.

– 8 –

The Quintessential Saint and the Preeminent Sinner

In the foreword to *The Golden People*, New York–based sportswriter Paul Gallico opined, "A writer . . . in the final analysis writes to earn a living. But often the subject matter he chooses, and the manner in which he presents it, is done for his own pleasure and escape."[1] His words reminded readers of the agency involved in the practice of writing. Sportswriters experienced some autonomy in how they covered sports icons, enjoying a level of freedom that historians have often overlooked.[2]

Gallico, however, paints an overly simplistic portrait of a journalist's ability to cover sports stars any way they chose. Sports reporters were bound by economic, cultural, and social forces. Cultural values, professional working conditions, interpersonal relationships, lingual conventions and forms, and the need to make a living inevitably structured their portrayals of celebrity athletes. Sports journalists and the men they covered enjoyed various degrees of independence; to a great extent, their freedom was based on the level of power they had obtained in their professions. It was the celebrity athlete, not the sports journalist, who claimed the most autonomy in their relationships, but ultimately, it was the sportswriter who had the last word.

In early 1914, there were rumors that war overseas was imminent. Social unrest caused by years of rule at the hands of expansionist monarchs and concerns over the lingering imperial impulses of European powers caused some countries to forge alliances with like-minded nation-states and to stockpile weapons. European powers had increased their military spending by 50 percent in the previous half-decade.[3]

Closer to home, war had already been declared in professional baseball. In 1912, two groups had attempted to organize professional leagues that were independent of the National Association of Professional Baseball Leagues. In 1913, John T. Powers formed the Federal League, an organization of six clubs in Chicago, Cleveland, Indianapolis, Pittsburgh, St. Louis, and Covington, Kentucky. Like their predecessors, they had struggled financially during their inaugural season, but they managed to complete the 120-game schedule.[4] Under new leadership the following year, they sought to lure away star talent from the National and American leagues with promises of higher salaries. They wanted to sign many of the seven hundred members of the Fraternity of Baseball Players of America, or the Baseball Players' Fraternity as it was referred to in most circles. Federal League leaders knew that many fraternity members were disgruntled with the current conditions in professional baseball. In particular, they had their sights set on the superstars of the Major Leagues. They did not consider, however, that by 1914, due in part to the work of the fraternity president, David Fultz, conditions were slowly improving in professional baseball.

Two years earlier, when the organization had formed, shortly after the Tigers' infamous player strike on behalf of their embattled teammate, Fultz and other fraternity leaders had begged Major League ownership for higher salaries, less restrictive reserve clauses, better protection against overzealous fans, and financial assistance for deserving ball players who had fallen on difficult times.[5] During summer 1913, Cobb, one of the organization's vice-presidents, had spoken with F. C. Lane about the latter demand. Lane reported on the details of their conversation in the September 1913 *Baseball Magazine*. "When Ty Cobb was last in New York I spent a very interesting evening in his company," he told readers. During their jaunt around Grand Central Station, he reported, Cobb had "regaled [him] with an inexhaustible store of reminiscence from his own meteoric career."[6] In addition to providing him with material for his next human-interest feature, he had received details about the plight of players going through hard times. Cobb had become a player advocate, and he hoped to find a sympathetic ally in Lane.

By 1913, Lane's *Baseball Magazine* had already proven itself to be a friend of the Players' Fraternity. It provided regular space for columns written by fraternity president David Fultz.[7] Consequently, it became an informal promoter of the fraternity and a de facto mouthpiece for the organization. It should come as no surprise then that Lane published Cobb's concerns about the misfortunes of underpaid athletes in "Why Players Fail: Scenes from the Real Life of the Diamond—Mental and Physical Troubles which Handicap the Player—The Undertow in Baseball."[8]

Over the next two decades, Lane continued to publish Cobb's thoughts on the players' struggles along with promotional features about the "Georgia Peach." Often these stories included editorial notes such as "revealed in" or "from" or "comprising an interview with Ty Cobb," which ran under the article's headline.[9] Information gathered in these interviews structured Lane's coverage of Cobb and was reflected in the human-interest features. With the aid of favorable publicity from sympathetic publications such as *Baseball Magazine,* Fultz and members of the fraternity were beginning to see results. As a consequence, only the more disgruntled members chose to risk their careers by jumping rosters to the rogue league. Most stars understood that rival leagues often failed and were not willing to risk being blacklisted by the Major Leagues.[10] Although the rebels may have tempted Cobb and Mathewson, they also chose to stay put. Many journalists were reporting that both were in the declining days of their careers, and they may have felt they had no choice.

Despite the prevailing opinion about the dwindling impact of the two icons, their chum Ring Lardner believed that both stars still had a few tricks up their sleeves. Of Mathewson, he wrote: "So, give him a chanc't. The year's young yet. Leave him get warmed up, then give him a good look. This spring was hard on the old soupers. You can't expect a birth that's been hurlin' the pill in the big show all these years to set the league afire. Don't talk like he was gone and ask me what kind of pitcher he was. . . . there ain't nobody else in the world that can stick a ball as near where they want to stick it as he can."[11]

Lane, too, was unwilling to give up on Mathewson; instead, he continued to celebrate the star's virtues. After the 1913 World Series, he had assigned sports correspondent F. L. Brunner to write a human-interest column on Mathewson and Philadelphia Athletics catcher Wally Schang.

Although Lane's editorial marks do not survive in archival records, his headline, "Hero Worship on the Diamond: The Big League Ball Player an Ideal Type of Athlete," tells modern readers a lot about his thoughts on the pitching veteran. He also penned the editorial note preceding the column, which stated in part: "Hero worship is the soul of baseball enthusiasm. It is a sane and wholesome trait in the National character, and the great stars of the diamond are in a large measure deserving of the popular admiration. Christy Mathewson is not alone master of the fade-away. He is master of himself as well."[12] In the article that follows, Mathewson is constructed as the nation's moral hero of manhood, a superman "with muscles of steel directed by an unclouded brain," whose name is "linked inseparably with clean living."

Lardner and Lane were right not to prematurely dismiss the two superstars. In 1914, Mathewson managed his twelfth straight twenty-plus-win season. His ERA may have ballooned to 3.00, but he still managed five shutouts, an impressive feat for any hurler.[13] He was doing so well by midseason that Lane decided to devote an entire issue of *Baseball Magazine* to the perennial favorite. That summer, he wrote Mathewson's father to request family photos. Gilbert Mathewson eagerly complied with the request. He entrusted Lane with "a mass of pictures of my family from which you may select anything that you think will interest your numerous readers," as well as newspaper clippings from his college and semiprofessional career.[14] For the December 1914 Mathewson Number, Lane wrote four stories and doled out assignments to three correspondents and two illustrators.

The end result was a mythmaking masterpiece. *Baseball Magazine* illustrator J. F. Kernan produced an iconic image of the broad-shouldered, blond-haired, blue-eyed Mathewson. The lines on his face signaled years of sun damage caused by pitching day after day before thousands of fans. In Kernan's illustration, an aging Mathewson was sitting alone in his squad's dugout—still sporting his baseball cap, uniform, and red New York Giants duster.[15] Within the magazine, Lane and his staff painted Mathewson as "the brainiest pitcher the diamond ever knew"—a heroic sportsman, who came from "blooded stock, imported from England."[16] He was one of the greatest pitchers who ever lived, but he was above all a Christian gentleman. Although sales figures for the issue do not exist, it must have been quite popular with subscribers because Lane followed it with a string of player-focused issues. Drawing on the same format, he honored stars such as Honus Wagner, Eddie Collins, Walter Johnson, Grover Cleveland Alexander, Sam Crawford, and Joe Jackson with special issues over the next two years.

At the beginning of 1914, Lane may have even considered creating an issue to celebrate Cobb's heroic virtues. During spring training, "Tyrus the Terrible" appeared to have altered his behavior. He was good-spirited with his teammates and even jolly in the company of reporters.[17] But by June, Cobb was up to his old antics. He lost his temper and beat an African American butcher's assistant over the head with the butt of his revolver. He later told reporters that he had done so to protect his wife's virtue. It seems that she had traded words with the local butcher over a spoiled piece of fish. It is unclear exactly what happened, but the outcome of the affair is a bit more certain; Cobb was arrested for disturbing the peace. He pleaded guilty and paid the fifty-dollar fine.[18]

A few weeks after the incident, he found himself in a terrible batting slump. He had only played in 45 out of Detroit's 102 games, and he trailed American League hitting leader "Shoeless Joe" Jackson by seventeen points in the title standings. Although most players would have been content with a .342 batting average, Cobb was unsatisfied. While "dining together before taking the out-of-town jump" in Chicago that summer, he lamented about his batting woes to Rice and Lardner. After listening to their playful razzing, he assured them he would "get busy" and told them to "watch [him] close up that gap this next week."[19] Unwilling to believe that "any odds were too great to be overcome," Rice later remembered, Cobb made eighteen hits in the next twenty-one at-bats, "under the heaviest sort of pressure in the stretch."[20] By season's end, with a batting average of .368, he had overtaken Jackson and Speaker to win his eighth league batting title.

Although a segment of sportswriters contended that Cobb and Mathewson were past their peak, the duo continued to be mainstays of newspaper sports pages, general-interest magazines, and specialty publications. Writers continued to cast the pair in mythic molds in these various media over the next few years. The platforms may have been different, but the end result remained the same: Cobb and Mathewson were the kings of the diamond.

Columns of "The Baseball Reporter"

By 1914, Rice's and Lardner's days as baseball beat reporters were nearing an end. Both attended games in New York and Chicago, but they no longer followed their assigned clubs day in and out. Instead, they worked on daily news columns—Rice on his "Sportlight" and Lardner on "In the Wake of the News." At the pinnacle of the man's world of sports journalism, they had gained an unprecedented level of access to baseball stars, access about which writers at small-town newspapers only dreamed. They drew on the material they gathered through informal chats with newsworthy figures for their syndicated columns, which were reprinted in hundreds of newspapers across the country.

Newspaper editors in the early twentieth century did not subject sports reporters to the stringent editorial standards that they imposed upon news writers.[21] As a result, prominent writers often were afforded more independence in the practice of journalism. This lack of standardization in the newsroom allowed them the creative space to celebrate the achievements of baseball's giants within their columns.

Rice and Lardner, like many of their colleagues, used poetry to construct larger-than-life heroes. Admirers of the meter found in Latin poetry, they used rhythms and rhymes to reminisce about the greatness of stars. On March 5, 1915, for instance, Rice wrote:

There are seven Browns in the Major Leagues
And four Smiths on the job
There are still five others by the name of Jones—
But there's only one Ty Cobb.[22]

Their pieces, however, did more than merely acknowledge two American originals; they celebrated the stars' long-term success in a number of columns. They both drew on common literary techniques to do so. In early 1914, for instance, Lardner borrowed from the "natural speech of the lowbrow" to remind his readers of Mathewson's perpetual greatness.[23]

Rice followed his cue the following year. He extolled Mathewson's longevity through humor and historical allusion. The fifteen-year veteran "must have bumped into the Fountain of Eternal Youth on one of his Florida jaunts," he joked in his February 1915 column.[24] Likewise, on April 3, 1915, he drew upon figurative language to illustrate Cobb's perennial success, writing "the safest way to beat out Cobb is to have him blown from the mouth of a cannon somewhere around the 13th of April."[25]

In the age of ballyhoo, the public expected an element of promotion in the sports and entertainment pages; however, in a profession increasingly defined by norms of objectivity, many of Rice's latter syndicated "Sportlight" columns took on a tone of detachment. Although he experienced some freedom in creatively crafting sports idols by using literary techniques, he was constrained by the necessity of appealing not only to his national audience but also to publishers, who controlled syndication negotiations and his bottom line. In order to please readers and publishers alike, his opinion columns had to avoid radical stances.

The words of *Harper's Weekly* editor Henry Mills Alden to author Henry James in 1890 retained a kernel of truth for members of the press in the early twentieth century. "Readers chose their books," he wrote, but the press is "pledged against offense to any of its patrons."[26] Rice often played it safe in his columns, straddling the line between developing interesting angles and stirring controversy. In the 1920s, he would take part in common debates such as who was the greater player, Cobb or New York slugger Babe Ruth. Instead of extolling the virtues of one star over the other, he celebrated the feats of both icons, writing "there's fame enough for both."[27]

Prior historical analyses of early twentieth-century baseball writing have constructed a binary of "gee whiz" and "aw nuts" sportswriting models.[28] An examination of Rice's columns reveals that sportswriting was a more complex subgenre. In his opinion columns, promotional poetry was blended with detached contextual references. Although his status as one of the best-known sports columnists in the nation afforded him a degree of creative freedom, in order to retain his good standing with sports celebrities, he had to conform to societal expectations. He often took cautious stances, reminding readers that "Time's dust-covered scroll" would turn in the final verdict about a player's greatness.[29]

Nevertheless, like the human-interest features of national magazine correspondents, portions of Rice's columns celebrated mainstream baseball stars. Publicity was a pervasive element in sports journalism, and in an era that increasingly celebrated heroes for their deeds, it was far from controversial to praise the success and longevity of two white, mainstream stars. It would have been much more radical to craft a Negro League baseball star such as James "Cool Papa" Bell as a hero.[30]

Freelance Features and Literary Journalism in American Magazines

In addition to the regular coverage they received in newspaper sports sections and specialty magazines, Cobb and Mathewson were becoming recurring figures in national general-interest magazines such as *Life*, *Literary Digest*, and *American Magazine*. Publishers increasingly called on freelance sportswriters to supply Americans with news of these baseball giants.

By the turn of the twentieth century, magazines had become "channels of national mass culture."[31] Publishers such as S. S. McClure and Frank Munsey established mass readership by transforming the traditional business model based on high subscription rates and a small cadre of local advertisers to one relying more heavily on advertising brand-name products of newly emerging national corporations. With an expanding base of national advertisers, both publishers dropped single-issue sale prices to a dime in 1893. Other magazines soon followed suit, sparking total monthly magazine circulations of more than sixty-four million by 1905. Monthly magazines, as historian Richard Ohmann notes, "had become the major form of repeated cultural experience for the people of the United States,"[32] and they increasingly included features about entertainment celebrities and sports figures. These magazines reproduced stories about mass culture and its icons with dependable frequency for millions of readers to share.

After 1912, Cobb and Mathewson frequently appeared in publications such as *American Magazine, Collier's, McClure's, Life, Good Housekeeping,* and *St. Nicholas,* reaching anywhere from eight thousand to more than one million readers.[33] Some magazines such as *Collier's, Life, McClure's,* and the *Saturday Evening Post* targeted general audiences, while others such as *Outing, The Delineator, Good Housekeeping, St. Nicholas,* and *Youth's Companion* targeted men, women, or children. The articles highlighting baseball's giants included brief mentions in full-length news articles, poetry, and fiction, as well as in-depth coverage in human-interest features, columns, book reviews, and obituaries.

In 1914, correspondents at general-interest magazines continued to ponder Cobb's and Mathewson's greatness. The pair had become cultural barometers for success. In April, for instance, *Puck* magazine humorist F. Dana Burnet called Russian ballerina Anna Pavlowa the "Ty Cobb of dancing" in his "The News in Rime [*sic*]" column.[34] Humorous references such as these served not only as a marker of greatness but as a cultural translator, providing general audiences with a comparative framework through which to understand Pavlowa's prestige. General-interest magazine contributors, however, were no longer content just to muse about the heroes' fame. They also provided full-length feature articles to publishers interested in profiting from the stars' continued popularity among middle- and working-class readers.

Sometimes editors utilized material submitted by readers. In late 1913, *American Magazine* editors decided to capitalize on Cobb's cultural caché by inviting subscribers to actively participate in telling his story. Readers delivered. They supplied an unlimited amount of free copy. In February 1914, sport enthusiasts B. F. Leventhal and Joseph A. Sexton had their memories of watching Cobb from the grandstands published in the magazine. Leventhal, like other mythmakers of the era, focused on Cobb's offensive prowess. He shared his memory of watching Cobb swipe three bases after a "lucky" bunt at Philadelphia's Shibe Park in June 1912. In a neighboring column, Sexton examined an aspect of Cobb's play that most sportswriters and fans overlooked. Sexton told of his "three-ringed circus catch" against the Philadelphia Athletics in July 1911.[35]

American Magazine, like other publications that republished well-known anecdotes of fans and professional journalists, served as a site of collective memory.[36] Like bricoleurs, they added layer upon layer of memory's matter on the pair's national portrait. Most writers simply added another coat of paint on the already thick patina. Others attempted to reclaim the image as their own. They endeavored to recast their molds. What they may not have realized, however, was that by 1914 the images of these two stars had been almost completely etched in stone.

That same year, magazine publishers were beginning to realize that middle-class women also were interested in the pair. That spring, *Delineator* women's magazine editor Marie Mattingly Meloney set out to provide her readers with an inside glimpse of the early years of the nation's big blond idol told by the woman that may have known him the best, his mother Minerva.[37] She culled an account of Mathewson's wholesome upbringing in Factoryville, Pennsylvania. In the profile, Meloney turned to many of the literary techniques that male sportswriters relied on. Following the cue of Greek bards, she told an epic hero's tale and borrowed the standard, archetypal plot line.[38] Mathewson had come from a humble birth; he had overcome many obstacles during his early career to achieve his iconic status; once at the pinnacle of his career, he had reacted to his triumphs and tragedies in the same manner—as a humble competitor, a good sportsman, the consummate Christian gentleman. His was the Victorian story of restrained manhood, and Mathewson was the definitive Christian.

Mothers, Meloney contended, should follow Minerva Mathewson's cue—they should train their sons to be upright Christian gentlemen, who would never shy away from life's toughest battles but would always respond to them with grace. Not all editors, however, had the time to make a personal trek to Factoryville or Royston; instead, they hired freelance writers to pen these human-interest accounts. The nation's cadre of sportswriters eagerly took up the quest. Over the next three years, they supplied publishers with an unlimited supply of stories about Mathewson and Cobb. Two of the biggest contributors of the reams of freelance material would prove to be Lardner and Rice.

By this time, both writers were experimenting with literary journalism, which had come into style at century's turn when Lincoln Steffens, *New York Commercial Advertiser*'s city desk editor, began experimenting with the anti-journalistic paradigm. He had set out to produce a "newspaper that shall have literary charm as well as daily information."[39] Although that "literary charm" was alive and well in the sports page, it had all but disappeared in the other sections of daily newspapers. It did, however, find a home in literary, humor, and general-interest magazines that attempted to attract a mass audience. Lardner and Rice had been using literary devices, such as metaphors, similes, meter and rhyme, in their sports columns and game recaps since before they made it to major media markets. Now they were experimenting with humor, characterization, and dialogue in a whole new way for literary and general-interest magazines.

After years of listening intently to dialect at train stations and hotel bars across the Midwest and Northeast, Lardner incorporated regional vernacular unreservedly in his fictional accounts of Jack Keefe, a brash young Chicago White Sox rookie, who often wrote letters home to his dear friend Al. As Lardner's biographer Jonathan Yardley aptly put it: "Jack Keefe is one of the great 'originals' in American fiction. . . . [He] is pig-headed, cocky, gullible, selfish, sentimental, naïve, stubborn, self-deceiving—and talented. He is a fountain of alibis, mangled axioms and witless repartee."[40]

Lardner introduced Jack to *Saturday Evening Post* readers in "A

Busher's Letters Home" on March 7, 1914. In the original and the five pieces that followed he often referenced two of the game's biggest stars. In doing so, he provided authentic flavor to his fictional accounts.[41] He also inadvertently tipped his hand to American readers; they learned about where his allegiances lay in the world of baseball. He idolized his heroes.

Readers would be able to see further evidence of his affection a year later when he penned a series of four articles about baseball for *American Magazine*. His hero-crafting chisel was in operation in the first two pieces—a tribute to Boston's "Miracle Braves," who had climbed from last place in the National League standings in late July to steal October's World Series the previous season, and "Some Team," an article about Ring's dream team, whose roster featured the likes of Cobb and Mathewson.[42] His idol-carving tool was in full operation later that summer when he etched tributes to his personal heroes.

In "Tyrus, the Greatest of 'Em All," Lardner's fictional veteran Chicago White Sox player begged the squad's rookie: "Sit down here a while, kid, and I'll give you the dope on this guy. . . . All of my life I been hearin' about the slow, easy-goin' Southerner. Well, Ty's easy-goin' all right—like a million-dollar tourin' car. But, if Ty is slow, he must be kiddin' us when he says he was born down South."[43]

Lardner then proceeded to tell some of the most infamous anecdotes about Cobb—his start with the Royston Rompers, his early struggles in the Major Leagues, his prowess on the base paths and behind the plate. He also sprinkled in some lesser-known stories. "Sometimes I pretty near think they's nothin' he couldn't do if he really set out to do it," Lardner's fictional Sox player told the rookie. "Before you joined the club, some o' the boys was kiddin' him over to Detroit. Callahan was tellin' me about it. Cobb hadn't started hittin'. One o' the players clipped the averages out o' the paper and took 'em to the park. He showed the clippin' to Ty."[44] Cobb, whose batting average had slipped to under .225, promised the player he would reach .325 in a week. "Well, it wasn't," Lardner's fictional Sox player told the newcomer. "No, sir! It was .326."

In the pieces, Lardner blended the fictitious dialogue of a veteran

Major Leaguer with facts and anecdotes about Cobb's career. Although he took fictional liberties with the above anecdote, the crux of the story was accurate. In summer 1914, hampered by minor injuries, Cobb had seen his batting average slump to .225. He was well behind league leaders Nap Lajoie and Joe Jackson. When Lardner pointed out the anomaly to Cobb in the presence of Rice, Cobb vowed that he would soon bring it up to .325. By season's end, his batting average was .368, and he had claimed his eighth consecutive league batting title.[45]

Lardner's fable-like ode to the "Georgia Peach" celebrated his intelligence, his skill, and his work ethic. Cobb, he wrote, did not need a lucky horseshoe; he made his own luck. Later known for his ability to humanize his subjects, Lardner did the opposite in this piece—he mythologized Cobb. He did not paint him as a villain like so many of his contemporaries; instead, he defended him against his critics. Cobb was right to hold out for higher salaries; he deserved them. And, he did not intentionally spike players; he was just a warrior in the heat of battle. Instead of crafting him as a villain or even as a trickster, Lardner placed him on a pedestal for Americans to emulate.

Lardner's idiosyncratic common speak was in rare form by August, when he described Mathewson's superb control. He wrote: "They's a flock o' pitchers that knows a batter's weakness and works accordin'. But they ain't nobody else in the world that can stick a ball as near where they want to stick it as he can. I bet he could shave you if he wanted to if he had a razor blade to throw instead of a ball."[46]

In the piece, like other writers of the era, he retold well known anecdotes such as those of Mathewson's 1905 World Series performance and the 1912 Snodgrass muff, but he did so with a literary flair that others lacked. Of Mathewson's three shutouts in the 1905 World Series, he wrote, "if goose eggs had of been worth a dollar a dozen, the Ath-a-letics could of quit playin' ball and toured the world in a taxi."[47] These mythic anecdotes were supplemented by figurative techniques. In "Matty," Lardner described Mathewson's longevity by manipulating an old cliché. "You've heard the old sayin' that a cat's got nine lives?" he wrote. "Well, boy, Matty makes a cat look like a sucker."

That same summer, Rice experimented with characterization and humorous dialogue in two pieces that he penned for *McClure's*. The two columns about a fictional baseball reporter provided insight into the daily life of a sports reporter. His fictional character was continually bombarded with conversations about baseball's greatest stars in his daily life. Whether with a mouthful of gauze in the dentist's chair or a handful of asparagus at the delicatessen counter, the reporter could not escape hearsay about Cobb and Mathewson.[48]

On each occasion, the baseball scribe, though frustrated by the inconvenience of the interruption, drew upon his observations in covering the duo to provide the bystanders with a new understanding of their prowess among other baseball greats. The baseball reporter, for instance, noted, "They may prove that other pitchers have more stuff than Mathewson; that others are harder to hit; but no man can ever prove that any other pitcher ever had Matty's control; for the cold, clammy record would bar his way."[49]

Lardner and Rice were experimenting with humor, characterization, and dialogue in their pieces—techniques that they put to good use in their literary journalism and in their fiction over the next decade; in the last instance, however, they were paying tribute to two of their favorite heroes. Like Rice, Lardner believed that the "champions and the way that they lived have something to say to all of us."[50] They believed that Americans could learn important cultural truths through popular baseball heroes, and they set out to teach their readers lessons about what it meant to be successful in American culture.

Other freelance magazine journalists were following Lardner's and Rice's cue, churning out article after article about the duo. They were all guilty of typecasting the pair into mythic molds. After 1914, the image they sketched of Mathewson would become etched in stone. He was more than one of the greatest pitchers ever to don a uniform; his fame had transcended sport. The nation's cadre of sportswriters had cast the Christian Gentleman as professional baseball's quintessential saint.

Mathewson, of course, was no saint. His wife would later tell reporters that he often smoked, sometimes drank, gambled, and used profanity.[51] He, like Cobb, on occasion brawled with fans. Once in 1904, he even punched an innocent lemonade boy.[52] Sportswriters forced him into the mold of baseball's flawless hero for the sake of their readers, who had come to idolize him. Many sportswriters were themselves mesmerized by the peerless pitcher. Others sought to give the public what it wanted. Some may have believed that doing so was harmless. Mathewson, though not perfect, was after all a great pitcher and an all-around good guy. Giving readers an icon was good for the game, and what was good for the game was good for business, and what was good for business was good for their own bottom lines. Plus, they may have reasoned, Mathewson might teach American boys how to become good men.

Cobb, meanwhile, was more difficult for sportswriters to define. In 1914, most scribes still agreed that he was one of the greatest—if not THE GREATEST—hitters to ever pick up a baseball bat. He was also lightning fast on the base paths and had a brilliant baseball mind. He was a phenom in the national pastime, but his multifaceted personality made it more difficult to cast him in the role of hero or villain. He was too complex for that. No sooner had Lane constructed the image of Cobb as a gentleman-hero than he made headlines for crawling into the stands and clobbering an innocent fan. His was hardly the face of a Victorian gentleman. He was no saint. Many sportswriters instead cast him as a villain. If Mathewson was baseball's archetypal saint, then Cobb, its other larger-than-life character, would be the Major Leagues' quintessential sinner. His friends, on the other hand, continued to portray him as an American hero. The more reliable sportswriters sketched him for what he was—an anomaly, a chameleon like trickster with an eerie knack of transforming just when sportswriters thought they had him figured out.

His pals may have been willing to overlook his flaws and portray him as a national hero, but most writers were not as kind. In June 1914, for instance, a *Literary Digest* correspondent included a lengthy anecdote about a hoax he played on baseball's other villain, New York Yankees first baseman "Prince Hal" Chase.[53] Cobb explained "how a lucky chance put a double charge into a trick that the Detroits loaded up for the Yankees." He orchestrated the scam with the help of Crawford, the article revealed, after overhearing Chase discussing playing strategies in the hallway of the Yankees clubhouse. "I sneaked out of the club-house without any one seeing me, and got hold of Crawford," he recalled. "'Sam,' I said. 'Chase is going to cross us on that bunt play to-morrow. Now, when we do it you dig for first base and I'll stop at second. They're going to try to get me at third. We'll both be safe, instead of your being out at first.'" "Baseball is not unlike a war," Cobb told readers, and "the heavy artillery" has "to meet trick with trick."

Even though Cobb and Mathewson played different characters in the mythic dramas penned by the era's journalists, the final act often included the same moral. After emphasizing physical keys to success, magazine coverage, such as the 1913 *Literary Digest* article, often focused on character traits that bred achievement.[54] Through figurative language and anecdotes, writers taught readers of Cobb's "fiery determination" and Mathewson's love of the game. These "Methuselahs" of baseball, as sportswriters referred to both athletes, claimed success through more than natural ability alone. The longtime veterans gained success by taking educated risks on the base paths and the mound—risks they learned from dutifully studying the science of baseball. They earned success through years of dedication and determination. It seemed that general-interest magazine coverage was on constant rewind—replaying the biggest plays of the era's greatest stars and retelling their heroic stories.

Advertising the Greatness of Baseball's Gods

National magazines such as *Collier's* and *McClure's* were not the only places to peruse human-interest features about Cobb and Mathewson. Baseball enthusiasts could also find coverage in specialty publications such as *Baseball Magazine.* Specialty sports magazines had existed since John Skinner's *American Turf Register* was introduced in 1829.[55] At the turn of the twentieth century, aficionados had obtained news about the national pastime through newspaper sports pages or from *Sporting Life* and *Sporting News,* two weekly journals established in the 1880s. The content of these two competing publications, however, centered on game coverage, not human-interest stories about the stars of the era.

Hoping to fill this void, Boston-based sportswriter Jacob Morse and a handful of investors launched *Baseball Magazine*, a monthly publication geared toward coverage of trends and personalities, in 1908. In the first issue, Morse wrote: "Baseball has never had a magazine of its own, while almost every other sport has a high class publication. So, the *Baseball Magazine* is supplying a long-felt need; in substance, the need of a monthly organ filled with the highest thought surrounding the game, well edited, well printed, and filled with first-class illustrations."[56] A key element of the journal's editorial mission was the implementation of human-interest features about notable stars. After Lane took the helm as editor in 1911, he did just that. He wrote and reworked approximately 150 stories about Cobb and Mathewson.

In his role as editor, Lane had more autonomy than did writers such as Rice and Lardner. As press historian Theodore P. Greene suggests, progressive magazine editors enjoyed more freedom then than at any point in history.[57] Unlike their predecessors, they were no longer reliant only on subscribers and local advertisers, and publishers had yet to insist upon "scientific" readership surveys. As a result, as long as annual readership levels remained steady, publishers gave many editors complete authority. Like other magazine editors, Lane served as the publication's gatekeeper—he had final say over what was included in human-interest features. He not only controlled the content, he also determined the form. He had the power to alter the style and the tone of articles.

Like Rice and Lardner, Lane did not have unlimited autonomy. The human-interest articles appearing in *Baseball Magazine* were structured by cultural and linguistic conventions, as well as social and economic factors. His portrayals of Cobb's and Mathewson's manhood within *Baseball Magazine* were bound by his understanding of manliness within American culture. His perspectives were shaped by national leaders such as psychologist G. Stanley Hall and former Rough Rider and President Theodore Roosevelt, who preached for Americans to adopt "the strenuous life, the life of toil and effort, of labor and strife," and "to lead clean, vigorous, healthy lives."[58] Roosevelt encouraged the "American boy" to participate in sports in order to "increase in physical and moral courage" and "to grow into the kind of American man of whom America can be really proud."[59]

His views also were influenced by the popular muscular-Christianity movement, which by the turn of the century was pervasive in American culture in texts such as Charles Kingsley's *Westward Ho!*, in messages of prominent speakers such as former baseball star Billy Sunday and football icon Amos Alonzo Stagg, and in the missions of popular organizations such as the Young Men's Christian Association and the Boy Scouts of America.[60] This blend of Victorian and modern constructions of masculinity exerted pressures on the ways in which Lane portrayed Cobb and Mathewson. For instance, like some national magazine correspondents, he constructed both icons as gentlemen. In a March 1912 editorial, he had celebrated Cobb as a "typical American gentleman";[61] likewise, he portrayed Mathewson as the paragon of manhood.[62]

In addition to being constrained by cultural norms and values, Lane was influenced by the same set of linguistic rituals that shaped the writing styles of other sports journalists. He often drew upon anecdotes, metaphors, and other literary conventions. Lane integrated cultural shorthand into human-interest articles, labeling Mathewson as the "master mechanic" and comparing Cobb's speed on the base paths to "lightning."[63] He retold anecdotes emphasizing Cobb's and Mathewson's success, such as Mathewson's "brilliant" performance in the 1905 World Series. Through these communicative rituals handed down from oral and print culture, Lane told stories about "kings" of the diamond, tales that taught lessons about manhood and success.[64] The very form of human-interest stories constituted positive portrayals.[65]

Lane may have portrayed Cobb and Mathewson as national heroes because of personal admiration or in order to maintain close rapport. He also may have celebrated the duo to turn a profit. *Baseball Magazine,* which was published continuously from 1908 until 1954, was a literary success, but that did not translate into a financial fortune.[66] So, shortly after Lane took the helm as editor in 1911, he attempted to appeal to wider audiences by expanding the editorial focus to other sports such as football and ice hockey; by centering coverage on human-interest features; and by creating special commemorative issues around teams, baseball stars, and events such as the World Series. His business strategy worked. By 1921, according to *N. W. Ayer & Son's American Newspaper Annual and Directory,* the publication had reached an audience of approximately seventy thousand, more than its weekly competitors *Sporting News* or *Sporting Life.*[67]

Cobb and Mathewson were receiving free promotion and accolades befitting a king (or a tyrant). They also were earning soft cash, easy money that came from their work as product endorsers or journalistic collaborators. It might not be the secret to their success on the ball field, but spending a few minutes on these projects could bring financial security after their playing days were over, and by 1914, Mathewson and Cobb knew that they could not play forever. They had learned this lesson all too well.

They both quickly accepted moneymaking opportunities. By 1914, Lane had established a friendly correspondence with Cobb and other baseball stars of the day. The editor often asked them to write back with their plans for the off season or to drop by the next time they were in the vicinity, but he soon approached Cobb on a different sort of business. The editor began to ask him if he might not like to endorse a few products for *Baseball Magazine*'s advertisers.

In response to Lane's request that he promote golf sweaters for Bradley Knitting Mills, Cobb replied on June 29, 1914, "I am always glad to do anything you ask of me and this gives me as much pleasure to comply with your wishes." He requested a complimentary "fancy golf sweater," in addition to any compensation he received.[68] Over the next few years, he answered Lane's requests to endorse products that ranged from Brunswick billiard balls to American Tobacco cigarettes. He quickly agreed to promote the billiard company, but he drew the line at cigarettes. In 1915, he wrote: "There is nothing that I know of that I ever refused to do for you but this is one instance I shall have to. . . . I am not a cigarette smoker and. . . . I can't see my way clear to recommend them."[69] Cobb had standards, even where easy money was concerned. Celebrities were flooded with requests to endorse products, and editors served as liaisons in the process.

In their off-season roles as product endorsers and stage actors, Mathewson and Cobb had to take time away from their families to smile in front of a camera. In their roles as player-correspondents, they had found that they could sometimes collaborate on articles even while they played the game that they loved. They just had to deliver a bit of inside dope. Sometimes they did not even have to do that. Their only responsibility was to stand behind what Wheeler or other reporters wrote.

By 1914, Cobb, who was beginning to profit from his stock investments in Coca-Cola and Ford Motor Company, realized that there were other intangible benefits to the ghosted material.[70] When Wheeler approached him to write his autobiography later that year, he said yes. Wheeler had done a fine job on Mathewson's *Pitching in a Pinch*. It had made them both a steady income, but it also had helped cement his image as the game's flawless hero. Cobb knew that Wheeler could not erase his warts, but he might be able to recreate himself in the autobiography. At the very least, he might be able to end the ugly rumors that he sharpened his spikes to intentionally injure players and to tell his side of the story about that unfortunate incident with the crippled New York Highlanders fan. He saw an opportunity to shape his image and make a buck, and he took it. He collaborated with Wheeler on his memoir—*Busting 'Em and Other Big League Stories*.

With the aid of Wheeler, he used the narrative forum to construct a positive public image. Creating a clean image meant reshaping his national identity as baseball's crafty trickster. National press coverage focused on his brawls with teammates, umpires, and fans; his habit of slashing infielders with razor-sharp spikes when stealing bases; and his practice of habitually holding out for higher salaries. In an effort to restore his image, Cobb and Wheeler attempted to downplay some of his past behavior or deny it outright, as in the case of rumors that he sharpened his cleats or intentionally spiked innocent infielders.

In "The Effects of Crowds on Big Leaguers," the collaborators denied wrongdoing and evaded responsibility for Cobb's scuffle with Claude Lueker in May 1912. They attempted to smooth over the sports community's collective memory by justifying his actions. After explaining the psychological role that rooters played in the minds of players, Cobb reminded readers that fans "have always 'ridden' me hard,"[71] and wrote that he wanted to "tell for the first time over my signature the real inside facts of that event."[72] He pointed out that Lueker verbally abused him by shouting racial slurs that made "my temper beg[i]n to go." He had avoided the rooter and tried to ignore the comments, he said. He went on to admit that he had "no recollection of . . . beating up my abuser," and he reminded readers that his actions in defense of his honor were not courageous; instead, he contended, they were caused by "blind fury."[73]

No longer at the *New York Herald,* Wheeler was not able to write the review for Cobb's autobiography, but he did everything else that he could to ensure its success. In his introduction to the book, he lauded Cobb as "an institution in baseball like the Presidency of the United States is in politics."[74] He praised Cobb's batting feats and wrote that, in addition to making "lightning look slow" on the base paths, Cobb was "the fastest thinker in the game." Now, the greatest student of the game had given readers a "breezy" account of the "real 'inside' life of the Big Leagues and baseball as it is played in fast society."[75]

No one was more fit to do so than Cobb, who was a "born reporter," "an intellectual blotter," who could have been "a star in the newspaper business." Despite Wheeler's and Cobb's best efforts, the memoir had little effect on his national image or his collective memory. He had become and would largely remain baseball's crafty trickster.

Published in 1914 by Edward J. Clode, *Busting 'Em* did not enjoy the literary or financial success of *Pitching in a Pinch.* Although it received an initial endorsement from the Boy Scouts' mouthpiece, *Boy's Life* magazine, the memoir, priced at one dollar, did not sell well.[76] It may have been that it was released too soon after Mathewson's memoir, or perhaps the reading public was beginning to grow weary of Wheeler's inside-baseball accounts. They may have even grown tired of Cobb. By summer 1914, other, more important things were on the minds of boys and men around the nation. The world was at war, and America would soon enter the fray.

In the meantime, disappointing sales would not keep Wheeler,

Cobb, and Mathewson from attempting other collaborative projects. That same year, Mathewson lent his name to Wheeler's new baseball series for boys. The duo had watched and read for years as Gilbert Patten, under the pen name Burt L. Standish, constructed a flawless American hero in Frank Merriwell. His rich Merriwell storyline evolved into more than two hundred dime novels and eventually crossed platforms into comic book, radio, and television, and film forms.[77] By the end of his career, more than 500 million copies of his books were in circulation. His was a lucrative media empire, but Patten saw very little of the profits. He wrote each book for $150, and he never claimed any of the royalties from his work.

By the mid-1910s, others were capitalizing on the sports-fiction craze. Ralph Henry Barbour was in the process of penning more than 150 children's sports books that, like the era's baseball coverage, emphasized achieving success through fair play.[78] In 1912, the Stratemeyer Syndicate, best known for giving America the Hardy Boys and Nancy Drew, began publishing Lester Chadwick's Baseball Joe series. Over the next sixteen years, Edward Stratemeyer, Howard R. Garis, and other anonymous writers would give American boys fourteen books that emphasized good sportsmanship above all and would have made Chadwick, the "Father of Baseball," proud.[79]

In 1914, Wheeler and Mathewson decided to engage in the children's genre. They hoped to capitalize on their cordial working relationship and Mathewson's well-known byline. Over the next four years, they gave American boys *Pitcher Pollack* (1914), *First Base Faulkner* (1915), *Catcher Craig* (1916), and *Second Base Sloan* (1917).[80] When Wheeler was not working on the series, he was running his powerful syndicate and writing feature stories for baseball stars. He could have continued like this forever. He and Mathewson might have fielded a whole roster of children's books if a war had not gotten in the way.

In the early twentieth century, sports journalists entered into symbiotic relationships with baseball icons. As Cobb wrote in *Busting 'Em*, "many ball players indulge in cards, and newspaper correspondents who travel with the club join in these games."[81] They also played golf, hunted, corresponded with, and visited star players in their homes. They did so, as Paul Gallico noted, to make a living.

As Gallico suggested, sports journalists experienced a degree of creative freedom in their narratives.[82] They could portray baseball icons in nontraditional manners. Writers controlled the selection of story material, as well as tone and style. Editors dictated story assignments, wrote editorial notes and headlines, and governed story structure.

Their agency, however, was bound by a number of economic, social, and cultural constraints. First and foremost, sports journalists were governed by profit-driven goals. In order to appeal to the widest audience base, they could not be too radical in their columns and feature articles. Likewise, they were limited by mainstream cultural norms and values. Cultural constructions such as those associated with manhood influenced their perspective about sports heroes and subsequently shaped their portrayal of Cobb and Mathewson. Journalistic norms such as the storytelling conventions embedded in newspaper columns, human-interest features, player-themed issues, and memoirs also influenced content. Finally, sports journalists were bound by the social structures that defined human-interest journalism. Story content was influenced by the need to maintain close rapport with baseball celebrities.

Employed in positions with varying degrees of agency, journalists crafted their favorite stars as national heroes. Sports journalists, who gained higher pay, job security, and even personal renown, were not the only ones who benefited from the relationships. Sports stars earned extra money by writing articles for specialty publications and lending their names to ghostwritten accounts. Above all, in collaborating with journalists, sports icons gained a degree of agency in their depictions. To an extent, Cobb and Mathewson dictated their portrayals by controlling interview material, writing first-person accounts, and entering into collaborative relationships.

An examination of newspaper columns, human-interest features, player-themed issues, and player memoirs reveals a new understanding of the pervasiveness of the promotional model within early twentieth-century sports journalism. As journalism historian W. Joseph Campbell contended, in the early twentieth century three paradigms—the activist model, the narrative model, and the detached model—reigned supreme in mainstream journalism.[83] Elements of these models were apparent in all forms of sports journalism from the detached newspaper column to the narrative-based human-interest story and the activist-player-themed issues. Ultimately, however, sports and entertainment journalism was marked by one common feature—ballyhoo.[84]

Regardless of the form, the promotional model dominated sports journalism. Even as the detached model became more pervasive in mainstream journalism, in the first three decades of the twentieth century, as F. C. Lane suggested in the July 1927 *Baseball Magazine,* sports journalists were baseball's biggest boosters.[85]

– 9 –

Baseball's Greatest Battle

In 1916, *Harper's Weekly* considered Mathewson's eternal fame in a brief biography. Even the serious news publication could not resist adding a touch of humor, comparing Mathewson, "the most famous of all, not excluding Ty Cobb, the Georgian," to Methuselah, a biblical patriarch who reportedly lived 969 years.[1] The tongue-in-cheek allusion was meant to provide a humorous take on the longevity of both superstars' fame, but it was fitting that they compared him to a biblical patriarch—he was after all the country's Christian Gentleman. Correspondents knew that Americans could use something to laugh about more than ever. They were on the brink of being engaged in a war to extend democracy, a war they hoped might end all wars.

In 1916, baseball stars were still playing America's favorite children's game. The year prior, Cobb had earned his ninth consecutive batting title. He had also set a Major League record for steals with ninety-six, a mark that would not be broken until 1962.[2] Even so, there were signs that Cobb was beginning to slip from his preeminent position. He was still good, but not good enough to win another batting title that season. Despite earning more than two hundred hits for the sixth time in his career, he lost his first league title in nearly a decade. His .371 batting average was nearly thirty points ahead of "Shoeless" Joe, but it was simply not enough to defeat Tris Speaker's sizzling bat.[3]

On the mound, thirty-five-year-old Mathewson was showing signs of age and fatigue. Over the next two seasons, he managed only twelve wins. His decline was so swift that, by July 1916, locked in a pennant battle, McGraw, his dearest companion in the baseball world, decided to do the unthinkable—he arranged a trade with

Cincinnati owner August Garry Herrmann.[4] The trade package included the once-prized hurler, rookie outfielder Edd Roush, and veteran third baseman Bill McKechnie for utility player Buck Herzog and outfielder Red Killefer. McGraw's decision grew not from malice or greed, but compassion. He knew that Cincinnati could give his friend what he and the Giants could not—an opportunity to manage. So it was on July 20, after packing his bags and cleaning out his locker in the Giants clubhouse, that Mathewson boarded a westbound train.

Wheeler wrote about the decision to trade the nation's big blond idol in the *New York Evening World.* The piece was republished in *Literary Digest* on August 12. His literary take on the incident included a vignette about Mathewson's last encounter with his teammates in the Giants clubhouse. When second baseman Larry Doyle invited Mathewson to play one last hand of cards, the journalist noted that "more tear drops trickled down the cheeks of the big athlete."[5] The scribe reported that Mathewson told Doyle in a "half-broken voice . . . 'This is the only locker I ever had in my life.'"

Lardner, who was still editing the *Chicago Tribune*'s "In the Wake of the News" column, responded to the announcement in rhyme:

> My eyes grow very misty
> As I pen these lines to Christy;
> Oh my heart is full of heaviness today.
> May the flowers ne'er wither Matty,
> On the grave in Cincinnati
> Which you've chosen for your final fadeaway.[6]

He was wrong about one thing, however; Mathewson had little choice in the matter. Nonetheless, he made the best of the decision.

A few weeks later he would make his final farewell from the mound. On September 4, Mathewson met his oldest foe—Chicago Cubs "Three Finger" Brown. In 1908, the duo had dazzled America's baseball-loving public with their classic pitchers' duels. Now, the men were just shells of their former selves. Both on slumping teams, the veterans had agreed to take their final bows together in a Labor Day match-up. It was billed in the newspapers as one last battle between two old warriors.[7] Americans in this era were obsessed with statistics, but the sportswriters forgot to search the record books in the buildup to the game. They failed to mention that a win for Brown would even his all-time record at twelve against Mathewson. Even so, the pregame publicity worked. "A great group of baseball rooters stood in the rain for an hour" before game time to claim tickets to see the pitching legends one last time, *Chicago Tribune* reporter I. E. Sanborn told his readers the following day.[8]

Mathewson's team rallied around their new manager. They handed him a ten-to-six lead going into the ninth inning, but the years of strain on his arm were beginning to show. His fastball had lost its edge. His famous fadeaway had faltered. He had already given up fourteen hits to the Cubs when, with two outs, he offered them one more. This time, Vic Saier connected on a two-run homer. On the next play, Mathewson showed one last glimpse of his old form, tricking Fritz Mollowitz into popping up on one of his fadeaways. The next day, the *New York Times* did not carry news of the final duel on its front page; instead, it was buried on page 12, under the headline "Matty Defeats Old Rival."[9] Stories of Mathewson's victories were no longer front-page items. News from the war front was the only above-the-fold story that day. After the game, the player-manager put away his pitching mitt for good. He would focus, instead, on leading his team from the dugout. That season, however, he noticed that something was not quite right about his squad. It seemed the first baseman Hal Chase was engaged in questionable behavior. He suspended "Prince Hal" the following season for "indifferent playing," a common euphemism for fixing games.

Mathewson and Cobb continued to make news, but another name joined theirs in the headlines of the sports pages. It was a manager, not a sportswriter, who discovered baseball's next hero. Baltimore Orioles manager Jack Dunn found George Herman Ruth on the playground of St. Mary's Industrial School for Boys in February 1914. Dunn signed Ruth on the spot. He took such a liking to the nineteen-year-old hurler that several Orioles took to calling Ruth "Jack's newest babe."[10]

The Babe did not stick around Baltimore for long. Dunn quickly sold the right-hander to Boston Red Sox owners John Taylor and

Joseph Lannin. Ruth delivered a victory in his first Major League appearance on the mound for the Sox on July 11, 1914. Sportswriters, however, took little notice of the young rookie in his first five appearances for Boston. The kid was good, but with a 3.91 ERA, he was not good enough yet. They sent Ruth down to the minors for the remainder of the season. In 1915, he would be back in the Boston uniform. Over the next three years, he would become a pitching mainstay for the club, delivering two consecutive twenty-plus win seasons and a league-low 1.75 ERA in 1916.

While Ruth made a name for himself on the mound, the nation loomed closer to war, and Major League baseball was doing all it could to help the cause on the homefront.[11] In 1915, some baseball clubs began introducing American men to ideas of military preparedness; the civilian soldiers participated in military drills and offered instruction to fans. By April 1917, when President Woodrow Wilson declared war on Germany, professional baseball was assisting Uncle Sam in other ways, too. League magnates donated balls, bats, and *Baseball Magazine* subscriptions to the troops. In addition to their patriotic displays, they also provided monetary assistance. Without too much public grumbling, they handed over entertainment taxes to the government. They also sponsored bond drives and auctioned off autographed memorabilia to raise money for the war efforts. In the end, that was not enough. Baseball had advertised its players as the "best fighters," and the nation needed its biggest stars for the war effort.

In the last instance, many writers agreed with Jerome Beatty of *Collier's,* who acknowledged in 1917 that organized baseball best contributed to the war effort by "recognizing how inconsequential it was compared to the 'real World Series'—the war."[12] Rice and Wheeler certainly did.

In late 1917, thirty-seven-year-old Rice turned down a *Collier's* offer of a dollar per word to head to the frontlines as a war correspondent; instead, he volunteered for duty as an enlisted man. On December 5, he traveled to Greenville, South Carolina, as a private in the First Tennessee. He excelled in training camp and was quickly promoted to second lieutenant. In April 1918, he shipped out with the

115th Field Artillery from Virginia aboard the *George Washington*. Four months later, it appeared as if he would march out to the frontlines when he suddenly received new orders.

Some higher-ranking official believed that his patriotic duty should be to serve as a journalist for the *Stars and Stripes*, the military's upstart daily newspaper. That summer, he would tour the front as a journalist. Rice, however, could not shake the feeling that he was letting down his friends and shirking his civic duty to serve as an enlisted man. By the end of the year, he had convinced his immediate commanders to transfer him back to his regiment. They did, but he would not stay in the trenches for long. In October, he would once again receive new orders. This time he was to serve as a press officer in the First Army Corps headquarters. He was reassigned twice more after the armistice was signed, but a diagnosis of chronic sinus trouble in December would prove to be his ticket home.[13]

En route, he ran into several of his old cronies from New York. In Bar Le Duc, he bumped into Damon Runyon, who was reporting from the field as a war correspondent for William Randolph Hearst's International News Service. He likely looked for Lardner, too, but Ring had already traveled home from the war front. He lacked his companion's stomach for war, but out of an understanding of the market's demands as much as a sense of patriotic duty, he agreed to head to the frontlines for *Collier's* in 1917. In 1918, he gave his readers *My Four Weeks in France*.[14]

On January 27, 1919, he would run into another of his chums. Wheeler would be his bunkmate on the USS *Rijndam* during his last leg home. During the war, First Lieutenant Wheeler had been responsible for seizing French horses for the artillery brigade; now, he and Rice were entrusted with making sure that the boys on the boat minded curfew during the two-week voyage home. Their easy assignment almost turned deadly, however, when a flu epidemic broke out on board.[15] Rice and Wheeler managed to arrive home unscathed, but they could not say as much for some of the men entrusted to their care. Little did Rice know then, but one of his dearest companions had suffered a fate similar to the men on board the *Rijndam* on his voyage to the warfront.

Following in the footsteps of Rice and Wheeler, two of baseball's greatest heroes had answered the call to duty during summer 1918. Only weeks before, military personnel had unleashed a new plan to combat the Axis Powers' use of mustard gas on the front lines. After the Germans first unleashed the Yellow Cross on Allied troops in July 1917, America's fighting men had been issued standard gas masks. These bulky tools proved to be more of a nuisance than a deterrent, so members of the U.S. military decided to take another approach.

They tasked Major General William L. Sibert with creating the Chemical Warfare Service, or the Gas and Flame Unit, as it was better known. Sibert announced to the press that it would be a super unit, comprised of men of strong minds and bodies. "We do not just want good young athletes," he told reporters. "We are searching for good strong men, endowed with extraordinary capabilities to lead others during gas attacks."[16]

Mathewson and Cobb fit Sibert's bill; they were two of the first to answer his request. They would be joined by thirty-eight-year-old Branch Rickey, a former big-league catcher who had only recently accepted a position as the manager of the St. Louis Browns.[17] Rickey would lead the special-forces unit. They were expected to turn the tide of trench warfare by implementing special flame tanks and gas grenades against enemy forces.

After accepting his commission in late August, Mathewson said goodbye to his wife and boarded a ship to France. Once on board, he was subjected to something much more severe than a simple case of seasickness. Like the *Rijndam* a year later, his ship was overrun by influenza. He had only just begun classes at Officer Training School in Chaumont when he had to be checked into the local hospital for ten days. No sooner had he recovered from the bout of serious illness and finished his training than he seemed destined to meet his maker once more.[18]

In September, he and Cobb were engaged in their final training exercises when the unthinkable happened. They were preparing a new group of military men on how to properly arm themselves against Germany's mustard gas when several soldiers, including

Cobb and Mathewson, missed the signal to place their gas masks on their faces. They both ingested a heavy dose of poison in the gas chamber. "Men screamed," Cobb later recalled, "when they got a whiff of the sweet death in the air. They went crazy with fear and I remember Mathewson telling me 'Ty, I got a good dose of the stuff. I feel terrible.'"[19] For weeks, Cobb had a horrible cough, and his lungs filled with liquid, but he felt he was saved by "divine providence." Mathewson was not so fortunate.

Two men died on the spot from inhaling a lethal dose of the poisonous gas. Mathewson appeared poised to join them. His system was already reeling from the case of influenza that he had caught on his journey to the frontlines. He was sent to the hospital to recover. In mid-December, a still-ailing Mathewson asked to return home in "order to resume my former occupation of managing a National League professional baseball club."[20] His request was granted on December 26. In February, he boarded the *Rotterdam* for his voyage home.

In the end, more than 440 major and minor league players had joined Mathewson and Cobb, but many more, including Ruth, avoided military duty by serving in the shipyards and on other war-related production work. As a result, they were condemned as draft-dodgers guilty of "yellow-hearted cowardice."[21] Sportswriter William Phelon was more accurate, however, when he wrote that professional baseball had "furnished a greater percentage of its personnel for military service than almost any other industry."[22] For now, Ruth may have been labeled a coward, but thanks to men such as Phelon, his status in the American imagination would change soon enough.

When Mathewson returned to the states, he was diagnosed with chronic bronchitis, and he entered a sanitarium in upstate New York. He had asked to be released from the remainder of his military duty so that he could rejoin the Reds as manager, but unsure that Mathewson would be around for the 1919 season, Cincinnati owner August Herrmann found a replacement in Pat Moran. All was not lost, however; McGraw offered Mathewson a position on the Giants management team. He was unwilling to desert his stalwart ace. Soon enough,

McGraw realized that his buddy had been right. Chase was undoubtedly throwing ball games.[23] Later that season, they would realize that Chase was not the only one.

While working as a post-season player-correspondent for Wheeler's Bell Syndicate, Mathewson took a seat in the press box to watch his old Cincinnati ball club take on the Chicago White Sox. He was joined there by the usual faces—Rice and Lardner, who had reclaimed their respective positions at the *New York Tribune* and *Chicago Tribune* after the war's end; *Sporting Life* editor Francis Richter; *Baseball Magazine* editor F. C. Lane; *Sporting News* editor J. G. Taylor Spink, who had taken over the "bible of baseball" after his father's death in 1914; and the current dean of sportswriters, Hugh Fullerton, who had been covering World Series match-ups since they started in 1903. They all may have had their favorite heroes, but they agreed on one thing—something about this particular World Series was not quite right.

Since the demise of the upstart Federal League in 1915, the culture of gambling in baseball, which had always existed, had become more pervasive. It now had the sport in a stranglehold. On the surface, however, this series appeared like any other world's championship.

Lardner, who had decided to take Wheeler up on his standing offer to work at Bell Syndicate after the series, was excited about seeing two of his old Chicago White Sox pals—manager Kid Gleason and pitcher Eddie Cicotte—in action.[24] His joy was shattered when he heard the rumors that the odds-on favorites might throw the series. Lardner was not naïve. He knew that gambling existed at the periphery of the sport. In 1916, he had even reported on rumors that members of the New York Giants had thrown games during their historic race for the National League pennant. Nonetheless, the avid baseball fan was not willing to admit to himself that gambling might exist nearer to the core of the sport, and that some of his favorite players—his personal heroes—were complicit in the corruption.

Before the series began, he along with Rice and Fullerton started to hear rumors that "the fix was in." They were so concerned that Fullerton went so far as to alert American League president Ban Johnson about the gambling threat the day before the series opener. The following day, he enlisted Mathewson to circle any questionable plays on his scorecard.[25] The baseball boosters-turned-investigative-journalists were right to be skeptical. Before the first game, the odds fluctuated wildly, and there were rumors that big-name gamblers such as Arnold Rothstein were tossing down huge sums of money on the series. What they could not have known at the time was that these very same gamblers, namely Abe Attell, Joseph "Sport" Sullivan, and "Sleepy" Bill Burns, had approached Chicago White Sox first baseman Chick Gandil about throwing the series.[26]

He agreed, and spoke to several of his teammates about the prospect. Some of his more straitlaced teammates such as Columbia University–educated second baseman Eddie Collins would never consent to doing anything to tarnish their own reputations or that of the game they loved so much. Gandil, instead, decided to approach several of his teammates who might listen—men that were so frustrated with the stingy ways of White Sox manager Charles Comiskey that they might be enticed to cash in on the gamblers' easy money.

He first approached Lardner's friend, pitcher Eddie Cicotte. He knew that he was ailing financially. The family man had purchased a farm and was in over his head. He also was still livid that Comiskey had convinced Gleason to pull him from his last scheduled start of the season in order to avoid paying him the $10,000 bonus that would have come with his thirtieth win. Cicotte initially turned down Gandil's offer, but he changed his mind. He knew that his arm would not hold out forever, and in the days before lucrative retirement plans, his family could use the money after his career was over.

After Cicotte agreed, Gandil managed to gain the consent of six other players—pitcher Claude "Lefty" Williams, outfielder Oscar "Happy" Felsch, shortstop Charles "Swede" Risberg, utility infielder Fred McMullin, and star outfield slugger "Shoeless" Joe Jackson. Third baseman Buck Weaver had attended the planning meeting but decided not to participate. The other men were to receive one hundred thousand dollars to be split among themselves for their part in the gambling scheme. To confirm that the fix indeed was in, Cicotte was to bean the first Reds batter.

Much to the chagrin of the sportswriters in press row, the pitcher who was known most for his control did just that. He went on to give up an uncharacteristic six runs in three and two-third innings, and the Reds handily defeated the Sox nine-to-one. After the game, a disenchanted Lardner approached his old pal back at the hotel. "What was wrong?" he reportedly asked the veteran pitcher. "I was betting on you today."[27] Cicotte could only shrug.

When Reds ace "Lefty" Williams lost four-to-two the following day, Lardner's worst fears were confirmed. That night the jaded columnist, perhaps a little tipsy on Irish whiskey, collaborated with some of his fellow journalists on a little song. The same songwriter who had penned "Gee, It's a Wonderful Game" in 1911 wrote another little ditty that night.[28] "I'm forever blowing ball games," went the lyrics adapted to the popular tune "I'm Forever Blowing Bubbles." It continued: "Pretty ball games in the air. I come for Chi., I hardly try, Just go to bat and fade and die. Fortune's coming my way, That's why I don't care. I'm forever blowing ball games, For the gamblers treat me fair." He then reportedly began performing his new tune down the aisles of the Chicago White Sox railroad car.

Over the next week, he and his cronies watched as the Reds won the nine-game series in eight games. Mathewson and Fullerton had circled seven suspicious plays. Shortly after the series, Fullerton led the charge: the White Sox had committed baseball's gravest sin, he reported. The news should not have come as a shock to the general public. Gambling had always been present in the national pastime. Even after National League president William Hulbert banned three members of the Louisville Grays for fixing games in 1877, allegations continued to circulate that Major League players were wagering on baseball.[29]

By the early twentieth century, the gambling culture surrounding baseball was pervasive. Early sports pages often carried daily odds for their readers, and when players were not on the baseball diamond, even saintly Mathewson bet on games of poker and rounds of golf.[30] It only made sense that players might be tempted to throw a game—to take a little something off a fastball, to muff an easy catch, or to whiff at what could have been a base hit. There was big money to be made for doing so, and players could use easy cash.

Until 1903, however, rumors of players fixing games had been just that—gossip. That all changed when Chicago Cubs ace hurler Jack Taylor took the mound for a post-season series against his crosstown rival. In his first appearance, he had dominated the Chicago White Sox, eleven-to-nothing. After dropping his next three starts against the club, he stood accused of throwing the series, the ultimate act of treachery.

In the off-season, he was traded away to Cincinnati by Cubs president Jim Hart, and although he notched his third consecutive twenty-win season for the Reds, accusations of foul play followed him. In late July, National Commission chairman August Herrmann conceded that Taylor "was not an honest ball player," but unlike Hulbert, he failed to evict the star pitcher for allegedly throwing games in St. Louis and Pittsburgh; instead, on February 20, 1905, he fined him three hundred dollars and sent him on his way.[31]

After the incident, Richter had written that the "disgusting Jack Taylor case" had "inflicted considerable injury upon the hitherto unsullied fame of base ball as the only absolutely honest professional sport."[32] Reporting that clubs in Pittsburgh, Boston, Philadelphia, Chicago, and St. Louis also had problems with the perilous evil, he warned that gambling was "growing to menacing proportions" in Major League baseball. It was "an ill wind that blows nobody good." "Something ought to be done," he pleaded.[33] Something should have been done, but it was not.

Later that season, Rice, covering his first World Series for the *Atlanta Journal,* reported on the widespread nature of gambling in New York and Philadelphia. Professional gamblers and the average fan were carelessly flinging down their dollars on the series. Rumors circulated that some members of the Philadelphia Athletics had agreed to fix the series. Rice and other sportswriters must have been a bit suspicious as the Giants, led by Mathewson, wiped the fields of the A's, but they did not dwell on the rumors in their reports. Even though it was common knowledge that New York Giants manager John McGraw had bet on his club during the series, Rice did not mention the detail to his Atlanta-area readers.[34]

Instead, he crafted a hero—Matty the marvelous. Rice, like most other sportswriters, did not want to dwell on the possibility. Neither did league officials. Professional baseball was entering one of its most profitable eras. It had done so by distancing itself from the culture of rowdyism that had ruined earlier professional leagues. Acknowledging the presence of gambling might drive throngs of middle-class fans away from the ballparks. It might spell doom for the financial fortunes of baseball magnates and their bards. As a result, everyone shut their eyes and hoped that the problem would go away. It did not.

Players such as Chase were reported to be willing to do anything for a buck, even gamble on the game that made them famous. Mathewson was undoubtedly aware of "Prince Hal's" reputation for corruption when he took over as Cincinnati's manager in August 1916, but soon he realized that Chase's penchant was not only costing the Reds to drop an occasional game, it was threatening to undermine his club and his beloved pastime. By 1917, Chase was casually asking teammates such as pitcher Jimmy Ring to throw games.

Mathewson knew that it had to stop. After watching Chase and second baseman Lee Magee engage in questionable behavior on several occasions during the 1918 season, he decided to act. In early August, shortly before he left for France, he suspended Chase for "indifferent playing and insubordination."[35] He even went so far as to collect testimony from individuals such as Lardner and McGraw, but when the case went up before National League president John Heydler in January 1919, several of the main witnesses, including Mathewson, who was overseas, did not appear, and Heydler was forced to let Chase off the hook.

The decision was ominous for baseball. In 1919, Chase, now in a Giants uniform, continued to bet on baseball. By September, at Mathewson's behest, McGraw decided to bench the veteran first-baseman for his corrupt behavior. Even so, "Prince Hal" found a way to profit from gambling. A month later, he served as a middleman in the infamous Black Sox scandal. He reportedly earned forty thousand dollars for his part.[36]

The following September, a Chicago grand jury would look into the matter of gambling on the 1919 World Series. After months of testimony, they eventually found the players not guilty, but baseball's squeaky-clean image had been tarnished in the national headlines. To forgo additional damage, professional baseball magnates turned to Judge Kennesaw Mountain Landis.

He would clean up the game. Landis banned the eight Black Sox players for life. He showed no mercy on baseball superstar "Shoeless" Joe, who had still managed to hit .375 for the series even after taking five thousand dollars for his part in the fix; nor did he show any leniency toward Buck Weaver, whose only sin was to fail to report his teammates after becoming aware of the plot.

After the series, Rice was indignant. It was a shame, he wrote, that hundreds of thousands of unknowing fans had handed over their hard-earned money to "see a flock of crooked mannequins worked by strings held by a group of crooked gamblers."[37] Still, he believed that the "majority of the players were honest" and good men. Over the next decade, he would continue to be one of baseball's biggest champions.

Unlike his fellow sportswriters, Lardner was deeply disillusioned by the incident. He knew that this was not the first incident of corruption, but he felt betrayed by the actions of his friends in the game's greatest showcase—the World Series. After 1919, he would continue to attend the event for Wheeler's Bell Syndicate, but his heart was not in it.[38] He was no longer in the baseball booster business; in fact, he would go on to condemn the production and worship of heroes. "Hero-worship," he wrote in 1922, "is the national disease that does most to keep the grandstands full and the playgrounds empty."[39] Over the next decade, he would continue to freelance for major national magazines, but he increasingly turned his attention to his other love—the stage.

After the 1919 Black Sox scandal, baseball needed a savior. Mathewson had served as one for his part in eradicating gambling from the national game. In the aftermath of the scandal, however, when they needed their quintessential saint most, it appeared that he was no longer available for the job. He returned to the Giants management staff for the 1920 and 1921 seasons, but his chronic bronchitis and its symptomatic cough lingered. In 1921, at the urging of his friends and family, he returned to the doctor. He was diagnosed with tuberculosis and entered a sanitarium in Saranac Lake, New York.

Once there, he was told that he only had six weeks to live. Mathewson was now engaged in the biggest fight of his life. "It was a different kind of struggle from any he had ever known," *Good Housekeeping* correspondent Lucian Cary told his readers. "It was the opposite kind of fight from the one he had fought so many hundreds of times on the diamond."[40] Baseball's war hero was now engaged in a battle for his life. His enemy had been baseball's perilous ills; now, it was the "white plague." In 1921, he had no time to be baseball's savior, and everyone knew that his old war buddy Cobb, though still a great hitter, was anything but a saint; instead, sportswriters looking for a great redeemer would find a temporary savior in a slugger by the name of Ruth.

-10-

A Triumphant Return

In the aftermath of the Black Sox scandal, America's sportswriters were looking for a savior. They found a temporary one in Babe Ruth. After being traded from the Red Sox in 1919, the Yankees' new star made a name for himself, but not as a pitcher as some sportswriters might have imagined based on his early career; instead, he became baseball's first home-run king.

During his last two seasons in Boston, Sox manager Ed Barrow had seen his hitting potential, so he played Ruth in the outfield when he was not pitching. That season, Ruth tallied a league-leading eleven homers; the following year, his twenty-nine home runs surpassed a Major League record set by Ned Williamson in 1884, a mark that many experts believed would never be beaten.[1] In New York, his prowess at the plate continued.

In late 1920, with news of the Black Sox scandal making front-page headlines across the country, he rewrote the record books once more. This time, he managed to belt out a staggering fifty-four home runs. His nearest competitor, St. Louis Browns first baseman George Sisler, only hit nineteen. Together, the pair had wiped Cobb off the Major League leaderboards. The following year, his fifty-nine home runs and .376 batting average led the Yankees to their first-ever league title.

During the series, Ruth sustained injuries to his elbow and knee. With their superstar not at his peak, the Yankees fell to their cross-town New York rival. The Giants had rallied to win the series for Mathewson, their beloved assistant manager who had recently been diagnosed with tuberculosis.

During the series, the national press had a chance to see what the slugger was made of. Ruth was becoming a baseball star, but he was not exactly the type of icon that sportswriters sought in the aftermath of the Black Sox debacle. The "Sultan of Swat," as sports bards would take to calling him after he demolished his own record with sixty home runs in 1927, was human. They soon learned that he was just as much of a sinner as Cobb. He would be suspended for the first six weeks of the 1922 season for breaking one of Landis's rules about post-season exhibition play.[2] Sportswriters began portraying Ruth for what he was, a larger-than-life figure.

He was so popular that New York Yankees owner Jacob Ruppert had to build a whole new stadium to accommodate his hero-worshipers. When the slugger drove a ball out of the park at the stadium's unveiling on opening day and then delivered the Yankees their first World Series in 1923, the venue became known as the "house that Ruth built."[3] Rice, Wheeler, and the other members of New York's press had no doubt: Ruth was a god in the world of sport.

In the meantime, Mathewson, the nation's much-beloved saint, had gone from a moment of joy as an assistant manager with the Giants during their 1921 pennant run to one of absolute terror when he was told a few days later by Dr. Edward Livingston Trudeau that he only had six weeks to live. As news of his imminent death spread, the baseball world rallied around its hero.

McGraw kept in close contact with his former ace. When the Giants clinched the pennant in Pittsburgh, he gave him a call to share the story. A roomful of reporters was on hand to take part in the intimate affair. They each could not resist sharing one last word or laugh with the peerless pitcher.

Weeks later, his old chums in the press box attempted to reach out with a final gesture of kindness to their pal. Knowing that Mathewson was overwhelmed with anxiety over his wife's welfare, they decided to hold a Christy Mathewson Day before the Giants' annual old-timers' game. Fred Lieb, the current president of the Baseball Writers' Association of America, served as chairman for the event.[4]

He orchestrated the production of a souvenir program. The specialty publication, which would sell at the stadium for a dollar, included anecdotes from his friends and foes around the league.

It also included a few yarns from his favorite sports bards. Even Lardner, who had become disillusioned with the national pastime, could not resist offering a few additional words of praise for his hero from the mound. In true literary fashion, he supplied a "You Know Me Al" letter for the occasion. In the piece, Gibbs told his dear friend that "the old boy was some pitcher."[5] He was more than that, their mutual pal Hugh Fullerton wrote. He was a bona fide national hero, who "played straight . . . asked no odds . . . and when he was beaten was the first to congratulate the victor."[6] In the end, Lieb sent Mathewson approximately fifty-five thousand dollars in proceeds from the event.

Against all odds, it appeared that Mathewson might be on the road to recovery. When his friends heard that he was in better health, members of the press flocked to see him. In August 1922, *Outlook* correspondent and Republican congressman Frederick Davenport told readers that Mathewson was winning his battle with the "white plague."[7] He was so much better by winter of that year that he decided he was ready to return to baseball.

At the urging of McGraw, Judge Emil Fuchs purchased the Boston Braves that winter, and on February 11, 1923, he announced that Mathewson would run the team as president. His would be a tough task; the Boston Braves had won only 53 out of their 153 games during the 1922 season.[8] Nevertheless, after his battle with death, Mathewson felt that he was up for the challenge. This was the material from which legends were made. The nation's sports bards crafted the story of a hero's triumphant return. After the Braves faced the Giants at the Polo Grounds in the 1923 season opener, Rice wrote of his hero's homecoming: "A king walked out of the shadows of the past into the brilliant spring sunshine of the Polo Grounds yesterday as 30,000 loyal subjects paid him the tribute of a roaring acclaim that no crowned monarch could ever know. . . . No name in baseball has ever meant the same as that of Christy Mathewson."[9]

Stories in general-interest magazines such as *Literary Digest* and

The Outlook and specialty publications such as *Good Housekeeping* women's magazine and *The Survey,* a public policy magazine, soon followed. They chronicled the war hero's victory over tuberculosis. In August 1923, for instance, *Good Housekeeping* correspondent Lucian Cary reminded readers why their husbands were so enamored of baseball's war hero. At age forty-three, Mathewson had recorded the biggest victory of his life after winning "his long fight with imminent death."[10] In the process of crafting what can only be described as a heroic god for the ages, Cary borrowed from the playbook of the sport's past mythmakers. He told his readers that Mathewson was above all a Christian gentleman. His pitching control was a metaphor for something greater. "He had control of his own temper and his own will," he wrote. "He was famous as a clean player, who never quarreled with umpires, never lost his head, never blew up."

Baseball had its saint back. It also had a sinner—in the form of one larger-than-life slugger. By 1925, some individuals in the baseball community believed that Ruth lacked character. In addition to intentionally defying the rules, he was guilty of engaging in life's excesses a little too much. He lived an exuberant life in New York's party scene. Simply put, he ate too much, drank too much, and skirted around too much. He also showed a general disregard for authority.

By September, his off-the-field antics were trying the patience of sportswriters and America's general public alike. It prompted a *Literary Digest* correspondent to paint Ruth as a rebellious and sniveling child. In the piece, he was cast as a sinner and Cobb as a saint. Cobb's was "the story of a determination to succeed, to be the first in the chosen endeavor of life."[11]

At least one person did not seem to mind Ruth's fall from the pedestal. Cobb, now acting as a player-manager for Detroit, hated Ruth. In particular, the regimented veteran despised his lack of discipline and his blatant disregard for his own health. On June 13 of the prior year, he had squared off with the slugger at Navin Field during a bench-clearing brawl, which ensued after Cobb ordered Detroit pitcher Bert Cole to hit New York outfielder Bob Meusel with the Yankees leading ten-to-six in the ninth inning.[12] Cobb would not remain in the role of saint for long. It was a position that could only truly be filled by one person in baseball.

In October, Mathewson was not at the World Series. He was not on the mound or in the dugout. He was not even in the press box. His Boston Braves had not made it to the series, and he was no longer collaborating with Wheeler. Matty was nowhere near Forbes Field when the Pittsburgh Pirates took on the Washington Senators in the 1925 series opener; instead, he was more than five hundred miles away. He was at his home in Lake Saranac, New York, near the sanitarium where he had spent his darkest days in the aftermath of World War I. He had traveled back there a few weeks prior. His persistent cough had resumed shortly after spring training, and he hoped that returning to his mountain retreat might help.

On the evening of October 7, he was once again engaged in the battle of his life. He had waged a valiant fight, but in the end, he died from complications of tuberculosis. Flags flew at half-staff at the following day's World Series game. At the moment when the first pitch was to fly through the air, Forbes Field was silent in mourning for one of the game's greatest legends. The start time had been delayed by ten minutes to offer a fitting tribute to the Christian Gentleman. After their moment of silence, the voices of players, managers, umpires, and fans rang out unanimously in the hymn "Nearer My God to Thee."[13]

The Senators defeated the Pirates later that night, but that would not be the leading story the next day. *New York Herald* sports editor W. O. McGeehan told his readers as much. "The death of Christy Mathewson makes the World Series seem a petty, piffling thing. The minds of the old timers went back to twenty years ago to the day when Christy Mathewson shut out the Athletics in a game that was all battle and melodrama."[14] The nation's cadre of sportswriters was bitter that their dear friend had been taken away in the prime of his life. "Always a cheerful and fair fighter," a sulking McGeehan wrote, "he lost a most unfair fight." Death had cheated Matty. The "white plague" had robbed his family, his friends, and the world of a dear man.

Though deeply disturbed by his death, McGeehan and his colleagues offered their readers a few words about what he had meant to the baseball community and to the nation. "It was not his prowess as an athlete that made him the idol of American manhood, young and old," McGeehan continued. "It was the character of the man. . . . He played for all that was in him, he fought the good fight and the clean fight. He was the incarnation of all those virtues with which we endow the ideal American." His was an appropriate eulogy for a man of Mathewson's stature—the king of baseball and an American war hero, but perhaps his dear friend Rice offered a more fitting tribute.

After reminiscing about Mathewson's magnificence on the mound and the more intimate moments of their friendship, Rice admitted that there was "little to be added to the epitaphs that will follow his body to the grave. He was a great pitcher, a great competitor, and a great soul. He was the only man I ever knew who in spirit and in inspiration was greater than the game."[15]

Mathewson's obituary appeared in newspapers across the nation from the *Scranton Times* and the *Boston Transcript* to the *New York World* and the *New York Times.* Over the next few months, eulogies followed in America's magazines. Wheeler reminisced about his relationship with Mathewson in *Literary Digest.* He was a clean sportsman, yes, but he was no prude, no mollycoddle. He was a man's man, "a hero of the diamond and of life."[16]

After his death in October 1925, magazine writers continued to cast Mathewson in the role of a moral hero. In its November 12, 1925, obituary, *Youth's Companion* described the character of the "idol of the baseball world."[17] He lived by example, the boy's magazine noted: "He never preached his code. He lived it. He never played a dirty trick. . . . He never quarreled with an umpire. He always gave all that was in him." Because of his courage, fellow players and fans respected the man who was "bigger than the game itself." *Literary Digest,* like other publications, reminded readers of his kindness to teammates, as well as his displays of sportsmanship in defeat. Comparing his "manly character" to that of George Washington, Theodore Roosevelt, and Frank Merriwell, tributes celebrated Mathewson's kindness, self-control, sportsmanship, and honesty.

Sportswriters contended that baseball would never be the same, but, even so, some practices continued much as they had before tuberculosis robbed the nation. Mathewson was baseball's saint, and his foil, much as he always had been, was Cobb. Over the next five years, freelance writers for the nation's general-interest and specialty baseball magazines offered another round of fable-like odes to baseball's quintessential sinner and it ultimate saint. Through these parables, the nation's bards taught young boys lessons about how to be strong, successful American men.

In Mathewson and Cobb, sportswriters offered two brands of manhood. In Mathewson, they found a type of restrained manhood that meshed with the country's lingering Victorian sensibilities. He was a moral hero, a gentleman, a "clean, right-living man."[18] In an age marked by anxiety about manhood, journalists did not want readers to get the wrong impression. "Don't get the idea Matty was a mollycoddle," Wheeler warned *Literary Digest* readers in 1921. "He was 100 per cent male he-man." He supported his claims with evidence: "He smoked a bit, drank a bit, at times gambled and swore."[19] Again, in a *Literary Digest* tribute, weeks after his death in 1925, Wheeler observed that, though he was a clean sportsman, "no prude was Matty."[20] Wheeler emphasized Mathewson's occasional foray with the bottle, his service during the war, his manly companionship on hunting trips, and his courage in death.

Likewise, sportswriter W. O. McGeehan described Mathewson as a "gentleman, sportsman, and soldier . . . the incarnation of all those virtues with which we endow the ideal American."[21] Coverage after Mathewson's death emphasized his status as a war hero of the American Expeditionary Forces in France and as the gentleman of the diamond. It credited him with changing baseball from a roughneck sport to a respectable pastime.

If Mathewson was portrayed as a gentleman on the mound, Cobb was the savage of the base paths. Writers such as Edward E. Purinton referenced him in columns with tips for molding boys into men.[22] Publications noted "his sardonic, confident look" and "his assured, daring, and successful style of play."[23] Writers painted him as a real man's man, a devil in spikes tearing down the base paths. He was the dashing, daring modern hero of manhood. His "fiery determination" was so extreme, wrote the era's correspondents, that "even old Father Time cannot head him off."[24]

A 1926 column in *Youth's Companion* might have summed up the coverage of Cobb the best: the "Georgia Peach," was a man "of action," "the most skillful, sure, and clever batsman," who is "always alive, always full of energy."[25] Cobb may have been a savage "maniac" on the baseball field, but he was a "gentleman by instinct"; he always regretted the "diamond unpleasantnesses [*sic*]" that his "fiery temperament" got him into.

Journalists largely portrayed Mathewson as a restrained gentleman and Cobb as a martial man's man by drawing on figurative language and anecdotes. In doing so, they crafted oversimplified types of a "Christian Gentleman" and a cultural trickster. These stories taught American boys to walk a fine line between being overtaken by their primal, savage urges or acting as "mollycoddles." Sports such as baseball, and by extension tales of baseball heroes, provided a space to tame the primeval sexual beast, creating a balance between the primitive and civilized man by "offering physical release while warding off anxieties about 'dirty' sexuality."[26]

In short, through human-interest coverage of Cobb and Mathewson, journalists helped construct common-sense notions of manhood at the height of the age of the bachelor.[27] Although, as historian Gail Bederman contends, constructions of masculinity are always in flux, during the early twentieth century, by-products of industrialization, most notably the extension of women into the public sphere, caused men to question and to reformulate conceptions of manhood.[28] These stories provide evidence of the transition from the Victorian notion of the self-reliant man of character to the successful modern businessman.

Magazine coverage of the pair did more than provide lessons about success, morality, and manliness; it also taught readers lessons about what it meant to be an American. Although magazine writers referenced the duo's humble upbringings, correspondents focused more on their status as national icons. Coverage of the "self-made men" emphasized the possibility of achieving the American dream through determination and hard work. Sportswriters supplied American readers with stories of the secrets of their success. Writers emphasized American ingenuity, noting their shrewd skill and inventiveness. For instance, in 1926, *Literary Digest* noted that Cobb concocted the fallaway slide to outwit his opponents,[29] and *Outing* called Mathewson's fadeaway pitch "the greatest deceiver ever used."[30]

Youth's Companion also celebrated both men as successful American heroes. The publication emphasized their skill, vitality, hard work, and sportsmanship. In 1926, for instance, the publication wrote that American boys "may easily find many less admirable heroes than Ty Cobb."[31] If, as folklorist Tristram Coffin says, "each age re-writes the past into a drama to fit its own purposes," in the first three decades of the twentieth century, national magazines largely portrayed Cobb and Mathewson as mythic idols to teach lessons about success, manliness, morality, and the American way.[32]

Other writing practices too, it seemed, had continued much as they had before the aftermath of the 1919 Black Sox scandal and Mathewson's death. Ghostwriters, for instance, had lingered in the national pastime. In 1921, promoter Christy Walsh joined Wheeler's Bell Syndicate in the custom. That season, Walsh signed a contract with baseball's newest sensation, New York Yankees slugger Babe Ruth. In addition to a thousand-dollar signing bonus, Walsh guaranteed Ruth a percentage of his earnings on future columns. He also promised him that he "would never have to touch a typewriter or pencil."[33] Like Bell Syndicate, the Christy Walsh Syndicate bankrolled a number of well-known sports journalists such as Damon Runyon and Ford Frick to pen columns for baseball stars such as Washington Senators pitcher Walter Johnson and St. Louis Cardinals second baseman Rogers Hornsby.[34]

Still, the "player-writer evil" remained contentious in the baseball writing community. After the institution of the commissioner system in 1920, ghostwriters for large syndicates reinstated the practice of writing articles for star World Series participants. By the mid-1920s, Lane's *Baseball Magazine*, like *Sporting Life* of a decade prior, reported on the ills of the system. In January 1926, *Baseball Magazine* correspondent Irving E. Sanborn crafted a five-page column considering how the Baseball Writers' Association of America might address the predicament. "If there were no bona fide player-writers, the problem would be fairly simple," Sanborn wrote of the longstanding quandary. "There are a few well-known stars, managers, or umpires, who actually pound out on a typewriter or into the ears of a stenographer, the World's Series' articles which appear under or over their names. And as a rule it is mighty good stuff."[35] The trouble was created by the "mass of fake stuff which pours over the telegraph wires before and during the World's Series, purporting to be written by well-known diamond stars . . . but which is really typed by writers who usually know less about baseball than the average bat boy does." These stories were based upon "haphazard conversations with celebrities . . . by freelance reporters," who failed to submit it to the baseball stars, Sanborn continued.

The articles were sold to "gullible or complacent publishers under the cloak of some 'syndicate' or other. Frequently the 'syndicate' is composed entirely of the freelance reporter himself, who seizes this chance to make a lot of easy coin by bunking the public." Although a veteran sporting editor could easily tell the difference between the authentic and fake player-author articles, he contended, the "credulous fan-reader [was] liable to accept the half-portion opinions of a second rate reporter as seriously as if they were those of some great player."

Sanborn was echoing the emerging concerns of a wide range of cultural critics from journalists such as Silas Bent, Malcolm Bingay, and Walter Lippmann to playwright Sinclair Lewis and Frankfurt School scholars such as Theodor Adorno, Herbert Marcuse, and Max Horkheimer. These individuals were concerned with the impact of mass-mediated messages on members of the bourgeoisie. Some individuals, such as Sanborn, contended that readers were passive dupes in danger of being easily swayed by the kitsch produced by individuals consumed with profit-driven motives of a consumer-capitalist regime.

The "player-writer evil" had risen to the level of crisis during the 1925 World Series when ghostwriters thousands of miles from Pittsburgh's Forbes Field authored articles for baseball stars heavily criticizing umpires. Even authentic player-writer stories, like the best of the phony ghostwritten stories, were partisan and prejudiced. A loyal player-writer could never tell his honest opinion, noted Sanborn, unlike "the good baseball scribe [who] not only can but does write things as he saw them, without thought, or fear, of favoring either side." He contended that sportswriters were neutral, detached chroniclers of action. As critics such as Bingay and Bent could attest, however, that could not have been further from the truth.[36] In order to eradicate the enduring predicament, Sanborn suggested a public education campaign "aimed at the publishers and editors of newspapers who fall for and pay for these phoney" stories or the barring of known frauds from professional baseball's press boxes.

Baseball Magazine considered the issue again in its June and November 1926 issues. In "Is Player-Writing an Evil?" correspondent James M. Gould reiterated that the problem was phony ghostwritten stories, not authentic player-written articles.[37] Even so, like Sanborn, he asserted that even authentic player-penned articles were inferior to those of professional reporters. Assuring readers that his colleagues did not "fear the invasion of ball-players" out of envy, he noted that it "takes a bit more than intelligence to write of baseball—it takes training." Although professional journalism training was still in its infancy, Gould attempted to distinguish the work of professional sportswriters from the drivel of ghosts. He did so because he was concerned that his way of life might be jeopardized by the popularity of ghosted material.

In November 1926, Sanborn covered the contentious issue once more, reiterating his educational campaign. He wrote: "It ought to be up to the publishers and sporting editors to see that their papers print only genuine articles. . . . there are, however, some editors who will buy and print phony player-articles. . . . Then, too, there are a few editors who will order their baseball reporters to deliberately fake stories by prominent players."[38]

Despite the condemnation of baseball magnates, suggested measures of the Baseball Writers' Association of America, and vigorous educational campaigns of the sporting press, the practice of ghostwriting continued.[39] As *Baseball Digest* correspondent Harold Rosenthal suggested in October 1960, “ghost-writing in baseball goes in cycles” that correspond to anticipated public appetites.[40] The public education campaigns of the Baseball Writers’ Association of America were not enough to curtail the custom, as Sanborn suggested in November 1926, because the practice was profitable for publishers.[41]

In an age of celebrity-focused, human-interest journalism, publishers were willing to ignore publicity and literary elements in sports journalism. Ghostwriters such as Wheeler and Walsh did more than collaborate with star baseball players on human-interest features; they served as unofficial press agents in the fledgling era of modern public relations. Until the Black Sox scandal, Major League baseball clubs had relied on publicity from sportswriters. So, too, did professional baseball stars.[42] In the age of self-exposure, celebrities entered into symbiotic alliances with human-interest journalists. Sportswriters transitioned from partners in collaborative journalistic endeavors to trusted advisors and pseudo-press agents, who offered antecedent public relations strategies to sports icons. While Ivy Lee, “the father of public relations,” was consulting the Rockefellers, Wheeler was advising Cobb and Mathewson in a similar, albeit unofficial, manner.[43]

By the mid-1920s, ghostwriting was becoming unpopular with some segments of professional journalism. Ghostwriting was among the “questionable” practices that sparked the formation of the American Society of Newspaper Editors in 1923.[44] Together with factions of the Baseball Writers’ Association of America, the new organization sought to dismantle what *Detroit News* managing editor Malcolm Bingay called an “ungodly union” between sportswriters and baseball celebrities. To diffuse what the former sports reporter termed “the rottenest condition in American journalism,” the American Society of Newspaper Editors sought to eliminate promotional copy through standardization in the sports department.[45] Under new detached models, sports reporters could no longer bypass “seasoned copy editors whose blue pencils assured the standardization and uniformity that veteran editors associated with the highest ideals of the profession.” The promotional player-author practice had created an ethical conflict of interest in an emerging detached world of journalism that centered on positivist conceptions of objectivity. This, along with the evolution of libel law after the 1950s, led to the gradual decline of the practice.[46]

For years, players such as Cobb had enjoyed free promotion from sympathetic sportswriters, "gee whiz" mythmakers, and journalistic collaborators. As his career came near to an end in 1926, Cobb would depend on these cozy relationships more than ever. At the end of that season, he unexpectedly retired. After issuing his letter of resignation to Navin, he told the nation's cadre of sportswriters that he was tired. He was disappointed with his lackluster performance as the Tigers' player-manager. He wanted to go out while he was still on top of his game. Cobb's reasons sounded logical enough. He had, after all, just completed his twenty-second year in the Major Leagues, but something in the way he said that he would miss the game and the equally unforeseen news that his friend Tris Speaker was retiring from his post as the manager of the Cleveland Indians told sportswriters that there was more to the story.

In September, *Chicago Tribune* reporters realized that there was much more to the news of Cobb's and Speaker's retirement.[47] Johnson had forced them out after reading two letters that pointed to their guilt in agreeing to fix a game during the 1919 season. Dutch Leonard, a disgruntled player who was released by Cobb in 1925, had furnished the letters to Johnson and Navin. Although the letters only made a vague allusion to gambling, which was at the time not illegal in professional baseball, Johnson had told Cobb and Speaker that their managing and playing days were over. They could leave quietly with their images intact, and they would never read about it in the headlines. They agreed, but *Chicago Tribune* reporters were not so generous. They threatened to publish the story they had unless Major League commissioner Judge Kennesaw Mountain Landis released details of the duo's retirement. He did and began an investigation of his own. In the hiatus, much to the chagrin of Johnson and Navin, the sportswriting world came to the defense of Cobb and Speaker. Even celebrities such as Will Rogers supported the pair. "If they had been selling out all of these years," he said. "I would like to see them play when they weren't selling out."[48]

Four months later, on January 27, Landis reversed Johnson's decision and reinstated Cobb and Speaker to their respective clubs. Speaker initially opted to remain in the grandstands, but Cobb decided to invoke baseball's infamous ten-day reserve clause and put himself on the free market. A number of Major League club managers including McGraw and Mack entered into a bidding war over the still-talented hitter.

In the end, Mack made him an offer he could not refuse. He played for the Philadelphia Athletics for two seasons, and he did not let down his loving fan base. In 1928, he posted a .323 batting average, but that season would be his last. He was ready to enter a new phase of his life. He entertained the idea of purchasing a ball club, but in the last instance, he decided to spend his remaining years managing his investments from his homes in Augusta, Detroit, and Atherton, California. Over the years, he also spent a good deal of time visiting with his sportswriting chums.

After Lane's retirement from *Baseball Magazine* in 1937, he had taken a position as the head of Piedmont College's History Department in the 1940s.[49] Located in the foothills of northeast Georgia, the university was not far way from Cobb's home in Augusta or from his business affairs in Atlanta. The two old pals exchanged invitations and friendly calls over the years.

Cobb also would visit with Rice frequently throughout the 1930s and 1940s. Rice had always kept a busy schedule, and it had not let up in the hiatus. If anything, it had only gotten busier. In addition to his syndication and freelance obligations, for a brief time, he had tried his hand at sports broadcasting. He had served as the play-by-play man for the first World Series to be broadcast over the airwaves in 1921. Radio, however, had not been for him. Over the next decade, he instead produced sports films and penned plays.[50]

Rice may have been busy, but he always made time for one of the men who had made him. In 1939, for instance, he arranged a golf outing with Cobb at Pebble Beach, and the two traveled to Greenville, South Carolina, to drop in on "Shoeless" Joe Jackson after the 1947 Masters Golf Tournament in Augusta.[51] On one occasion, Cobb invited Rice, along with fellow journalists Gene Fowler and Henry McLemore, to his California home. En route from the San Francisco airport to his Menlo Park estate, he made a confession to Grantland.

As Rice recalled in his autobiography, "'Grant,' he said suddenly stopping near the end of the runway while a giant transport buzzed us, 'Do you remember the wire you received back in 1904 . . . about the phenom from Royston. . . . And do you remember a flock of post-cards from all over Alabama and Georgia, telling you what a hot shot I was . . . all signed with different names?' In the parked car, he admitted his promotional tactic. When Rice asked him why, he responded: 'Because I was in a hurry. We were both youngsters on the way up. I didn't know it then but I was trying to put you onto your first big scoop!'"

Perhaps no one in the baseball community had understood the value of promotion better than Cobb. As he grew older, he continued to use his friendships with American sportswriters to his advantage; some relationships, however, were showing signs of strain. On March 27, 1952, Rice wrote an unflattering column about him. It suggested that his criticism of modern baseball stemmed from his envy of Ruth's fame. On May 5, in frustration, Cobb penned an angry letter to Rice. He wrote that Rice should not have published the unflattering comments "upon the grounds of our friendship."[52]

If Lardner had still been alive, he might have defended Cobb. He, like Cobb, lacked an appreciation for the home-run era ushered in by what he called the "Br'er Rabbit" ball.[53] Lardner, however, had died some nineteen years earlier of complications from heart disease caused by years of heavy drinking. Rice would join him two years later. Shortly after finishing a column about Willie Mays and the All-Star Game on his faithful Royal typewriter, he died at his desk of heart failure on July 13, 1954.[54]

In the ensuing years, Cobb found that he still had some friends in the sportswriting community, but some were beginning to forsake him. In the aftermath of his death seven years later, the nation would find out just who his true friends were. Al Stump was not one of them. After ghosting an autobiography of Cobb shortly before his death, Stump wrote a damning portrait of Cobb, which appeared in the December 1961 issue of *True Men's Magazine*. In "Ty Cobb's Wild 10-Month Fight to Live," Cobb's former ghost presented him as an alcoholic, paranoid megalomaniac who suffered from a severe bout with pancreatic cancer. After the controversial piece was published, Cobb's remaining friends in the world of sports rushed to his defense in J. G. Taylor Spink's *Sporting News*.[55] In the following months, Spink published approximately fifty articles and editorials offering favorable images of Cobb. Wheeler's byline was not among those published in baseball's bible. Neither was Lane's.

The last remaining working writer of the bunch was Wheeler. He had been the first in the press box in 1907, and he was the last man standing. Like Rice, he had remained a dominant force in the journalism profession. In the mid-1920s, he had written freelance articles for national magazines while handling the day-to-day operations of his Bell Syndicate and serving as the executive editor of *Liberty* magazine. In 1930, he had taken a position as the general manager of the North American Newspaper Alliance, which had absorbed his Bell Syndicate. From this post, over the next thirty-three years, he continued to direct some of the nation's finest journalists, from Rice to Ernest Hemingway.[56] In the end, his obituary in the *Ridgefield* [Connecticut] *Press* may have summed his life up best. Like Rice, he was a man who had "never quit newspapering, permanently, until his death" on October 13, 1973.[57]

Lane, however, had quit "newspapering" long before. After his stint in the History Department at Piedmont College, he and his wife Emma traveled around the world. They circumnavigated the globe six times, and he wrote books of geography, nature, and poetry over the next three decades.[58] In their twilight years, he and his wife settled in Cape Cod; he died in a nursing home at age ninety-eight on April 20, 1984. He was far removed from his days as the editor of *Baseball Magazine.*

When Lane left his post at *Baseball Magazine* in 1937, "gee whiz" baseball reporting was in a period of dormancy. It had begun its decline in the aftermath of the 1919 Black Sox scandal, but despite the best efforts of the American Society of Newspaper Editors and newspaper critics such as Silas Bent and Malcolm Bingay, who had demanded an end to the "unholy union" in sport, it had lingered in American culture throughout the Roaring Twenties. The champions of detached journalism, however, would have the last word during the bleak days of the Great Depression. Americans were not in the mood for sports heroes anymore, and even if they were, newspapers did not have space for the grandiose language of Rice and the crop of imitators that had sprung up around him.

Washington Post columnist Shirley Povich became the face of the next generation of sportswriters. When Povich began his career as a sportswriter covering the Senators for the *Washington Post* in 1924, he admitted to being "a hero worshipper," but he told Holtzman that he soon learned to detach himself. "You say to yourself, 'They're ballplayers. Let them play the game. I'm a reporter.'"[59] His pal Red Smith agreed. "I've tried not to exaggerate the glory of athletes," he told Holtzman. "I'd rather, if I could, preserve a sense of proportion."[60]

In the early twentieth century, editors such as Harvey Woodruff of the *Chicago Tribune* had begun rotating their beat reporters from team to team to preserve a sense of detachment for the sake of objectivity. By the 1920s, editors were drilling the concept of detachment into their reporters' heads. *New York Times* sportswriter John Drebinger recalled to Holtzman that his editors constantly reiterated the worthiest mission of journalism. They "banged it into our heads . . . never show any prejudice or bias. . . . Always report objectively. . . . Above all don't slant your stuff!"[61] As Povich acknowledged, cheerleading lingered into the middle of the twentieth century. It lingers still. However, the writers of Povich's generation attempted to adhere to standards of objectivity—to be detached journalists capable of writing an investigative exposé when actions or events warranted one. They wrote succinctly and looked down on the "maudlin balderdash" of the previous generation. As Smith told Holtzman, above all they wanted to be remembered as good reporters, "good and honest and accurate."[62]

-11-

The End of the "Gee Whiz" Era

Like many Americans, young Dick Russell and Furman Bisher "devoured" sports news in the early twentieth century. Sprawled out on floors of post offices and living rooms, they enjoyed daily encounters with the sports page. They also perused general-interest magazines and specialty publications for features about their favorite stars. In an era before radio gained a pervasive presence in American culture, the sports scribe crafted feature stories about the national pastime's stars for a baseball-crazed nation.

Sportswriters played a complex cultural role. They did more than merely transmit information about baseball stars to sports enthusiasts. As communication theorist James Carey suggests, they acted as cultural storytellers, interpreters with the power to shape reality.[1] They translated actions on the baseball diamond into allegories that taught character lessons. They influenced not only the lives of the individuals about whom they wrote, but the lives of their readers as well. They simultaneously exerted pressure on the images and legacies of baseball stars and instructed readers in cultural dos and don'ts with their myth-narratives.[2] Through these simple archetypal story frames, they taught crucial lessons about the American way of life. They offered moral exemplars of manhood that might help individuals of all social milieus to succeed in American culture. Using cultural shorthand, national magazine correspondents cast Cobb and Mathewson into a binary of sinner and saint to instruct readers about cultural acceptability. Cultural norms, values, and mores, however, were not always clear-cut. During an era in which Victorian and modern norms collided, writers sent mixed messages about manhood and success. They told their readers that real men were expected to take daring risks while at the same time behaving as proper gentlemen. Sports journalists claimed a degree of creative freedom through the process of writing, but in the last instance, they were bound by economic, cultural, and social factors. Consequently, they produced innocuous American heroes of manhood for mainstream audiences.

A symbiotic relationship existed among publishers, editors, writers, and baseball's elite, and the production of sports heroes for a nation consumed with hero-worship was the simple byproduct of that alliance.[3] Avoiding a functionalist account,[4] it can be said that ballyhoo prevailed in sports journalism for a season, but in the end, detachment emerged, albeit unevenly.

The evolution of the public sphere in the eighteenth and nineteenth centuries created a new public fascination with the private lives of the famous.[5] The press had included biographies of prominent American icons since the colonial era, but beginning in the late nineteenth century, newspaper and magazine publishers attempted to profit on the perceived public interest in celebrity profiles.[6] Biographies had long presented leaders of business and industry as men of character, exemplars to be emulated, but by the mid-nineteenth century, individuals were beginning to recognize them for what they were—in many cases self-promotional stories that masked the foibles of the rich and famous. Since the real self was not on display in public venues, celebrity journalists were the only hope of gaining insight into the character of cultural icons. Consequently, top reporters began to seek out the minutiae of the private lives of American icons. Only leading reporters, however, were able to gain entry into the inside circle of celebrities.[7]

In the man's world of sports, journalists entered a close community of magnates, club owners, managers, officials, players, and other sportswriters.[8] Sportswriters and players engaged in close contact with one another by virtue of the relatively small size of the profession and the operational structure of the two industries.[9] Reporters traveled, dined, and lodged with baseball icons. They even enjoyed leisure activities together. They did so in part, as Rice suggested, for companionship in a grueling profession that required days on the road away from family and friends. They also forged friendships with stars to cull inside information for their human-interest stories—to give readers a peek into the private lives of sport celebrities.

Although they shared almost daily interaction with sportswriters, stars did not have to fear investigative exposés into their private affairs. Gallico contended that prominent writers were constrained by personal relationships with sports celebrities.[10] Afraid of losing their insider status, they did not dare unearth controversial gossip. He wrote that, in the last instance, writers were "handcuffed" by their desire to remain in inside circles. "It's not easy to break bread with a person, play golf with him, be received in his home as a friend and sometimes a trusted advisor, then go down to the office and write a signed story critical of the man," he lamented.[11]

Through writing, sports journalists enjoyed a degree of agency in how they crafted baseball stars. Sportswriters and editors had the power of story selection and presentation. Even so, these portrayals were bound by more than a writer's "pleasure and escape."[12] Sports journalism was governed by the cultural conventions of American society and the journalistic profession. Mainstream cultural values such as those associated with success and manhood shaped the perspectives of sports reporters. Editors and writers, for instance, were influenced by the pervasiveness of the muscular-Christianity movement in American culture.

Because sportswriters penned features at for-profit magazines and newspapers, they were encouraged to produce copy that appealed to the masses. Consequently, journalists avoided stances that were too controversial; instead, they crafted heroes from common archetypal structures, which had existed across cultures since ancient times.[13] They drew upon the familiar frames and story arcs of the hero, the villain, and the trickster, and wove their stories together with metaphors and allusions. The more skilled writers experimented with characterization and dialogue. They relied upon these literary techniques to instruct their readers.

Drawing on certain story structures and forms undoubtedly influenced content.[14] The newly emerging detached journalistic model dictated that Rice's newspaper columns maintain a more neutral, balanced tone.[15] While the activist model pervasive in magazine journalism allowed room for promotional human-interest features, player-themed magazine issues and memoirs took on a promotional tone that mirrored their form.

Media historian W. Joseph Campbell contends that three basic paradigms governed journalism in the early twentieth century, but these detached, narrative, and activist models did not exist in isolation of one another.[16] The epistemologies that undergirded the models coexisted in newsrooms and influenced the practice of journalism. Rice's columns provide evidence of the overlaps and ruptures in journalistic paradigms. Instances of hero-worship coexisted in the same journalistic space as neutral references to an icon's accomplishments.[17] Regardless of the format, however, the promotional model was pervasive in the era's sports journalism.

The promotional model was founded upon an "unholy union" among sportswriters, club owners, managers, and players. Under these mutually beneficial relationships, upper-echelon sportswriters earned high salaries and national renown, and baseball celebrities gained free promotion as well as a degree of autonomy in their portrayals. As player-correspondents, Cobb and Mathewson earned "soft money" as self-promoters.[18] They also used these journalistic formats as promotional forums to shape their national images. It was not unusual for the press to promote individuals, issues, or organizations. In the age of "seedbed" public relations strategies,[19] baseball magnates relied upon the press to promote the industry.[20] Professional writers constructed baseball heroes to turn a profit.

Journalists celebrated Cobb and Mathewson as national idols. Correspondents at national magazines cast them into cultural roles of sinner and saint to teach readers character lessons. Folklorist Tristram Coffin writes that each age constructs a "drama to fit its own purposes";[21] in the early twentieth century, sportswriters taught lessons about success, manliness, morality, and what it meant to be an American. Magazines did not offer profiles of unblemished American icons as guides to blindly emulate; instead, they offered more nuanced portraits that educated Americans about basic character lessons. For example, in their discussions of Cobb's fallaway slide and Mathewson's fadeaway pitch, sports scribes instilled the idea that successful Americans were inventive, taking clever risks, which were rewarded. The media's celebration of baseball heroes, as sports media historian Bruce Evensen notes, was "a commentary on a generation's search for significance during a period in American history when for many the world seemed increasingly insensible."[22]

In the first three decades of the twentieth century, waves of immigrants and rural migrants flooded American cities. Leaders, intellectuals, and writers sought to make the nation a great melting pot. President Theodore Roosevelt, for instance, hoped to unify the nation through sports such as football and baseball. This surge in nationalism was evident not only in the promotional rhetoric surrounding sport, but also in the move toward immigration restriction and the standardization of American culture in the public and private realms.[23] As the role of church and family began to erode in an increasingly modern age, sport became a powerful ideological tool. The sporting press became a national educator, crafting heroes to teach American-ness. Sportswriters constructed baseball stars as self-made icons, as symbols of American exceptionalism, who pulled themselves up by their bootstraps. The sporting press celebrated Cobb and Mathewson as self-made men, who succeeded through a mixture of individualism and teamwork.

The production of sports heroes did more than inform immigrants about what it meant to be an American. Sportswriters taught readers what it meant to be successful. The early twentieth century marked the coming of age of the American success story. By century's turn, "hymns to American middle-class concepts of success"[24] were no longer confined to Horatio Alger's dime novels; instead, success stories were pervasive in American journalism.[25] Newspapers and magazines were filled with human-interest stories about leaders of industry and ingenuity such as J. P. Morgan, J. D. Rockefeller, and Henry Ford as well as heroes of action—war heroes such as Sergeant Alvin C. York, heroes of adventure such as Charles Lindbergh, and sports heroes. A new cast of successful sports heroes joined Cobb, Mathewson, and Ruth. The list of athletic greats included football icons Knute Rockne and Red Grange, golfing legend Bobby Jones, boxer Jack Dempsey, and tennis stars Bill Tilden and Helen Wills. Even the funny pages would come to feature fictional stories of successful heroes. During the Great Depression, superheroes such as Batman and Superman would appear alongside the heroic exploits of Little Orphan Annie.[26] In their portraits of these icons and their roads to success, the press celebrated traits associated with business acumen such as self-reliance, along with those associated with religious piety and manliness such as wholesomeness and tenacity.

In an age of lingering Victorian cultural norms, sportswriters constructed Mathewson as an honest and fair player, who displayed good sportsmanship under all circumstances.[27] They recognized his successes such as his remarkable performance in the 1905 World Series, but they celebrated him even more in defeat. Crafted by sportswriters as a moral hero on a par with George Washington,[28] Mathewson was often asked to speak to young boys about "clean living and fair play."[29]

Shortly after the release of the memoir *Pitching in a Pinch* in 1912, the Boy Scouts of America endorsed the volume as one that would not only "entertain" but also "train" young boys.[30] Later that year, G. P. Putnam's Sons released a special Boy Scouts edition of the book. In their 1914 *Handbook for Scout Masters,* the Boy Scouts advertised the volume as one "guaranteed . . . to provide clean, wholesome, vigorous stories."[31] Mathewson may have been depicted as "clean," but magazine writers such as Wheeler assured readers that he was a "100 per cent male, he-man."[32] Likewise, although the national media crafted Cobb as a primeval savage on the base paths, sports promoters such as Wheeler and Lane provided a caveat. Despite his "fiery temperament," Cobb was ultimately a "gentleman."[33]

In an era of an inescapable encounter with modernity and world war marked by a "crisis in masculinity,"[34] Mathewson and Cobb were constructed as heroes of restrained and martial manhood.[35] Historian Amy S. Greenberg argues that the two models of manhood emerged in the late nineteenth century. She constructs a binary of manhood; however, the paradigms did not exist in isolation from one another. The fluidity of these cultural constructions is evident within the cultural contradictions in sports coverage. Within the same editorial space, Cobb is celebrated as a "real" man in touch with his savage, primeval self, as well as a "gentleman." These paradoxes within coverage provide evidence of the fluidity of cultural constructions of masculinity.[36]

In an age that sought simplicity in heroic figures,[37] the national media cast the icons into cultural roles as America's preeminent sinner and its quintessential saint. Mass-mediated heroes and villains are symbols for tensions within social orders, such as the inevitable encounter with modernity in the early twentieth century. In an increasingly modern world, sportswriters drew upon ancient types to cast Mathewson and Cobb into roles that taught moral lessons about right and wrong. Material rewards, they argued, could be earned by trickery on the base paths, but true success could be won regardless of victory or defeat by being a good sport, someone who is always fair, honest, loyal, and kind.

The media's celebration of both idols reveals a cultural struggle over residual and emergent traditions. Mathewson was a successful pitcher and valiant war-hero, who claimed victory over death, but in the last instance, he was the ultimate self-reliant man of character. Press coverage emphasized his wholesome Protestant upbringing and his virtuous character. He was a throwback to the Victorian era. Cobb, on the other hand, was a self-made man who gained success not only by being a dedicated student of the game but by taking measured risks. He, too, was a war hero, and he fought with the same tenacity on the diamond. He was a real man's man, a modern American hero. In baseball, both men found a space to tame the primeval sexual beast, while learning important cultural values such as teamwork that would serve them well in the modern world. Sportswriters argued that America's youth could learn these same lessons through baseball, and if they did not have time to play the game, they could pick them up by studying the local sports page or a specialty sports publication.

Magazine depictions of baseball's sinner and saint reflect the religious overtones of a larger cultural struggle that defined the Progressive Era. "Today, the distinction between the righteous and sinners is the main thing, for upon a lively consciousness of that distinction rests the hope of transmitting our institutions undecayed, of preserving our democratic ideals, of avoiding stratification and class rancor," renowned American sociologist Edward Ross wrote in *Sin and Society* (1907).[38]

Magazine writers warned against worshipping the greedy gods of finance; instead, they encouraged readers to forge a new path.[39] Press profiles no longer merely sketched out a road to success for readers to follow. Instead, they crafted portraits of heroes and villains in human-interest features that often mirrored characters in ancient parables and fables.

In the Progressive Era, the press encouraged Americans to abide by a new type of moral individualism. Thus, they painted Cobb as a sinister villain during the moments when he held out for higher paying contracts or when he seemed to disregard the welfare of his team for his own individual pursuits. Meanwhile, they celebrated Mathewson as a saint for always putting his team first, such as when he blamed himself instead of Snodgrass for the 1912 World Series loss.

By the Roaring Twenties, however, many Americans had grown tired of Puritanical harangues. In 1919, philosopher Morris Raphael Cohen observed that baseball had become America's national religion, and the press portrayed Cobb and Mathewson as gods.[40] Baseball and its cast of stars became a secular religion in the modern nation.[41] During the decade, the press began to shift their focus from considerations of the character of cultural icons to discussions of their personalities.[42] The moral range among baseball heroes illustrated the secular shift. As sports historian Donald Mrozek wrote, "A Christy Mathewson revered for his upstanding personal life, and a Ty Cobb admired despite his seeming indifference to humane concerns."[43] The common theme emphasized in press accounts of Cobb and Mathewson was their road to success marked by a stark level of tenacity and discipline to the science of baseball.

National magazine coverage of Cobb and Mathewson reveals a continuing devotion to Victorian values such as the Protestant work ethic, as well as a celebration of cunning and risk-taking in a modern world. Both sets of norms were valued in an emerging consumer-capitalist society. Press coverage of the two baseball stars appealed to the modern nation's fascination with statistics and quantifiable deeds.[44] Cultural historian Warren Susman argued that "the mechanization of life generally, when combined with the mounting effort to rationalize all aspects of man's activities, produced a particular middle-class delight in what could be measured and counted."[45] In an era marked by pervasive scientism, Cobb and Mathewson were celebrated as national heroes for their remarkable deeds on the baseball diamond, deeds that could be counted, measured, and compared. The duo's quantifiable success translated into portrayals as self-made men. National magazines constructed both as intelligent students of the scientific game, who turned calculated risks into rewards.[46]

In the last instance, press coverage of the two icons perpetuated a common-sense logic of sport that emphasized its usefulness as a cultural tool, which instilled ideal values such as rugged individualism, teamwork, sportsmanship, discipline, hard work, self-reliance, and a love for one's country. The positive sporting creed was an especially potent construct in America's modern capitalist society, which relied on an achievement-driven workforce. As Frankfurt School cultural critic Theodor Adorno suggested, however, mediated coverage of sport appeared "to restore to the body some of the functions of which the machine has deprived it" only to "train men all the more inexorably to serve the machine."[47]

Although most national magazine correspondents cast Cobb and Mathewson as national hero and trickster, some writers avoided typecasting the duo. Dayton Stoddard and C. E. Van Loan, for instance, flipped the stereotypes, portraying Cobb as a national hero and Mathewson as a trickster, who cunningly swindled a rookie with his master fadeaway pitch.[48] Likewise Rice, Lane, and Wheeler celebrated Cobb as a national hero. These contradictions in coverage not only provide evidence of the potential agency in the practice of writing, they also illustrate the fluid nature of cultural types. Conceptions of hero, villain, and trickster are not static classifications. They are social constructions mutually constituted in cultural interactions that are subject to change over the course of time. On September 19, 1925, *Literary Digest* illustrated the fluctuations of heroic cultural status: "On [baseball diamonds], national heroes are created with more rapidity and louder acclaim than anywhere else in the country, yet how precarious their position, how fickle the popular favor on which they live! The roar of applause in the bleachers turns with incredible ease into howls of disapproval. And hands that one year are waved in greeting to a mighty man of the baseball field, the next will show their thumbs turned down on him."[49]

Writing about the paradoxes embedded in heroic accolades, the article "Spanking Baseball's Baby and Petting Its Paragon" celebrates Cobb as a flawless ideal, "the story of a determination to succeed, to be the first in the chosen endeavor of life." Meanwhile, it casts Ruth as a sniveling child rebelling against baseball's rules of conduct.

The mediated portrayals of Cobb and Mathewson also reveal the fluidity of the cultural values that are celebrated. Many correspondents decried Cobb's cunning on the base paths, but in his columns, Rice instead praised Cobb as an astute student of the game. Likewise, *Youth's Companion* portrayed him as a "daring" man of "action" willing to work hard.[50] In December 1926, a correspondent wrote that Cobb was "always alive, always full of energy and subtlety, a player who had wit and humor and a personality that gave color and brilliance to every play he made—the d'Artagnan of the ball field."[51]

Mathewson may have been gone in December 1926, but he was not forgotten. After his long battle with tuberculosis ended in October 1925, Rice's old newspaper, the *New York Herald-Tribune,* wrote that Mathewson's legacy would last as long as baseball was played. Praising him for more than his prowess on the mound, the publication suggested that he was the "the incarnation of all those virtues with which we endow the ideal American."[52] *Youth's Companion* added that "every true sportsman in America paid . . . tribute [to the man who] was bigger than the game itself."[53]

Mathewson was bigger than the game itself, and his reputation lived on in the years after his death. In 1930, fiction writer Merritte

Parmelee Allen penned "Christy Mathewson's Glove" for *St. Nicholas* boy's magazine.[54] Within the fictional story, "Coach Wade," a former teammate of Mathewson's, teaches "Cal," the captain of a high-school baseball team, that winning is not everything by sharing anecdotes about Matty's career. "Some day there may be a greater player—though I doubt it—but there will never be a finer gentleman," Coach Wade told Cal in a pre-season pep talk. "He showed us that it takes a bigger man to lose than to win. We admired him in victory but we loved him in defeat." In 1983, Eric Rolfe Greenberg wrote *The Celebrant,* a piece of historical fiction, centered on the lives of a fictional immigrant family living in New York City and their interactions with Mathewson.[55] More recently, a play by Eddie Frierson, the one-act *"Matty": An Evening with "The Big Six,"*[56] was produced. In the collective memory of baseball enthusiasts, Mathewson is remembered as a moral hero—"a model of boyhood," known for his manly character and good sportsmanship in victory or defeat.[57] In the end, *Playground Magazine* was right when it lamented in December 1925 that "one of the supreme gentlemen of sport has died, leaving the world to a fine memory and at least a momentary heartache."[58]

The press's long farewell to Mathewson marked a temporary decline in production of moral sports heroes. In the first three decades of the twentieth century, the sporting press may have emphasized deeds above virtues,[59] but in a culture still anchored to its Puritan roots, they considered questions of character. They taught moral lessons through their coverage of baseball's Christian Gentleman and its crafty villain. As Susman suggests, in the 1920s the nation shifted from a "culture of character" to one consumed with personality.[60] Leaving behind discussions about moral character, the sporting press celebrated prominent personalities as characters. The human-interest, celebrity-style journalism of the early twentieth century reflects this new appeal. So, too, does America's fascination with Ruth in the Roaring Twenties.

In an increasingly secular world, sportswriters of the "Golden Age of Sports Writing" penned column after column celebrating the "Great Bambino," the "Sultan of Swat," not only for his hitting prowess but also for his colorful personality. In his autobiography, Rice wrote that Ruth and the other sports heroes of the 1920s "had something more than mere skill or competitive ability. They also had in record quality and quantity that indescribable asset known as color, personality, crowd appeal, or whatever you may care to call it."[61] Ruth was the ultimate sports hero in the modern world.[62]

By the mid-1920s, Ruth's fame had temporarily overshadowed that of Cobb and Mathewson. Historian Ken Sobol wrote that "more citizens of America, young and old, knew his name . . . than had ever heard of Ty Cobb."[63] Ruth maintained a pervasive presence in the national media. In addition to regular coverage in the sports pages and baseball magazines, the "Great Bambino" received regular media attention in general-interest magazines and on the radio. The exuberant hero of boyhood earned spots in national advertising campaigns, in vaudeville shows, on barnstorming tours, and even in the movies.[64]

Ruth was a brand of sports icon that historian Susan Drucker referred to as a pseudo-hero.[65] He achieved fame for his home-run slugging abilities, but by decade's end, he was, in the words of Daniel Boorstin, "known for his well-knownness."[66] He was not a sports hero; he was a sports celebrity. He had been "shaped, fashioned, and marketed as heroic" by the mass media.[67] He had been packaged as such to fill empty space—blank newsprint and dead airwaves—space that was positioned alongside advertisements for national products such as Coca-Cola, space that needed to be filled with entertaining content to attract the attention of the masses. Celebrities or pseudo-heroes, Boorstin contended, overshadowed and sullied the feats of the authentic hero—men and women who gained fame because of virtuous achievements that should be valued in American culture.

Ruth, however, could not count on the media to provide an unlimited supply of good press. Neither could any sports star. By the 1920s, the era of unbridled promotion in sportswriting was drawing to a close. More than a decade after the height of journalistic muckraking, Lardner and Hugh Fullerton helped uncover the 1919 Black Sox scandal.[68] With the aid of Mathewson, they introduced the "aw nuts" model of sportswriting. The promotion of baseball and its cast of stars, however, did not end when newly appointed baseball commissioner Kennesaw Mountain Landis banned "Shoeless" Joe Jackson and seven other Chicago White Sox from the sport, but it definitely changed. By the mid-1920s, members of the Baseball Writers' Association of America and the newly formed American Society of Newspaper Editors, such as *Detroit Press* managing editor Malcolm Bingay, called for an end of the unholy alliance between professional sports organizations and the press.[69] Bingay argued that publishers had created a Frankenstein monster in the promotion-driven sports pages and advocated for the system's demise.[70]

With sports stars no longer assured of good press, they began to hire press agents. Following the lead of Ruth, who hired Christy Walsh as his agent in 1921, baseball stars relied upon agents to serve as personal gatekeepers.[71] They served as middlemen between the press and celebrities. They advocated for promotional coverage. They also facilitated interviews, advertising endorsements, and special appearances, all of which served to further detach sportswriters from athletes.[72] Writers no longer felt as compelled to portray stars as heroes in order to maintain close rapport. After an unflattering story, they could avoid baseball stars and make amends later by appealing to the gatekeeper.

The beginning of the Great Depression witnessed the demise of "gee whiz" promotion in sportswriting. The collapsing economy meant smaller newspapers and less space devoted to sport.[73] The verbose style of Rice was no longer realistic. Poetic odes to sports heroes seemed less relevant in the more "serious" age.[74] The Great Depression undermined many of the prior cultural norms and values, such as those linking success to the Protestant work ethic.[75] This end of an era of innocence in American culture was reflected in the temporary death of "gee whiz" sports journalism.

Although modern sports journalism retained elements of promotion, by the 1930s sports stories became more standardized, and sportswriters no longer attempted to hide a player's flaws. As detachment emerged in the sporting press, the practice of mythmaking became more prevalent over the airwaves, where play-by-play announcers such as Red Barber and Graham McNamee forged heroes for a new generation of Americans in the 1940s and 1950s.[76] The more detached sporting press still crafted heroes of Joe DiMaggio and more recently Nolan Ryan and Cal Ripken,[77] but they did so with a greater sense of realism. The era of blind romanticism in sports journalism died during the stark days of the Great Depression.

Our historical understanding of a particular time and place is always limited. Our comprehension of the past is bound by the surviving records that documented past cultures and ways of life. Business correspondence, diaries, and memoirs that provide insight into the practice of journalism are scant, forcing reliance upon the limited remaining business correspondence of Lane and published memoirs of Cobb, Mathewson, Rice, Lardner, and Wheeler for a grasp of working relationships among sportswriters and baseball celebrities. Archival holdings are not necessarily complete, and published memoirs bring a set of inherent challenges to analysis. Historical studies also are governed by a scholar's own subjectivities. As cultural historian Raymond Williams wrote: "We 'see' in certain ways—that is, we interpret sensory information according to certain rules—these rules and interpretations—are, as a whole, neither fixed or constant. We can learn new rules and new interpretations, as a result of which we shall literally see in new ways."[78]

Future research on the production of sports heroes in the early twentieth century might explore audience reception of these cultural constructions by analyzing letters to the editor, letters, and scrapbooks. There is a dearth of historical studies on audience reception of mediated messages,[79] and such a study would provide a new appreciation of the negotiation of cultural norms and values. Mediated portrayals of sports icons were mutually constituted in cultural constructions of manhood. Future studies might examine sports-focused juvenile literature such as the Frank Merriwell series to gain new insights into the mediated construction of boyhood and manhood throughout the course of the twentieth century. The production of heroes was not limited to sports stars or to the first three decades of the twentieth century. Other studies might examine the practice of hero-crafting in other time periods and in other mediated platforms. Further studies on the role of the press as a promotional vehicle might explore the collaborative practice of ghostwriting in various cultural industries, from sports to business and politics.

In the first three decades of the twentieth century, sportswriters crafted heroes for a baseball-crazed nation fascinated with celebrities and fame. Although America's love affair with baseball extended across all sexes, classes, and ethnicities, the mainstream media's celebration of heroes did not. The mainstream sporting press cast only white men into roles as national idols. To do so, sportswriters forged friendships with baseball stars, but retaining rapport with celebrities meant ignoring their flaws. Today, the sports media still churn out heroes for a nation consumed by celebrity and fame. More than a half-century after the dismantling of baseball's color line, the twenty-first-century sports media celebrate African Americans, Asians, and Latinos along with their white counterparts. However, in a sport that banned female participants, baseball idols remain heroes of manhood.[80]

Today's sports heroes do not remain on their pedestals forever. In a twenty-four-hour news cycle, the sports media no longer hide an idol's imperfections. Instead, after fifteen minutes of fame, heroes are meticulously deconstructed. The twenty-first-century sports media hoist star athletes on a heroic pedestal, only to surreptitiously knock them off their cultural perch.

In an earlier era, before tales of the "Sultan of Swat" and "Joltin' Joe" DiMaggio flooded the air waves, sportswriters crafted "your father's idol."[81] Before the comic-book superheroes of the late 1930s, they created supermen of "action" with "muscles of steel" for a modern world.[82] Sports journalists penned daily odes to Dead Ball Era stars such as Cobb and Mathewson. They celebrated the deeds and virtues of these heroes of youth in newspaper columns, human-interest features, player-themed issues, and ghostwritten memoirs in an era of ballyhoo. And, "though heroes have a habit of sliding from the pedestal,"[83] in the early twentieth century, sports journalists crafted "kings of the diamond" who continue to linger in the American imagination.[84]

Epilogue

NOSTALGIA FOR A BYGONE ERA

Growing up in the sleepy mill town of Denton, North Carolina, Furman Bisher took pleasure in watching mill-league greats leg out triples while serving as the batboy and scorekeeper for his town's squad. When he was not watching baseball, he was reading about his heroes—the "Georgia Peach" and Pittsburgh Pirates outfielders Paul and Lloyd Waner—in the pages of the *Greensboro Daily News.*

"All of my life my ambition was to be a sportswriter," ninety-one-year-old Bisher admitted in early October 2009 in my office at the Grady College of Journalism and Mass Communication in Athens. In this aim, Bisher succeeded. After returning from serving in World War II, he took a job with the *Charlotte News.* From this post, he gained fame in the sports world for obtaining the first and only interview with "Shoeless" Joe Jackson after the 1919 Black Sox scandal.

By 1950, he had made it to the big time—a position as sports editor of the *Atlanta Constitution.* One of his first assignments in the field was to cover Ty Cobb Day, hosted by Atlanta Crackers owner Earl Mann to honor the baseball idol in 1952. Bisher met the "Georgia Peach" for the first time that day; six years later, he landed one of the biggest interviews of his young career.

In spring 1958, the *Saturday Evening Post* correspondent traveled to Cornelia, Georgia, for a three-day interview with the ailing baseball legend. "I knew him pretty well," the columnist recalled. "So, I went up to see him. Each morning, I would knock on his door . . . and each morning, he would say, 'Now, what is it that you are here for?' And we would have to start over again. . . . We had three wonderful days." They drove up to Chenocetah Mountain, the site of Cobb's future home near his birthplace in The Narrows. "He was real sentimental," Bisher remembered. "And, he took me by the hand and said, 'As soon as I get finished, I am going to give you a key to this house, and anytime you want to bring your family up here, you can.'"

Bisher's article, focusing on the seventy-one-year-old Cobb's plan for his twilight years, ran weeks later in the *Post*'s June issue. Upon receiving his fifteen-hundred-dollar freelance payment, he sent a check to the Ty Cobb Educational Foundation, a scholarship program for Georgia youngsters. "About two weeks later, I got a letter from him, about three-and-a-half pages in green ink, and it started out 'Dear Bisher' . . . berating me because I didn't send him more money," he chuckled, noting that he sold that very same letter for more than two thousand dollars in recent years.

Over the next five decades, Bisher contributed hundreds of articles to national magazines, from the *Sporting News* to the *Saturday Evening Post.* He covered everything from the World Series to the Kentucky Derby as a columnist and sports editor at the *Atlanta Journal-Constitution.*

Bisher retired from that world less than two weeks after our 2009 interview. On October 12, he typed his farewell column for the *Atlanta Journal-Constitution* on his beloved Royal typewriter. For fifty-nine years, he had served in various roles as reporter, editor, and columnist at the newspaper, along with noted journalists such as Ralph McGill, Terry Kay, Celestine Sibley, and Lewis Grizzard.

By the end of November, he had officially checked out of retirement. He penned a Thanksgiving Day sports column for the *Atlanta Journal-Constitution,* shortly thereafter inking a deal to serve as a columnist with the *Gwinnett Daily Post,* where he filed occasional columns about baseball, football, and golf.

During our visit, Bisher recalled a conversation he once had with a legendary sports journalist. "Red Smith and I were covering a Falcons game a few years ago," he said. "After the game, I was driving Red back to the motel. It was a cold, miserable December day, and as he started to get out, I said 'Well, another cold, wet day in the press box,'. . . . Red put his arm on my shoulder and said, 'Another cold, wet day in the press box, God I love it.'"

Bisher loved the world of the press box and was not ready to say farewell. Like his predecessors, he continued to "peck away" on his typewriter until the very end, which came on March 18, 2012. In an obituary, *New York Times* reporter Lynn Zinser called Bisher a "Southern institution," but the legendary sportswriter was more than that.[1]

He was an American original. He wrote with a strong voice—a poetic panache. In an age when it became increasingly unfashionable to do so, he crafted flawless American heroes out of (extra)ordinary athletes on his reliable Royal typewriter. He, like his southern-born predecessor Grantland Rice, believed in the value of sport and sports heroes. He saw in both the potential to teach the American public values such as hard work and dedication.

In my office in October 2009, he reminisced about the joys of sportswriting in the 1940s, '50s, and '60s. "In the early part of the century, before big salaries came into being, [sports stars] interacted more" with sportswriters, he recalled. "The difference was we were all making about the same amount of money back then. Now, [most sports stars] are aloof. . . . They don't have a lot of time for you. They have their big projects going, their own foundations, and that kind of thing. It's a totally different world." Today's sports world, as Bisher admitted, is "different" from the one he encountered as a fledgling reporter in the late 1930s. He recalled a closer community of sports journalists, who often overlooked a player's flaws.

In 2014, rose-colored glasses are out of fashion in sportswriting. Sports journalists still mass-produce heroes. They cast athletes who excel in their sport, such as eighteen-time Olympic gold medalist Michael Phelps, four-time Masters Tournament champion Tiger Woods, three-time World Series champion Curt Schilling, and single-season home-run leader Barry Bonds, as national heroes. Unlike sportswriters of old, they do not turn a blind eye to their personal peccadilloes. Instead, operating on a twenty-four-hour news cycle, they painstakingly deconstruct heroes involved in controversies such as extramarital affairs and substance abuse, accusing them of tarnishing sport's clean image. As Bisher reminds us, sports journalists might help craft heroes, but "they can also ruin a few."

Sportswriter Frank Deford contends that the ferocity of the sports media's assault on athletes in comparison to media treatment of controversial entertainment stars suggests that the nation holds athletes to higher standards than the average celebrity. "We love sports, and we're envious of those who play them so well," he said in March 2010 in his weekly radio commentary for NPR's "Morning Edition." "So when an athlete, like [Tiger] Woods, fails as a human being, we respond more with anger than disappointment that he has dared tarnish something we do so adore. It's almost as if we expect politicians and entertainment celebrities to be venal and flawed, but despite all historical evidence to the contrary, we keep expecting better from athletes."[2]

Whether the American public expects more from athletes and what that reveals about American society are debatable, but one thing is certain: in the twenty-first century, the sports media still crown kings of the diamond, but in a twenty-four-hour news world, baseball stars are only kings for a day. In a world where modern baseball heroes do not remain on the pedestal for long, the ghosts of two of the Dead Ball Era's best-known heroes linger in our collective memories. Institutions such as the National Baseball Hall of Fame and the Library of Congress preserve their images. Whole towns celebrate their accomplishments.[3] We also remember them in popular culture—in music, in literature, in film, and in the press.

In recent years, Big Six has resurfaced in American memory in documentaries and biographies, fictional works, and even plays. Still, his name and image remain most indelibly fixed in the minds of baseball aficionados. In the early twentieth century, the American public knew Mathewson for his honesty, kindness, compassion, and sportsmanship. As these Victorian-era mores became less valued in American society, so too did his image. Once a national icon, Mathewson has become irrelevant to the average American. When Mathewson's name is harkened in popular memory, it is as a throwback to a simpler time.

Cobb, on the other hand, has become a fixture in popular culture. Since his death in 1961, his name has become synonymous with scoundrel, a sinister villain in national lore. The "angry genius in spikes" has been celebrated as such in books, museums, and even in popular films such as *Field of Dreams* (1989) and *Cobb* (1994).[4] Perhaps his image continues to be etched more vividly in American memory for what it reveals about the modern man. In the early twentieth century, Cobb became a symbol of virulent, rugged manhood. He was well known for his relentless drive and determination to succeed at all costs. That message still resonates with the American public, and the image of his eccentric personality remains fixed in American memory.

Nevertheless, in a modern era in which sports commentators bemoan the erosion of teamwork and sportsmanship, it might be fitting to return to early twentieth-century press accounts about these kings of the diamond. It might even be expedient for sportswriters to cast aside sensational human-interest stories for examinations of character and to consider these morality tales once more.

Notes

PROLOGUE

1. Amber Roessner, "Baseball and the Mill: Remembering the Mill Leagues," *Gainesville Times,* July 1, 2004, archive.gainesvilletimes.com/news/stories/20040701/localsports/12934.shtml (accessed May 15, 2012).

2. Lori Amber Roessner, "Hero-Crafting in *Sporting Life,* an Early Baseball Journal," *American Journalism* 26 (Spring 2009): 39–65.

3. Grantland Rice, *The Tumult and the Shouting: My Life in Baseball* (Berkeley: University of California Press, 1954), 169.

4. Ibid., 3.

5. Raymond Williams, *The Long Revolution* (New York: Chatto & Windus, 1961), 63.

6. In 1857 William Trotter, editor of the *Spirit of the Times,* called baseball the "noble American game" (cited in Allen Guttmann, *From Ritual to Record: The Nature of Modern Sports* [New York: Columbia University Press, 1978], 95).

7. Ring Lardner, "Tyrus, the Greatest of 'Em All," *American Magazine,* June 1915, 19 (Readers' Guide Retrospective Index).

1. CONSTRUCTING HEROES

1. Ina Russell to Richard B. Russell, February 18, 1912, p. 1, Winder Papers, Series D II-1–2, Richard B. Russell Collection, Richard B. Russell Library for Political Research and Studies, University of Georgia Libraries, Athens. Preceding this reference, his mother Ina sent a clip of the September 27, 1911, sports edition of the *Atlanta Constitution,* which included a reference to Cobb, in a letter package. See Ina Russell to Richard B. Russell, September 27, 1911, insert, Winder Papers, Series D II-2–3.

2. Memorabilia such as ticket stubs, scrapbooks, and newspaper clippings can be found in the Winder Papers, Series D. Richard B. Russell's rare T206 baseball card collection is also available for viewing online at baseballcards.galib.uga.edu/ or with special permission through the Richard B. Russell Library for Political Research and Studies, University of Georgia Libraries, Athens.

3. George Horace Lorimer, "Our One Perfect Institution," *Saturday Evening Post,* October 31, 1908, 24.

4. Thomas Carlyle, *On Heroes, Hero-Worship, and the Heroic in History: Six Lectures* (New York: Oxford University Press, 2008), 216.

5. Ralph Waldo Emerson, *Works* (New York: Oxford University Press, 2006), 145.

6. Dixon Wecter, *The Hero in America: A Chronicle of Hero Worship* (New York: Scribner, 1972). See also Orrin E. Klapp, *Heroes Villains, and Fools: Reflections of the American Character* (Irvington, N.J.: Irvington Publishers, 1962).

7. Carl Jung, *The Spirit in Man, Art and Literature* (Princeton, N.J.: Princeton University Press, 1971).

8. Joseph Campbell, *The Hero with a Thousand Faces* (New York: New World Library, 2008).

9. Joseph Campbell, *Creative Mythology,* vol. 4 of *The Masks of God* (New York: Viking Penguin, 1968), 621.

10. Campbell, *The Hero with a Thousand Faces,* 388.

11. Wecter, *The Hero in America,* 8.

12. Carlyle, *On Heroes,* 18.

13. Daniel J. Boorstin, *The Image: A Guide to Pseudo-Events in America* (New York: Vintage Books, 1992), 168.

14. Susan Drucker and Robert Cathcart, eds., *American Heroes in a Media Age* (New York: Hampton Press, 1994), 41-43.

15. Jeanne C. Reesman, ed., *Trickster Lives: Culture and Myth in American Fiction* (Athens: University of Georgia Press, 2001), xii.

16. Ty Cobb and Christy Mathewson were members of the first class of stars inducted into the National Baseball Hall of Fame in 1936. Cobb received 222 out of the 226 press votes as the first inductee (John D. McCallum, *Ty Cobb* [New York: Praeger Publishers, 1975], xi). A number of sports historians have isolated Cobb and Mathewson as two of the Dead Ball Era's most recognizable heroes. For examples, see Harold Seymour and Dorothy Seymour Mills, *Baseball: The Golden Age* (New York: Oxford University Press, 1971), 107–11, 115–16; David Voigt, *American Baseball: From the Commissioners to Continental Expansion* (Norman: University of Oklahoma Press, 1970), 52-57, 59. In addition to recognition as two of the era's most prominent heroes in two of the oldest academic treatments of baseball, Cobb and Mathewson have been identified as prominent icons of the era in secondary sources such as, on Mathewson: Frank Deford, *The Old Ball Game: How John McGraw, Christy Mathewson, and the New York Giants Created Modern Baseball* (New York: Atlantic Monthly Press, 2005); Michael Hartley, *Christy Mathewson: A Biography* (Jefferson, N.C.: McFarland & Co., 2004); Ray Robinson, *Matty, an American Hero: Christy Mathewson of the New York Giants* (New York: Oxford University Press, 1993); Philip Seib, *The Player: Christy Mathewson, Baseball, and the American Century* (New York: Thunder's Mouth Press, 2004); on Cobb: Charles C. Alexander, *Ty Cobb* (New York: Oxford University Press, 1984); Richard Bak, *Ty Cobb: His Tumultuous Life and Times* (Dallas, Tex.: Taylor Publishing Co., 1994); Dan Holmes, *Ty Cobb: A Biography*

(Westport, Conn.: Greenwood Press, 2004); McCallum, *Ty Cobb;* Don Rhodes, *Ty Cobb: Safe at Home* (Guilford, Conn.: Globe Pequot Press, 2008); Tom Stanton, *Ty and the Babe* (New York: St. Martin's Press, 2007); Al Stump, *Cobb* (Chapel Hill, N.C.: Algonquin Books, 1994).

17. My focus is on the practice of hero-crafting in mainstream, mass-circulating newspapers and magazines, which had reached national audiences since the late nineteenth century. Radio sports broadcasts were beginning to gain popularity in the 1920s; however, as media historian Marc Fisher observes, radio did not become a mass medium until 1927 when the first truly affordable radio sets came on the market. Later that year, as sports media historian Bruce Evensen points out, the Jack Dempsey–Gene Tunney heavyweight bout of September 1927 became a national mass-mediated phenomenon. Still, due to the fears of professional baseball club and newspaper owners, national radio coverage of baseball did not become pervasive until the 1930s. See Bruce Evensen, *When Dempsey Fought Tunney* (Knoxville: University of Tennessee Press, 1996), x–xi; Marc Fisher, *Something in the Air: Radio, Rock, and the Revolution That Changed America* (New York: Random House, 2007), xiv; Tony Silva, *Baseball over the Air: The National Pastime on the Radio and in the Imagination* (New York: McFarland, 2007).

18. For examples of references in popular sheet music, see Anna Caldwell, James O'Dea, Mabel Hite, and Mike Donlin, *Stars of National Game* (New York: Jerome H. Remick Co, 1908); Doc White, R. N. Lardner, and Chas Miller, *Gee! It's a Wonderful Game* (New York: Jerome H. Remick Co, 1911). A quick search of H. W. Wilson's *Reader's Guide to Periodical Literature* reveals more than fifty articles about Cobb and Mathewson in early twentieth-century national magazines. Many of the headlines include heroic accolades such as "king," "greatest of them all," and "champion." In addition to their pervasive presence in the headlines of the popular press, Cobb and Mathewson were referenced in popular literature, from poetry to short stories. See Merritte Parmelee Allen, "Christy Mathewson's Glove," *St. Nicholas,* April 1930 (Readers' Guide Retrospective Index), 430–33; Clifford Hollander, "The Millionaire Kid," *McClure's Magazine,* May 1919, 18 (American Periodical Series). For more examples of Cobb references in popular literature see, "Depth of Ignorance," *Life,* July 3, 1913, 35 (American Periodical Series); Helen Van Campen, "The Woes of Two Workers," *McClure's Magazine,* September 1913, 198 (American Periodical Series). For more examples of Mathewson references in popular literature, see Billy Sunday, "Letters of a Japanese School Boy," *Life,* February 18, 1915, 276 (American Periodical Series). Mathewson and Cobb were also featured in vaudeville shows and Broadway plays such as *The College Widow* (Cobb, 1911–12) and *The Girl and the Pennant* (Mathewson, 1913), black-and-white films such as *Somewhere in Georgia* (Cobb, 1917), *Breaking into the Big Leagues* (Mathewson, 1912), *The Umpire* (Mathewson, 1914), *Love and Baseball* (Mathewson, 1914), and in radio interviews such as the "Coca-Cola Top-Notchers" program in 1930 (Cobb). For an example of radio interviews, see: Grantland Rice, "Coca-Cola Top-Notchers," 1930,

Michigan State University, www.youtube.com/watch?v=jzkEphQAi7U (accessed January 11, 2010). Cobb and Mathewson would go on to star in several early silent films. Mathewson would appear in three films in the 1910s—*Breaking into the Big Leagues* (1912), *The Umpire* (1914), and *Love and Baseball* (1914)—and in 1917, Cobb would star in sportswriter-turned-screenwriter Grantland Rice's *Somewhere in Georgia.*

19. For examples, see the *Youth's Companion,* January 30, 1908, 58 (American Periodical Series); *Baseball Magazine,* October 1923, 530.

20. See, for example, Jerome Holtzman, *No Cheering in the Press Box* (New York: Henry Holt & Co., 1973), 2–6.

21. William F. Kirk, "When 'Matty' Was a Boy," *Sporting Life,* December 14, 1912, 2.

22. Cobb was often lauded in poetry by Grantland Rice. To gain insight into his treatment in children's magazines, see Ted Hathaway, "Cobb as a Role Model," *Nine* 11 (Fall 2003): 64–72.

23. Robinson, *Matty,* 220.

24. Cited in Ronald A. Mayer, *Christy Mathewson: A Game-by-Game Profile of a Legendary Pitcher* (Jefferson, N.C.: McFarland, 2008), 1.

25. Ty Cobb, Quotes, The Official Web Site of Ty Cobb, www.cmgww.com/baseball/cobb/quotes.html (accessed January 11, 2010).

26. See for example, Lardner, "Tyrus, the Greatest of 'Em All," 19; Alexander, *Ty Cobb,* 3.

27. Alexander, *Ty Cobb,* 3–5.

28. Although other notable stars of the Dead Ball Era received regular coverage in local newspaper sports sections and specialty baseball magazines, they did not gain as much attention in newspapers and magazines that reached national audiences. A search of H. W. Wilson's *Reader's Guide to Periodical Literature,* for instance, reveals more than fifty articles about Cobb and Mathewson in national, general-interest magazines, but only uncovers a total of fifteen articles about Tris Speaker, Johnny Evers, Frank Chance, Cy Young, Walter Johnson, Napoleon Lajoie, and Honus Wagner between 1900 and 1928.

29. See, for example: Benjamin G. Rader, "Compensatory Sports Heroes: Ruth, Grange and Dempsey," *Journal of Popular Culture* 16, no. 4: 11–22; Rader, *American Sport: From the Age of Folk Games to the Age of Televised Sport* (New York: Prentice Hall, 2004), 142–59.

30. Sut Jhally, *The Spectacle of Accumulation: Essays in Culture, Media, and Politics* (New York: Peter Lang, 2006), 129.

2. THE SPORTING PRESS

1. Henry Chadwick, "Base Ball," *Brooklyn Eagle,* October 18, 1859, 3. Brooklyn Public Library, eagle.brooklynpubliclibrary.org/Default/Skins/BEagle/Client.asp?Skin=BEagle (accessed March 10, 2010).

2. Ibid.

3. Steven A. Riess, *Touching Base: Professional Baseball and American Culture in the Progressive Era* (Urbana: University of Illinois Press, 1981), 15.

4. David Block, *Baseball Before We Knew It* (Lincoln: University of Nebraska Press, 2005), 10–20.

5. Andrew J. Schiff, *"The Father of Baseball": A Biography of Henry Chadwick* (Jefferson, N.C.: McFarland Press, 2008), 12.

6. Ibid., 13.

7. Cited ibid., 88.

8. Ibid., 95.

9. Cited in Dean A. Sullivan, *A Documentary History of Baseball, 1825–1908* (Lincoln: University of Nebraska Press, 1995), 48.

10. Cited in Schiff, *"The Father of Baseball,"* 93.

11. Ibid., 98.

12. The NABBP was one of the first centralized sports associations in the United States. See Schiff, *"The Father of Baseball,"* 95–100; George B. Kirsch, *The Creation of American Team Sports: Baseball and Cricket, 1838–72* (Urbana: University of Illinois Press, 1989), 62–65; Benjamin Rader, *Baseball: A History of America's Game* (Urbana: University of Illinois Press, 2002), 21-27; Harold Seymour and Dorothy Seymour Mills, *Baseball: The Early Years* (New York: Oxford University Press, 1960), 15–20.

13. Peter Morris, *A Game of Inches: The Stories Behind the Innovations That Shaped Baseball: The Game Behind the Scenes* (Chicago: Ivan R. Dee, 2006), 136.

14. Cited in William J. Ryczek, *Baseball's First Inning: A History of the National Pastime through the Civil War* (Jefferson, N.C.: McFarland Press, 2009), 173.

15. Ibid., 168–73.

16. Cited ibid., 173.

17. Morris, *A Game of Inches,* 88.

18. Cited in Sullivan, *A Documentary History of Baseball,* 92.

19. Schiff, *"The Father of Baseball,"* 139.

20. Jerold J. DuQuette, *Regulating the National Pastime: Baseball and Antitrust* (New York: Greenwood Publishing, 1999), 4.

21. Ryczek, *Baseball's First Inning,* 170.

22. Alfred Henry Spink, *The National Game* (Carbondale: Southern Illinois University Press, 1911), 356; W. Joseph Campbell, *Yellow Journalism: Puncturing the Myths, Defining the Legacies* (Westport, Conn.: Praeger Publishers, 2001), 6–10; Michael Emery, Edwin Emery, and Nancy Roberts, *The Press and America: An Interpretative History of the Mass Media,* 9th ed. (Boston: Allyn and Bacon, 2000), 157; John Nerone, "The Mythology of the Penny Press," *Critical Studies in Mass Communication* 4 (1987): 397; W. David Sloan and James D. Startt, *The Media in America: A History,* 4th ed. (Northport, Ala.: Vision Press, 1999), 221–45.

23. David Quentin Voigt, *American Baseball: From Gentleman's Sport to the Commissioner System* (Norman: University of Oklahoma Press, 1966), 94.

24. Schiff, *"The Father of Baseball,"* 158.

25. Margot Lamme and Karen Russell, "Removing the Spin: Toward a New History of Public Relations," *Journalism & Communication Monographs* 11, no. 4 (Winter 2010); William B. Anderson, "Crafting the National Pastime's Image: The History of Major League Baseball Public Relations," *Journalism & Communication Monographs* 5, no. 1 (Spring 2003).

26. Morris, *A Game of Inches,* 118.

27. The National League engaged in monopolistic practices such as establishing restrictive territorial rights to curtail rival clubs and creating a reservation clause to mandate that players were property of a club until traded, sold, or released. During the last two decades of the nineteenth century, rival leagues such as the American Association (1881), the Union Association (1884), and the Player's League (1890) threatened its stronghold. These competing leagues offered cheaper admission prices and more lucrative player contracts. In 1883, delegates from the National League and the American Association formulated the National Agreement, which promised mutual respect for all rosters and minimum player salaries. For nearly a decade, the two leagues coexisted. In 1891, the embattled American Association merged with the National League, forming one unified league composed of twelve clubs (Rader, *Baseball,* 43–78; Seymour and Mills, *Baseball: The Early Years,* 73–171).

28. Morris, *A Game of Inches,* 320.

29. See for example, John Rickards Betts, "Sporting Journalism in Nineteenth-century America," *American Quarterly* 5, no. 1 (Spring 1953): 54; Howard P. Chudacoff, *The Age of the Bachelor: Creating an American Subculture* (Princeton, N.J.: Princeton University Press, 1999), 187–90; William A. Harper, *How You Played the Game: The Life of Grantland Rice* (Columbia: University of Missouri Press, 1999), 6–9; Kirsch, *The Creation of American Team Sports,* 203; Richard Orodenker, *The Writers' Game: Baseball Writing in America* (New York: Twayne Publishers, 1996), 26–34; Riess, *Touching Base,* 15–25; Seymour and Mills, *Baseball: The Early Years,* 345–58; Voigt, *American Baseball: From the Commissioners to Continental Expansion,* ix–xi.

30. Confectionary companies would follow their cue at the turn of the century (Morris, *A Game of Inches,* 112–13).

31. Morris, *A Game of Inches,* 117–51.

32. By 1900, the space devoted to sport increased to 9 percent of total newspaper content. See Betts, "Sporting Journalism in Nineteenth-century America," 54; Harper, *How You Played the Game,* 11; Orodenker, *The Writers' Game,* 27–33; Riess, *Touching Base,* 15; Seymour and Mills, *Baseball: The Early Years,* 69; Voigt, *American Baseball: From Gentleman's Sport to the Commissioner System,* 194–95.

33. Janet M. Cramer, *Media, History, Society: A Cultural History of U.S. Media* (Malden, Mass.: Wiley-Blackwell Publishing, 2009), 120–21; Hanno Hardt and Bonnie Brennen, eds., *Newsworkers: Toward a History of the Rank and File* (Minneapolis: University of Minnesota Press, 1995), 1–29.

34. Voigt, *American Baseball: From Gentleman's Sport to the Commissioner System,* 90–96. In 1908, the recently established Baseball Writers' Association of America bemoaned the dreary conditions of press boxes exposed to the elements. Leonard Koppett, *The Rise and Fall of the Press Box* (Toronto: Sports Media Publishing, 2003), 10–11.

35. Emery, Emery, and Roberts, *The Press and America,* 179.

36. Anderson, "Crafting the National Pastime's Image," 7–43; Orodenker, *The Writers' Game,* 31; Seymour and Mills, *Baseball: The Early Years,* 352; Voigt, *American Baseball: From the Commissioners to Continental Expansion,* 95.

37. Emery, Emery, and Roberts, *The Press and America,* 179.

38. Voigt, *American Baseball: From Gentleman's Sport to the Commissioner System,* 93; Voigt, *American Baseball: From the Commissioners to Continental Expansion,* 95. Voigt notes that publishers paid reporters an average of $7.50 per thousand words. Many were paid by the word, resulting in a verbose style. In 1910, journalists made significantly more than the average American, who earned roughly $14.40 per week. They were not paid as much as other working professionals, however. As cultural historian Richard Ohmann notes, in 1900 the average millworker earned an annual salary of approximately $500, but an engineer earned $2,000. Richard Ohmann, (*Selling Culture: Magazines, Markets and Class at the Turn of the Century* [New York: Verso, 1996], 170).

39. Cramer, *Media, History, Society,* 120–21; Hardt and Brennen, eds., *Newsworkers,* 48–74, 110–34.

40. Evensen, *When Dempsey Fought Tunney,* 49.

41. Ibid.; Cramer, *Media, History, Society,* 121–122; Emery, Emery, and Roberts, *The Press and America,* 180; Ted Curtis Smythe, "The Reporter, 1880–1900: Working Conditions and Their Influence on News," *Journalism History* 7 (1980): 5.

42. Jean Hastings Ardell, *Breaking into Baseball: Women in the National Pastime* (Carbondale: Southern Illinois University Press, 2005), 192.

43. Ibid., 33. Not until the Jazz Age, however, did a small contingent of female sportswriters such as Margaret Goss and Jane Dixon become regular employees on sports staffs of large metropolitan dailies. See David Kaszuba, "They Are Women, Hear Them Roar: Female Sportswriters of the Roaring Twenties" (unpublished thesis, Penn State University, 2003, 47 127.

44. Block, *Baseball: Before We Knew It,* 225; Harper, *How You Played the Game,* 2–7; Orodenker, *The Writers' Game,* 26–31; Pat Washburn and Joe Lowe, "The Beginning of American Sports Journalism, 1733–1857," presentation at American Journalism Historians Association Annual Meeting in Birmingham, Ala., October 2009.

45. Voigt, *American Baseball: From Gentleman's Sport to the Commissioner System,* 94.

46. Hazel Dicken Garcia, *Journalistic Standards in Nineteenth-Century America* (Madison: University of Wisconsin Press, 1989), 3–28; David T. Z. Mindich, *Just the Facts: How "Objectivity" Came to Define American Journalism* (New York: New York University Press, 1998), 5; Michael Schudson, *The Power of the News* (Cambridge, Mass.: Harvard University Press, 1995), 55–59.

47. James W. Carey, *Communication as Culture: Essays on Media and Society* (London: Unwin Hyman, 1989), 13–36. By 1900, according to journalism historian W. Joseph Campbell, three primary paradigms dominated American journalism—the activist model, the narrative model, and the detached model (*The Year That Defined American Journalism: 1897 and the Clash of Paradigms* [New York: Routledge, 2006], 5–9).

48. William B. Anderson, "Does the Cheerleading Ever Stop? Major League Baseball and Sports Journalism," *Journalism & Mass Communication Quarterly* 78, no. 2 (Summer 2001): 355–82; Anderson, "Crafting the National Pastime's Image," 7–43; Kirsch, *The Creation of American Team Sports,* 203; Orodenker, *The Writers' Game,* 131; Steven A. Riess, *City Games: The Evolution of American Urban Society and the Rise of Sports* (Champaign: University of Illinois Press, 1989), 66; Riess, *Touching Base,* 15–25; Seymour and Mills, *Baseball: The Early Years,* 351.

49. Charles Ponce de Leon, *Self-Exposure: Human-Interest Journalism and the Emergence of Celebrity in America, 1890–1940* (Chapel Hill: University of North Carolina Press, 2002), 244.

50. Seymour and Mills, *Baseball: The Early Years,* 351.

51. Edwin Shuman, cited in Karen Roggenkamp, *Narrating the News: New Journalism and Literary Genre in Late Nineteenth-Century American Newspapers and Fiction* (Kent, Ohio: Kent State University Press, 2005), xiii.

52. The "story" model had its roots in the entertainment focus of the penny papers and later the "new" journalism of the 1880s and 1890s (Campbell, *The Year That Defined American Journalism,* 5–9).

53. Richard D. Mandell, *Sport: A Cultural History* (New York: Columbia University Press, 1984), 185.

54. Drucker and Cathcart, eds., *American Heroes in a Media Age,* 80–85. Celebrity-style journalism served to "make the famous more real," as journalism historian Stuart Allan suggests, thereby offering greater intimacy in the everyday lives of readers. By providing the "real story" of a celebrity's personal life, human-interest journalism sought to eliminate social distance by making the remote seem familiar. See Stuart Allan, ed., *Journalism: Critical Issues* (New York: Open University Press, 2005), 22.

55. Campbell, *The Hero with a Thousand Faces,* 1949; Betty Houchin Winfield and Janice Hume, "The American Hero and the Evolution of the Human Interest Story," *American Journalism* 15, no. 2 (1998): 79.

56. Riess, *Touching Base*, 6–9; Roessner, "Hero-Crafting in *Sporting Life*," 39–65; Seymour and Mills, *Baseball: The Golden Age*, 93.

57. Donald J. Mrozek, *Sport and American Mentality* (Knoxville: University of Tennessee Press, 1983), 128; Ponce de Leon, *Self-Exposure*, 252.

58. Riess, *Touching Base*, 26–39. In 1900, Ban Johnson, a former Cincinnati sportswriter and the president of the most dominant minor league—the Western League—capitalized on rumors of a revival of the American Association. With the tacit consent of National League president Nick Young, Johnson changed his league's name to the American League and placed clubs in several eastern cities from which the National League had recently pulled out. On January 28, 1901, he announced the formation of the American League with clubs in Baltimore, Boston, Chicago, Cleveland, Detroit, Milwaukee, Philadelphia, and Washington. Over the next two years, he took advantage of a poorly timed National League salary cap and raided league rosters. In 1903, the two leagues declared peace and signed a national agreement. They promised to respect league rosters, formed a three-man national commission to oversee Major League affairs, and instituted an annual World Series between league pennant winners. Between 1903 and 1920, Major League baseball prospered, attracting millions of fans to ballparks across the country.

59. Ibid., 15. Although national championships existed intermittently in the nineteenth century, the National Agreement between the rival National and American leagues culminated in the introduction of the World Series in 1903. The World Series quickly proved to be a fan favorite, challenging mediated attention given to national election coverage.

60. Ibid., 30–38. Even as Progressive Era reforms resulted in shorter work weeks and more discretionary time, increased ticket costs made blue-collar attendance a rare treat instead of a frequent occurrence. Ticket prices increased from 25 cents for American Association match-ups in 1882 to a 50-cent minimum for Major League games in 1902. By 1910, ticket prices ranged from 50 cents for bleacher seats to one dollar for reserved seats. By 1920, the prices of reserved and box seats had escalated to $1.25 and $1.65, respectively. These prices were quite expensive when compared to other amusements popular with the working class, such as nickelodeons.

61. Mrozek, *Sport and American Mentality*, 166.

62. Riess, *Touching Base*, 15.

3. ENTER CHRISTY MATHEWSON AND TYRUS COBB

1. Mrozek, *Sport and American Mentality*, 166–72.

2. Cited in Lawrence Ritter, *The Glory of Their Times: The Story of the Early Days of Baseball Told by the Men Who Played It* (New York: HarperCollins, 1992), 51.

3. Cited in Mayer, *Christy Mathewson*, 3.

4. Ty Cobb, Quotes, Official Web Site.

5. Robert H. Boyle, *Sport: Mirror of American Life* (Boston: Little, Brown, and Co., 1963), 241.

6. Factoryville Borough, www.factoryville.org (accessed January 11, 2010).

7. Cited in Seib, *The Player*, 5.

8. Robinson, *Matty*, 9; Seib, *The Player*, 4.

9. Cited in Seib, *The Player*, 6.

10. Cited in Robinson, *Matty*, 13.

11. Mrs. William Brown Meloney, "My Boy," *The Delineator*, June 1914, 8–9 (Readers' Guide Retrospective Index).

12. Seib, *The Player*, 5.

13. Hartley, *Christy Mathewson*, 11; Robinson, *Matty*, 15–18.

14. Seib, *The Player*, 9.

15. Tristram Coffin, *The Old Ball Game: Baseball in Folklore and Fiction* (New York: Herder and Herder, 1971), 136–52.

16. Seib, *The Player*, 12–13.

17. Robinson, *Matty*, 16.

18. Ibid., 17; Seib, *The Player*, 14.

19. Robinson, *Matty*, 22–23.

20. Cited ibid., 26.

21. Seib, *The Player*, 21.

22. Robinson, *Matty*, 31.

23. Cited in Mayer, *Christy Mathewson*, 20.

24. Cited in Robinson, *Matty*, 32.

25. Hartley, *Christy Mathewson*, 19–31.

26. Robinson, *Matty*, 57–58. See also Lucian Cary, "Mathewson's Biggest Victory," *Good Housekeeping*, August 1923, 48 (Readers' Guide Retrospective Index); "Matty's Record for 1913," *Literary Digest*, December 20, 1913, 1238 (Readers' Guide Retrospective Index); "The Fight of a Clean Sportsman," July 19, 1922, 481.

27. Ren Mulford Jr., "A Red Desert," *Sporting Life*, October 21, 1905, 3.

28. Cited in Robinson, *Matty*, 66.

29. "Giants Win Ball Honors," *Los Angeles Times*, October 15, 1905, sec. 3: 1.

30. Alexander, *Ty Cobb*, 9.

31. Ibid., 7–14.

32. Ty Cobb and Al Stump, *My Life in Baseball: The True Record* (Lincoln: University of Nebraska Press, 1961), 9.

33. Rhodes, *Ty Cobb*, 27.

34. Cited in Alexander, *Ty Cobb*, 11.

35. Ibid., 12.

36. Dennis Abrams, *Ty Cobb* (New York: Infobase Publishing, 2008), 15.

37. Cited in Rhodes, *Ty Cobb*, 26.

38. Ibid., 4.

39. Ibid., 5.

40. Ibid., 8.

41. Cited in Alexander, *Ty Cobb,* 17.

42. Stump, *Cobb,* 68.

43. Cited in Rhodes, *Ty Cobb,* 15.

44. Stump, *Cobb,* 79.

45. Cited in Alexander, *Ty Cobb,* 20. Just after midnight on August 9, 1905, Cobb's mother Amanda, believing she heard an intruder, fired two rounds from a double-barreled shotgun at William Herschel. He died shortly thereafter. Controversy surrounded his death. Some townsfolk claimed that William had discovered that Amanda was having an affair and hoped to catch her in the act that summer's eve (Stump, *Cobb,* 92–94).

46. Stump, *Cobb,* 242.

47. Cobb and Stump, *My Life in Baseball,* 53.

48. Holmes, *Ty Cobb,* 15–16.

49. Cited in Cobb and Stump, *My Life in Baseball,* 19.

50. Holmes, *Ty Cobb,* 98.

4. THE MAKING OF A GENTLEMAN, A PEACH, AND A SPORTSWRITER

1. Harper, *How You Played the Game,* 78; Charles Fountain, *Sportswriter: The Life and Times of Grantland Rice* (New York: Oxford University Press, 1993), 67–68.

2. Harper, *How You Played the Game,* 78; Joel Shrock, *The Gilded Age* (Westport, Conn.: Greenwood Press, 2004), 271.

3. Harper, *How You Played the Game,* 88–89; Fountain, *Sportswriter,* 69–70; Holmes, *Ty Cobb,* 8; McCallum, *Ty Cobb,* 20–21; Rice, *The Tumult and the Shouting,* 18–19.

4. Rice, *The Tumult and the Shouting,* 18–19.

5. Harper, *How You Played the Game,* 88–89; Holmes, *Ty Cobb,* 8.

6. Cited in McCallum, *Ty Cobb,* 20–21.

7. Rice, *The Tumult and the Shouting,* 18–19.

8. Cited in Harper, *How You Played the Game,* 10.

9. Rice, *The Tumult and the Shouting,* 32.

10. Cited in Harper, *How You Played the Game,* 119.

11. Emery, Emery, and Roberts, *The Press and America,* 179; Harper, *How You Played the Game,* 120, 225–26; Rice, *The Tumult and the Shouting,* 35–38.

12. Orodenker, *The Writers' Game,* 31–33; Holtzman, *No Cheering in the Press Box.*

13. Cited in Harper, *How You Played the Game,* 123.

14. Alexander, *Ty Cobb,* 70. With a 1.89 career ERA, Joss still ranks second in Major League history.

15. Ibid., 38.

16. Cited ibid., 42.

17. Ibid., 38.

18. Cited in Jonathan Yardley, *Ring: A Biography of Ring Lardner* (New York: Rowman & Littlefield, 2001), 63.

19. Ibid., 38.

20. Cited in Alexander, *Ty Cobb,* 54.

21. Ibid., 57.

22. John N. Wheeler, *I've Got News for You* (New York: E. P. Dutton & Co., 1961), 1–25.

23. Robinson, *Matty,* 79.

24. Alexander, *Ty Cobb,* 34.

25. Cited in Gordon H. Fleming, *The Unforgettable Season* (Lincoln: University of Nebraska Press, 2006), 38.

26. Less than three months after he accepted the position at the *Chicago Inter-Ocean,* he received an offer from Hearst to serve as the sports department's desk man for his Chicago morning paper for twenty-five dollars per week (Yardley, *Ring,* 60–75).

27. Cited in Robinson, *Matty,* 87.

28. Cited in Fleming, *The Unforgettable Season,* 44.

29. Ibid., 61.

30. Ibid., 69.

31. Yardley, *Ring,* 60–75.

32. Ibid.

33. Alexander, *Ty Cobb,* 66.

34. "Cobb's Ambition," *Sporting Life,* April 4, 1908, 5.

35. Alexander, *Ty Cobb,* 13.

36. Robinson, *Matty,* 97.

37. Ibid., 98.

38. Ibid., 99.

39. Cited in Fleming, *The Unforgettable Season,* 245.

40. Ibid., 300.

41. Alexander, *Ty Cobb,* 73.

42. Spink, *The National Game,* 344. Another such group—the National Base Ball Reporters' Association—had formed in 1887, but it had proven unsustainable.

43. Cited in Craig Depken, "Baseball Writers Association," Division of Labor, October 15, 2008, divisionoflabour.com/archives/005244.php (accessed May 1, 2012).

44. Robinson, *Matty,* 110.

45. Alexander, *Ty Cobb,* 71.

46. Nie, "The Giant and the Giants," *Baseball Magazine* 2, no. 1 (November 1908): 7–9.

47. Jacob Morse, "The Aftermath," *Baseball Magazine* 2, no. 2 (December 1908): 1–6.

48. Yardley, *Ring,* 90.

49. Robinson, *Matty,* 116.

50. Alexander, *Ty Cobb,* 83.

51. Ibid., 79.

52. Yardley, *Ring,* 95.

53. F. C. Lane, *Batting* (New York: Society for American Baseball Research, 2001), 3.

54. Alexander, *Ty Cobb,* 97.

55. Harper, *How You Played the Game,* 169.

5. GATHERING THE "INSIDE DOPE"

1. Cited in Harper, *How You Played the Game,* 169.

2. Ardell, *Breaking into Baseball,* 191–93; Kaszuba, "They Are Women, Hear Them Roar." Few women dared to enter the male sphere of sportswriting at the turn of the twentieth century, and those who did struggled to infiltrate the tight-knit man's club.

3. Rice, *The Tumult and the Shouting,* 38–39, 314–33.

4. Wheeler, *I've Got News for You,* 19–28; Holtzman, *No Cheering in the Press Box,* 1–33.

5. Harper, *How You Played the Game,* 175.

6. Fred Lieb, *Baseball as I Have Known It* (Lincoln: University of Nebraska Press, 1996), 25–35.

7. Charles C. Alexander, *John McGraw* (Lincoln: University of Nebraska Press, 1995), 126.

8. Lieb, *Baseball as I Have Known It,* 35–37.

9. Larry D. Masch, *Rube Marquard: The Life and Times of a Baseball Hall of Famer* (New York: McFarland, 1998), 73–74.

10. "1911 New York Giants Schedule," *Baseball Almanac,* www.baseball-almanac.com/teamstats/schedule.php?y=1911&t=NY1 (accessed July 17, 2012).

11. Anderson, "Crafting the National Pastime's Image," 7–43; Orodenker, *The Writers' Game,* 31; Seymour and Mills, *Baseball: The Early Years,* 352; Voigt, *American Baseball: From Gentleman's Sport to the Commissioner System,* 95.

12. Harper, *How You Played the Game,* 175.

13. Lieb, *Baseball as I Have Known It,* 36.

14. Koppett, *The Rise and Fall of the Press Box,* 187; Smythe, "The Reporter, 1880–1900," 1–10.

15. Mike Vaccaro, *The First Fall Classic: The Red Sox, the Giants, and the Cast of Players, Pugs, and Politicos Who Reinvented the World Series in 1912* (New York: Anchor Books, 2009), 3.

16. Smythe, "The Reporter, 1880–1900," 1–10.

17. Silas Bent, *Ballyhoo: The Voice of the Press* (New York: Boni & Liveright, 1927), 96–97.

18. Orodenker, *The Writers' Game,* 31.

19. Holtzman, *No Cheering in the Press Box,* 2.

20. Harper, *How You Played the Game,* 185.

21. Yardley, *Ring,* 128.

22. Robinson, *Matty,* 132.

23. Ibid.

24. Cited in Fountain, *Sportswriter,* 121.

25. Rice, *The Tumult and the Shouting,* 45, 291.

26. Grantland Rice, *New York Herald-Tribune,* October 9, 1925, in *Bucknell Alumni Monthly,* November 1925, 4, Christy Mathewson Player File, National Baseball Hall of Fame Library, Cooperstown.

27. Rice, *The Tumult and the Shouting,* 291.

28. Alexander, *Ty Cobb,* 125.

29. John Wheeler, "'Matty' as the Champion of the Friendless," *Literary Digest* December 26, 1925, 36.

30. Rice, *The Tumult and the Shouting,* 45.

31. Wheeler, "'Matty' as the Champion of the Friendless," 36.

32. Lane, *Batting,* 3.

33. Paul Gallico, *The Golden People* (Garden City, N.Y.: Doubleday, 1965), 14.

34. Ibid.

35. Rice, *The Tumult and the Shouting,* 291.

36. Cited in Wheeler, *I've Got News for You,* 99.

37. Cited in Schudson, *The Power of the News,* 80.

38. Edward Lyell Fox, "Baseball as the Players See It," *Outing* 58, no. 2 (May 1911): 147.

39. Cited in Robinson, *Matty,* 124.

40. Cited in Paul Dickson, *Baseball's Greatest Quotations: An Illustrated Treasury of Baseball Quotations and Historical Lore* (New York: HarperCollins, 2008), 437.

41. Masch, *Rube Marquard,* 137.

42. "1911 National League Standings and Expanded Standings," *Baseball-Reference.com,* www.baseball-reference.com/leagues/NL/1911-standings.shtml (accessed July 17, 2012).

43. Sullivan, *A Documentary History of Baseball,* 153.

44. Addie Joss, Rich Blevins, and Gary Mitchem, *Addie Joss on Baseball: Collected Newspaper Columns and World Series Reports* (New York: McFarland, 2012).

45. Stoney McLinn, "The Works of Ty Cobb," January 5, 1939, 4, Ty Cobb Player File, National Baseball Hall of Fame Library.

46. John P. Tierney, *Jack Coombs: A Life in Baseball* (New York: McFarland, 2008), 84.

47. Wheeler, *I've Got News for You,* 11–17.

48. Francis Richter, "The Decisive Factors," *Sporting Life* 58, no. 6 (October 14, 1911): 4.

49. Hartley, *Christy Mathewson,* 179.

50. Robinson, *Matty,* 128.

51. Ibid.

52. Ty Cobb, "Mathewson's Headwork Superior in Pitchers' Battle, Says 'Ty' Cobb," *New York Herald,* October 15, 1911, Ty Cobb Scrapbook, B1.710.83, p. 368, National Baseball Hall of Fame Library.

53. Robinson, *Matty,* 129.

54. Cited in Dean A. Sullivan, comp. and ed., *Middle Innings: A Documentary History of Baseball, 1900–1948* (Lincoln: University of Nebraska Press, 1998), 55.

55. Cited in Norman Macht, *Connie Mack and the Early Years of Baseball* (Lincoln: University of Nebraska Press, 2007), 526.

56. Orodenker, *The Writers' Game,* 33.

57. Francis Richter, "Notes and Comments," *Sporting Life* 58, no. 8 (October 28, 1911): 7.

58. Cited in Sullivan, *Middle Innings,* 55.

59. Cited in Robinson, *Matty,* 129.

60. Richter, "Notes and Comments," 7.

61. Grantland Rice, "The Sportlight," *Atlanta Constitution,* Christy Mathewson Player File.

62. John Wheeler and Christy Mathewson, *Pitching in a Pinch: Baseball from the Inside* (New York: G. P. Putnam's Sons, 1912), 261.

63. Fountain, *Sportswriter,* 122.

64. Robinson, *Matty,* 129–30.

65. John B. Foster, "Comment upon the Brooklyn Team and the World's Series," *Sporting Life,* October 28, 1911, 7 (LA84 Foundation).

66. Edward J. Gerrity, "This Is My Town," John N. Wheeler Player File, National Baseball Hall of Fame Library; Wheeler, *I've Got News for You,* 11–13.

67. "Ty Cobb on the Job as Our Sporting Editor," *Knoxville Sentinel,* Ty Cobb Scrapbook, B1.710.83, p. 328.

68. Wheeler and Mathewson, *Pitching in a Pinch,* 52.

69. Ibid., 55.

70. Ibid., 62.

71. Ibid.

72. Ibid., 63.

73. Ibid., iii.

74. Ibid., iv.

75. Cited in Wheeler, *I've Got News for You,* 13.

76. Deford, *The Old Ball Game,* 129.

77. "Best Sellers of the Week," *Boston Daily Globe,* June 3, 1912, 7; *Public Libraries* (Boston: Harvard University Library Bureau, 1912), 17: 407.

78. Hartley, *Christy Mathewson,* 197.

79. Wheeler, *I've Got News for You,* 21–23.

80. Carey, *Communication as Culture,* xviii.

81. Lawrence Ritter, oral history interview with Sam Crawford, March 27, 1964, National Baseball Hall of Fame Library.

82. Rice, *The Tumult and the Shouting,* 23–24.

83. Cited in Evensen, *When Dempsey Fought Tunney,* 1996, 49; Bent, *Ballyhoo,* 1927, 121–22.

6. CRAFTING KINGS OF THE DIAMOND

1. Lane, *Batting,* 3.

2. Ibid., v–xi.

3. F. C. Lane to Max Bishop, October 24, 1930, p. 1, F. C. Lane Papers, 1911–1936, Series I-1-2, National Baseball Hall of Fame Library.

4. Ty Cobb to F. C. Lane, January 2, 1912, "Ty Cobb: A Personal Letter," *Baseball Magazine,* March 1912, 6 (LA84 Foundation).

5. Rob Edelman, "Ty Cobb, Actor," Society for American Baseball Research, sabr.org/research/ty-cobb-actor (accessed May 1, 2012).

6. Ibid.

7. Cobb to Lane, January 2, 1912, "Ty Cobb: A Personal Letter," 6.

8. It appears that Cobb's first correspondence with Lane occurred in late 1911 or early 1912, shortly after he took over as the sole editor of *Baseball Magazine.* In a letter dated January 2, 1912, Cobb responded to Lane's request for material for the March Ty Cobb issue. The handwritten letter, along with a first-person column, was subsequently published in the issue (Ty Cobb to F. C. Lane, 1911–1927, F. C. Lane Papers, 1911–1936, Series I-1-3; Cobb to Lane, January 2, 1912, "Ty Cobb: A Personal Letter," 6).

9. "History," McSorley's Old Ale House, www.mcsorleysnewyork.com/history_01.html (accessed May 1, 2012).

10. Bill Burgess, "*Baseball Magazine,*" Bulletin, www.baseball-fever.com/showthread.php?91324-Baseball-Magazine&daysprune=-1 (accessed May 10, 2010).

11. Gerrit Albertus Beneker, Artnet, www.artnet.com/artists/gerrit+albertus-beneker/biography-links (accessed May 1, 2012).

12. Ty Cobb to F. C. Lane, Tuesday, undated, p. 1, F. C. Lane Papers, 1911–1936, Series I-1-3.

13. Ty Cobb, "Reminiscences of a Big League Player," *Baseball Magazine,* March 1912, 7–9 (LA84 Foundation).

14. Cover, *Baseball Magazine,* March 1912.

15. Howell Foreman, "When Ty Cobb Was a Boy," *Baseball Magazine,* March 1912, 5.

16. Hugh Jennings, "My Opinion of Tyrus Cobb," *Baseball Magazine,* March 1912, 16.

17. John J. Evers, "Ty Cobb from the Viewpoint of a National Leaguer," *Baseball Magazine,* March 1912, 14.

18. F. C. Lane, "Editorials," *Baseball Magazine,* March 1912, 3.

19. Allan, ed., *Journalism,* 22.

20. James Landers, *The Improbable First Century of Cosmopolitan Magazine* (Columbia: University of Missouri Press, 2010), 38–171.

21. Burgess, "*Baseball Magazine.*"

22. Ibid. During his last two seasons in the majors, Joss battled a sore arm and a case of pleurisy.

23. Alexander, *Ty Cobb,* 94.

24. Ibid.

25. Ibid.

26. Ibid., 105.

27. Ibid.

28. Lieb, *Baseball as I Have Known It,* 59.

29. F. C. Lane, "Ty Cobb vs. Ban Johnson," *Baseball Magazine,* June 1912, 8–11.

30. Rhodes, *Ty Cobb,* 57.

31. Accounts vary about the exact timing of the incident. Historian Charles Alexander, for instance, argues that the brawl occurred at the end of the third inning. Meanwhile, Al Stump notes that it took place at the end of the sixth inning. See Alexander, *Ty Cobb,* 105; Stump, *Cobb,* 206.

32. Holmes, *Ty Cobb,* 59.

33. Alexander, *Ty Cobb,* 105.

34. Francis Richter, "Revolt," *Sporting Life,* May 25, 1912, 1.

35. Alexander, *Ty Cobb,* 107.

36. Ibid., 106–7.

37. Ibid., 107.

38. "Play Ball," *The Independent,* April 10, 1926, 409 (American Periodical Series).

39. Richter, "Revolt," 1.

40. Holmes, *Ty Cobb,* 58–61.

41. Alexander, *Ty Cobb,* 109.

42. Ibid., 108.

43. Wheeler, *I've Got News for You,* 11–17.

44. Cited in Vaccaro, *The First Fall Classic,* 40.

45. Ibid., 7.

46. Harper, *How You Played the Game,* 187.

47. Ibid.

48. Vaccaro, *The First Fall Classic,* 78.

49. Ibid.

50. Mayer, *Christy Mathewson,* 221.
51. Cited in Harper, *How You Played the Game,* 188.
52. Vaccaro, *The First Fall Classic,* 100.
53. Cited ibid., 153.
54. Ibid., 169.
55. Ibid.
56. Ibid., 230.
57. Ibid., 225.
58. Christopher Bell, *Scapegoats: Baseballers Whose Careers Are Marked by One Fateful Play* (New York: McFarland, 2002), 25.
59. Cited in Yardley, *Ring,* 39.
60. Richard Bak, *New York Giants: A Baseball Album* (New York: Arcadia Publishing, 1999), 56.
61. Cited in John Billheimer, *Baseball and the Blame Game: Scapegoating in the Major Leagues* (New York: McFarland, 2007), 40.
62. Cited in Harper, *How You Played the Game,* 191.
63. Ibid.
64. Ibid., 192.
65. Ibid., 193.
66. "Matty," *Literary Digest,* November 16, 1912, 932–33 (Readers' Guide Retrospective Index).

7. GHOSTS AND GHOULS

1. *Life,* December 26, 1912, 2544 (American Periodical Series).
2. Harold Kellock, "The New Column," *The Bookman: A Review of Books and Life,* June 1916, 440 (American Periodical Series).
3. Alexander, *Ty Cobb,* 113.
4. Ibid., 269.
5. Francis Richter, *Sporting Life,* February 13, 1913, 1, 4.
6. Cited in Alexander, *Ty Cobb,* 112.
7. Ibid.
8. Ibid., 113.
9. Yardley, *Ring,* 131.
10. Ibid., 132.
11. Harper, *How You Played the Game,* 224.
12. Wheeler, *I've Got News for You,* 11–17.
13. Yardley, *Ring,* 164.
14. For example, see Christy Mathewson, "Pitching in a Pinch," *Sporting News,* February 6, 1913, 7; February 18, 1913, 8; February 20, 1913, 7.
15. Deford, *The Old Ball Game,* 130.
16. Seib, *The Player,* 66.
17. "The Girl and the Pennant," *Life,* November 1913, 791.

18. Wheeler, *I've Got News for You,* 14.

19. Other articles written under Cobb's byline included "Trick Plays and How to Make Them" (July 1916) and "Place Hitting" (October 1917). Based on the content, as well as writing tone and style, it is clear that they were written by Lane or one of his correspondents (*Baseball Magazine,* July 1916, 25–28 [LA84 Foundation]).

20. "Ty Cobb Sporting Editor for the Journal on Friday," *Atlanta Journal,* Ty Cobb Scrapbook, B1.710.83, p. 394.

21. "Farrell Facts," *Sporting Life,* February 1, 1913, 11 (LA84 Foundation).

22. "Johnson Jolt," *Sporting Life,* March 15, 1913, 8 (LA84 Foundation).

23. William Peet, "The Public Exploitation of Expert Reputation," *Sporting Life,* March 15, 1913, 8 (LA84 Foundation).

24. A. Herrmann, "Player-Scribe," *Sporting Life,* March 29, 1913, 14.

25. Wheeler, *I've Got News for You,* 1961, 14.

26. "National League News in Short Metre," *Sporting Life,* July 26, 1913, 20.

27. "Red Sox Troubles," *Sporting Life,* August 9, 1913, 2.

28. "The Player-Author," *Sporting Life,* August 16, 1913, 3.

29. "Cobb Bound by No Rules," *Sporting Life,* September 20, 1913, 3.

30. Ibid.

31. Ibid.

32. Alexander, *Ty Cobb,* 115.

33. Robinson, *Matty,* 154.

34. "Depth of Ignorance," 35.

35. "Why 'Matty' Lasts," *Literary Digest,* August 23, 1913, 209–10 (Readers' Guide Retrospective Index).

36. Robinson, *Matty,* 154.

37. Ibid., 156.

38. Cited in Deford, *The Old Ball Game,* 193.

39. Francis Richter, "A World Series Menace," *Sporting Life,* October 4, 1913, 4.

40. "The Player Authors," *Baseball Magazine,* November 1913, 51.

41. F. C. Lane, in *Baseball Magazine,* November 1913, 51.

8. THE QUINTESSENTIAL SAINT AND THE PREEMINENT SINNER

1. Gallico, *The Golden People,* 14.

2. Tom Pendergast, *Creating the Modern Man: American Magazines and Consumer Culture, 1900–1950* (Columbia: University of Missouri Press, 2000), 1–25.

3. David Fromkin, *Europe's Last Summer: Who Started the Great War in 1914* (New York: Alfred K. Knopf, 2004), 94.

4. Robert P. Wiggins, *The Federal League of Base Ball Clubs: The History of An Outlaw Major League, 1914–1915* (New York: McFarland, 2008).

5. Ibid., 45–51.

6. F. C. Lane, "Why Players Fail," *Baseball Magazine,* September 1913, 30 (LA84 Foundation).

7. Although it is unclear from archival sources whether *Baseball Magazine* served as the official advocate for the Baseball Players' Fraternity, it is obvious from the regular columns written by fraternity president David Fultz that the magazine was an informal promoter of the organization. For example see, David L. Fultz, "The Baseball Players' Fraternity and What It Stands For," *Baseball Magazine,* November 1911, 29–31, 124, 126.

8. Lane, "Why Players Fail."

9. For example, see Ty Cobb, "The Greatest Batter I Have Ever Seen," *Baseball Magazine,* November 1924, 537–60; Cobb, "The Supreme Athletic Effort of All Time," *Baseball Magazine,* January 1925, 341; Cobb, "How Young Pitchers Are Spoiled," *Baseball Magazine,* August 1925, 396.

10. Wiggins, *The Federal League of Base Ball Clubs,* 45–51.

11. Cited in Robinson, *Matty,* 155.

12. F. L. Brunner, "Hero Worship on the Diamond: The Big League Ball Player an Ideal Type of Athlete," *Baseball Magazine,* April 1914, 49–51 (LA84 Foundation).

13. Robinson, *Matty,* 167.

14. G. B. Mathewson to F. C. Lane, October 14, 1914, p. 1, F. C. Lane Papers, 1911–1936, Series I-1-12.

15. J. F. Kernan, cover, *Baseball Magazine,* December 1914. After his death in October 1925, the magazine offered readers an opportunity to purchase a reprint of the famous cover to frame "for your study or den" (Kernan cover ad, *Baseball Magazine,* December 1925, inside front cover).

16. F. C. Lane, "Mathewson's Folks," *Baseball Magazine,* December 1914, 38 (LA84 Foundation).

17. Alexander, *Ty Cobb,* 118.

18. Ibid., 119.

19. Grantland Rice, "The Durable Cobb," *Collier's,* April 3, 1926, 24 (Readers' Guide Retrospective Index).

20. Ibid.

21. Evensen, *When Dempsey Fought Tunney,* 49.

22. Rice, "The Sportlight," *Washington Post,* March 5, 1915, 8 (ProQuest Historical Newspapers).

23. Robinson, *Matty,* 155.

24. Rice, "The Sportlight," *Washington Post,* February 26, 1915, 8.

25. Ibid., 9.

26. Cited in Amy Tucker, *The Illustration of the Master: Henry James and the Magazine Revolution* (Palo Alto, Calif.: Stanford University Press, 2010), 32.

27. Rice, "The Sportlight," *Atlanta Constitution,* January 14, 1922, 6.

28. Orodenker, *The Writers' Game,* 9–15.

29. Rice, "The Sportlight," *Atlanta Constitution,* January 14, 1922, 6.

30. Brian Carroll, "Early Twentieth-Century Heroes: Coverage of Negro League Baseball in the Pittsburgh Courier and the Chicago Defender," *Journalism History* 32, no. 1 (Spring 2006): 34–42.

31. Ohmann, *Selling Culture,* 15, 25–30.

32. Ibid.

33. As Ohmann argues, the point is not to establish arbitrary circulation minimums that constitute mass-circulating magazines. Even magazines that lack a million readers can be considered mediums for the masses when they center on mass culture. See *Selling Culture,* 15–16; N. W. Ayer, *N. W. Ayer & Son's American Newspaper Annual and Directory* (Philadelphia: N. W. Ayer & Son, 1912, 1915, 1923, 1924, 1925, 1927).

34. F. Dana Burnet, "The News in Rime," *Puck,* April 4, 1914, 9 (American Periodical Series).

35. B. F. Leventhal, "Two Glimpses of Ty Cobb," *American Magazine,* February 1914, 78 (Readers' Guide Retrospective Index); Joseph A. Sexton, "Two Glimpses of Ty Cobb," *American Magazine,* February 1914, 78 (Readers' Guide Retrospective Index).

36. Journalism historians argue that the press, through its storytelling capability, plays an important role in shaping public memory on national and local levels. For examples, see Jill A. Edy, *Troubled Pasts: News and the Collective Memory of Social Unrest* (Philadelphia: Temple University Press, 2006); Janice Hume, "Press, Published History, and Regional Lore: Shaping the Public Memory of a Revolutionary War Heroine," *Journalism History* 30 (Winter 2005): 200–209; Caroline Kitch, *Pages from the Past* (Chapel Hill: University of North Carolina Press, 2005); Michael Schudson, *Watergate in American Memory: How We Remember, Forget, and Reconstruct the Past* (New York: HarperCollins, 1992).

37. Meloney, "My Boy," 8, 45.

38. Campbell, *The Hero with a Thousand Faces,* 1–171.

39. Cited in Campbell, *The Year That Defined American Journalism,* 99.

40. Yardley, *Ring,* 165.

41. Ibid.

42. Ibid., 37.

43. Lardner, "Tyrus, the Greatest of 'Em All," 19.

44. Ibid.

45. Rice, "The Durable Cobb."

46. Ring Lardner, "Matty," *American Magazine,* August 1915, 26 (Readers' Guide Retrospective Index).

47. Ibid.

48. Grantland Rice, "The Grand Old Batting Eye," *McClure's,* June 1915, 19, 52 (American Periodical Series); Rice, "The Shoes of Mathewson," *McClure's,* July 1915, 23, 61 (American Periodical Series).

49. Rice, "The Shoes of Mathewson," 23, 61.

50. Rice, *The Tumult and the Shouting,* xvi.

51. "'Matty's' Tribute from the Fans," *Literary Digest,* January 15, 1921, 52 (Readers' Guide Retrospective Index).

52. Robinson, *Matty,* 65.

53. "Ty Cobb on the Batting Art," *Literary Digest,* June 27, 1914, 1558–63 (Readers' Guide Retrospective Index).

54. "Why 'Matty' Lasts," 209–10.

55. Roessner, "Hero-Crafting in *Sporting Life,*" 39–65; Washburn and Lowe, "The Beginning of American Sports Journalism, 1733–1857."

56. Burgess, "*Baseball Magazine.*"

57. Theodore P. Greene, *America's Heroes: The Changing Models of Success in American Magazines* (New York: Oxford University Press, 1970), 169–73.

58. Theodore Roosevelt, *The Strenuous Life: Essays and Addresses* (Boston: Harvard University, 1905), 1, 3.

59. Ibid., 155, 160.

60. Donald E. Hall, ed., *Muscular Christianity: Embodying the Victorian Age* (New York: Cambridge University Press, 1994); Tony Ladd and James A. Mathisen, *Muscular Christianity: Evangelical Protestants and the Development of American Sport* (Grand Rapids, Mich.: Baker Books, 1999); Clifford Putney, *Muscular Christianity: Manhood and Sports in Protestant America, 1880–1920* (Cambridge, Mass.: Harvard University Press, 2001), 1–300.

61. Lane, "Editorials."

62. For example, see Brunner, "Hero Worship on the Diamond"; F. C. Lane, "The Secret of Christy Mathewson's Success," *Baseball Magazine,* October 1916, 65 (LA84 Foundation).

63. "Christy Mathewson's Great Record," *Baseball Magazine,* June 1913, 64 (LA84 Foundation).

64. In October 1916, for instance, he described the "Secret of Christy Mathewson's Success" as his "wizardly, uncanny" control. See F. C. Lane, "Who Is the Greatest Player in the History of Baseball," *Baseball Magazine,* January 1912, 27–34 (LA84 Foundation); Lane, "The Secret of Christy Mathewson's Success," 65–70.

65. Hayden White, *The Content of the Form: Narrative Discourse and Historical Representation* (Baltimore: Johns Hopkins University Press, 1987).

66. Burgess, "*Baseball Magazine*"; Lane, *Batting,* vi.

67. Ayer, *N. W. Ayer & Son's American Newspaper Annual and Directory* (1921).

68. Ty Cobb to F. C. Lane, June 29, 1914, pp. 1–2, F. C. Lane Papers, 1911–1936, Series I-1-3.

69. Ty Cobb to F. C. Lane, May 17, 1915, p. 1; Cobb to Lane, April 14, 1922, pp. 1–3; Cobb to Lane, September 13, 1927, pp. 1–2, all in F. C. Lane Papers, 1911–1936, Series I-1-3.

70. Alexander, *Ty Cobb,* 155.

71. Ty Cobb and John N. Wheeler, *Busting 'Em, and Other Big League Stories* (New York: E. J. Clode, 1914), 26.

72. Ibid., 28.

73. Ibid., 29.

74. Ibid., 5.

75. Ibid., 6.

76. Franklin K. Matthiews, "Books Boys Like Best," *Boy's Life,* December 1914, 31.

77. Boyle, *Sport,* 241.

78. Ibid.

79. Trey Strecker, *Dead Balls and Double Curves: An Anthology of Early Baseball Fiction* (Carbondale: Southern Illinois University Press, 2004), 162–71.

80. Deford, *The Old Ball Game,* 129.

81. Cobb and Wheeler, *Busting 'Em and Other Big League Stories,* 174.

82. Gallico, *The Golden People,* 14.

83. Campbell, *The Year That Defined American Journalism,* 5–9.

84. Bent, *Ballyhoo,* 32.

85. F. C. Lane, "Was Ty Cobb a Managerial Failure?" *Baseball Magazine,* July 1927, 339.

9. BASEBALL'S GREATEST BATTLE

1. F. B. Adams, "Plutarch Lights of History, No. 6: Christy Mathewson," *Harper's Weekly,* April 15, 1916, 395 (Readers' Guide Retrospective Index).

2. Alexander, *Ty Cobb,* 126–28.

3. Ibid.

4. Robinson, *Matty,* 173.

5. "Sentiment and 'Matty,'" *Literary Digest,* August 12, 1916, 363–65 (Readers' Guide Retrospective Index).

6. Cited in Robinson, *Matty,* 176.

7. Sullivan, *Middle Innings,* 38.

8. Cited ibid., 38.

9. "Matty Defeats Old Rival," *New York Times,* September 5, 1916, query.nytimes.com/mem/archive-free/pdf?res=F50614FE3F5F13738DDDAC0894D1405B868DF1D3 (accessed June 10, 2012).

10. Wayne Stewart, *Babe Ruth: A Biography* (New York: Greenwood Publishing, 2006), 28.

11. Robert Elias, *The Empire Strikes Out: How Baseball Sold U.S. Foreign Policy and Promoted the American Way Abroad* (New York: New Press, 2010), 77–94.

12. Ibid., 81.

13. Harper, *How You Played the Game,* 240–44.

14. Yardley, *Ring,* 193.

15. Harper, *How You Played the Game,* 240–44.

16. Todd W. Anton and Bill Nowlin, *When Baseball Went to War* (New York: Triumph Books, 2008), 34.

17. Murray Polner, *Branch Rickey: A Biography* (New York: McFarland, 2007), 75–76.

18. Robinson, *Matty,* 190–94.

19. Cited in Anton and Nowlin, *When Baseball Went to War,* 36.

20. Cited in Robinson, *Matty,* 194.

21. Cited in Elias, *The Empire Strikes Out* 84.

22. Ibid., 85.

23. Robinson, *Matty,* 186–87.

24. Yardley, *Ring,* 212–16.

25. Robinson, *Matty,* 190; Eliot Asinof, *Eight Men Out: The Black Sox and the 1919 World Series* (New York: Henry Holt and Co., 1963), 46.

26. Asinof, *Eight Men Out,* 232–33.

27. Cited in Yardley, *Ring,* 214.

28. Ibid.

29. Sullivan, *A Documentary History of Baseball,* 101.

30. Seib, *The Player,* 118.

31. Daniel E. Ginsberg, *The Fix Is In: A History of Baseball Gambling and Game Fixing Scandals* (New York: McFarland, 2004), 71.

32. Francis Richter, "Current Comment," *Sporting Life,* February 18, 1905, 1.

33. Ibid., 2.

34. Harper, *How You Played the Game,* 160. McGraw won four hundred dollars for betting on his club.

35. Cited in Robinson, *Matty,* 187.

36. Asinof, *Eight Men Out,* 159.

37. Cited in Harper, *How You Played the Game,* 279.

38. Yardley, *Ring,* 216.

39. Ibid., 217.

40. Cary, "Mathewson's Biggest Victory," 48, 174.

10. A TRIUMPHANT RETURN

1. Stewart, *Babe Ruth,* 42.

2. Ibid., 57.

3. Ibid., 65.

4. Robinson, *Matty,* 206.

5. Cited in Yardley, *Ring,* 40.

6. Cited in Hartley, *Christy Mathewson,* 155.

7. Frederick M. Davenport, "Christy Mathewson," *The Outlook,* August 30,

1922, 704–5 (American Periodical Series/Readers' Guide Retrospective Index).

8. Hartley, *Christy Mathewson,* 167.

9. Grantland Rice, *Journal of the Outdoor Life* 20 (1923): 290.

10. Cary, "Mathewson's Biggest Victory," 48, 174.

11. "Spanking Baseball's Baby and Petting Its Paragon," *Literary Digest,* September 19, 1925, 58–66 (Readers' Guide Retrospective Index).

12. Stanton, *Ty and the Babe,* 99.

13. Hartley, *Christy Mathewson,* 165.

14. W. O. McGeehan, *New York Herald,* republished in "A Tribute to Mathewson," Christy Mathewson Memorial Stadium Dedication, September 30, 1989, 9.

15. Grantland Rice, *New York Herald,* republished in "A Tribute to Mathewson," 9.

16. "Taps for 'Matty,'" *Literary Digest,* October 24, 1925, 42 (Readers' Guide Retrospective Index).

17. "Christy Mathewson," *Youth's Companion,* November 12, 1925, 802 (American Periodical Series).

18. "Why 'Matty' Lasts," 209–10.

19. "'Matty's' Tribute from the Fans," 52.

20. "Taps for 'Matty,'" 42.

21. McGeehan, *New York Herald,* republished in "A Tribute to Mathewson," 9.

22. Edward E. Purinton, "The American Boy," *The Independent,* December 18, 1916, 495–97 (American Periodical Series).

23. "Ty Cobb of the Detroit Tigers," *Outing Magazine,* July 1910, 343 (American Periodical Series).

24. "Why Ty Cobb Is Tired—and Retired," *Literary Digest,* November 20, 1926, 60 (Readers' Guide Retrospective Index).

25. "The Georgia Peach," *Youth's Companion,* December 9, 1926, 966 (American Periodical Series).

26. Varda Burstyn, *The Rites of Men: Manhood, Politics and the Culture of Sport* (Toronto: University of Toronto Press, 1999), 96.

27. Chudacoff, *The Age of the Bachelor.*

28. Gail Bederman, *Manliness & Civilization: A Cultural History of Gender and Race in the United States, 1880–1917* (Chicago: University of Chicago Press, 1995), 6.

29. "Why Ty Cobb Is Tired—and Retired," 60. The fallaway slide is an aggressive, unconventional sliding technique, in which a runner slides away from the base using his hand to tag the base to avoid being put out.

30. C. E. Van Loan, "Making Good in the Big League," *Outing,* June 1910, 319 (American Periodical Series).

31. "The Georgia Peach," 966.

32. Coffin, *The Old Ball Game,* 76.

33. Rader, *American Sport,* 147.

34. Jonathan Eig, *Luckiest Man: The Life and Death of Lou Gehrig* (New York: Simon & Schuster, 2005), 112.

35. Irving E. Sanborn, "Problems That Confront the Baseball Writers Association," *Baseball Magazine,* January 1926, 343–45, 378.

36. Bent, *Ballyhoo*; Evensen, *When Dempsey Fought Tunney,* 49–52.

37. James M. Gould, "Is Player-Writing an Evil?" *Baseball Magazine,* 301–2.

38. Irving E. Sanborn, "What Shall Be Done with the Phony-Player-Writer?" *Baseball Magazine,* November 1926, 564.

39. The practice fell out of favor in the 1970s after the release of Jim Bouton's *Ball Four.* Bouton's vivid chronicle of his experiences traveling with the New York Yankees during the 1969 season was heavily criticized by those inside baseball, who argued that he broke an unwritten code among players and writers. The practice gradually declined after the 1970s but is still visible in player blogs ghosted by professional writers. See Frederick J. Day, *Clubhouse Lawyer: Law in the World of Sports* (Lincoln, Nebr.: iUniverse, 2004), 303–14; Howard Good, *Journalism Ethics Goes to the Movies* (New York: Rowman & Littlefield, 2008), 78–79.

40. Harold Rosenthal, "Ghosts Find World Series Their Happy Haunting Grounds," *Baseball Digest,* October 1960, 48.

41. Sanborn, "What Shall Be Done with the Phony-Player-Writer?" 564.

42. Wheeler and Walsh engaged in antecedent public relations strategies outlined by Cutlip, Russell, and Lamme such as crafting promotional literature and serving as publicity advisors. See Scott Cutlip, *Public Relations History: From the 17th to 20th Century: The Antecedents* (Hillsdale, N.J.: Erlbaum, 1994); Lamme and Russell, "Removing the Spin."

43. Cutlip, *Public Relations History*; Scott Cutlip, *The Unseen Power: Public Relations, a History* (Hillsdale, N.J.: Erlbaum, 1994), 59.

44. Evensen, *When Dempsey Fought Tunney,* 49–52.

45. Ibid., 49.

46. Good, *Journalism Ethics Goes to the Movies,* 78–79; Day, *Clubhouse Lawyer,* 303–14.

47. Ginsberg, *The Fix Is In,* 196–213.

48. Ibid., 205.

49. Lane, *Batting,* 3.

50. Harper, *How You Played the Game,* 313.

51. Rice, *The Tumult and the Shouting,* 26–29.

52. Ty Cobb to Grantland Rice, May 5, 1952, pp. 1–7, Grantland Rice Papers, Series I-1-1, Jean and Alexander Heard Library, Special Collections, Vanderbilt University, Nashville.

53. Yardley, *Ring,* 412.

54. Harper, *How You Played the Game,* 509.

55. Amber Roessner, "Remembering the Georgia Peach: Popular Press, Public

Memory, and the Shifting Legacy of an (Anti-) Hero," *Journalism History* 36, no. 2 (Summer 2010): 83–95.

56. Wheeler, *I've Got News for You.*

57. "John N. Wheeler," *Ridgefield Press,* October 13, 1973, www.baseballfever.com/showthread.php?57538-Meet-The-Sports-Writers/page10 (accessed May 1, 2012).

58. Lane, *Batting,* 3.

59. Cited in Holtzman, *No Cheering in the Press Box,* 126.

60. Ibid., 259.

61. Ibid., 217.

62. Ibid., 244.

11. THE END OF THE "GEE WHIZ" ERA

1. Carey, *Communication as Culture,* 13–36. If, as American philosopher John Dewey contended, society exists "in communication," through the dramatic act of writing, sports scribes told stories that had the power to shape reality.

2. Jack Lule, *Daily News, Eternal Stories: The Mythological Role of Journalism* (New York: Guilford Press, 2001).

3. Hardt and Brennen, eds., *Newsworkers,* 7.

4. Tim P. Vos, "Historical Mechanisms and Journalistic Change," *Journalism History* 30, no. 1 (April 2013): 36–43.

5. Jurgen Habermas, *The Structural Transformation of the Public Sphere: An Inquiry into a Category of Bourgeois Society* (Boston: MIT Press, 1991).

6. Campbell, *The Year That Defined American Journalism,* 5–9; 69–117; Greene, *America's Heroes,* 38.

7. Ponce de Leon, *Self-Exposure,* 89.

8. Ardell, *Breaking into Baseball,* 192. Baseball may have been the national pastime, but sportswriting was largely a male profession. Before the passage of Title IX in 1972, fewer than seventy-five women were employed in sports departments.

9. Koppett, *The Rise and Fall of the Press Box,* 187.

10. Cited in Ponce de Leon, *Self-Exposure,* 99.

11. Ibid., 90.

12. Gallico, *The Golden People,* 14.

13. Campbell, *The Hero with a Thousand Faces.*

14. White, *The Content of the Form.*

15. For example, see Rice, "The Sportlight," *Atlanta Constitution,* March 5, 1915, 8; Rice, "The Sportlight," *Atlanta Constitution,* May 8, 1928, 10.

16. Campbell, *The Year That Defined American Journalism,* 5–9.

17. Rice, "The Sportlight," *Atlanta Constitution,* August 17, 1928, 8.

18. Peet, "The Public Exploitation of Expert Reputation."

19. Cutlip, *Public Relations History.*

20. Anderson, "Crafting the National Pastime's Image," 7–43.

21. Coffin, *The Old Ball Game,* 76.

22. Evensen, *When Dempsey Fought Tunney,* xii.

23. Ibid., 161.

24. Warren I. Susman, *Culture as History: The Transformation of American Life in the Twentieth Century* (New York: Random House, 1973), 244.

25. Ponce de Leon, *Self-Exposure.*

26. Mark Inabinett, *Grantland Rice and His Heroes: The Sportswriter as Mythmaker in the 1920s* (Knoxville: University of Tennessee Press). Few women appeared in these tales; Wills and Little Orphan Annie were the exceptions.

27. For example, see Adams, "Plutarch Lights of History, No. 6: Christy Mathewson," 395; Cary, "Mathewson's Biggest Victory," 174; "'Matty's' Tribute from the Fans," 52; "Why 'Matty' Lasts," 209–10.

28. For example, see "Christy Mathewson," *Playground,* December 1925, 517.

29. Riess, *Touching Base,* 26.

30. Christy Mathewson and John N. Wheeler, *Pitching in a Pinch: The Boy Scouts Edition* (New York: G. P. Putnam's Sons, 1913).

31. Boy Scouts of America, *Handbook for Scout Masters* (Boston: Harvard University, 1914), 353.

32. "'Matty's' Tribute from the Fans," 52.

33. "Spanking Baseball's Baby and Petting Its Paragon," 58.

34. Bederman, *Manliness & Civilization,* 6.

35. For example, see "Christy Mathewson," *Playground,* December 1925, 517; "'Matty's' Tribute from the Fans," 52; Purinton, "The American Boy," 495–97; Wheeler, "'Matty' as the Champion of the Friendless," 36; "Why Ty Cobb Is Tired—and Retired," 60.

36. Amy S. Greenberg, *Manifest Manhood and the Antebellum American Empire* (New York: Cambridge University Press, 2005).

37. Evensen, *When Dempsey Fought Tunney,* xii.

38. "The old standards are passing. The old gods are dying," noted an *American Magazine* editorial in November 1906. Cited in Greene, *America's Heroes,* 232.

39. Greene, *America's Heroes,* 236.

40. Riess, *Touching Base,* 39.

41. Susman, *Culture as History,* 123.

42. Ibid., 141–42.

43. Mrozek, *Sport and the American Mentality,* 176.

44. Susman, *Culture as History,* 141–42; T. J. Jackson Lears, *No Place of Grace: Antimodernism and the Transformation of American Culture, 1880–1920* (Chicago: University of Chicago Press, 1981), 10.

45. Susman, *Culture as History,* 141–42.

46. For examples, see Cary, "Mathewson's Biggest Victory," 174; Leventhal,

"Two Glimpses of Ty Cobb," 78; "Ty Cobb on the Batting Art," 1558–63; "Why Ty Cobb Is Tired—and Retired," November 20, 1926, 56.

47. Cited in Susman, *Culture as History,* 11.

48. Van Loan, "Making Good in the Big League," 319; Dayton Stoddard, "What Baseball Has Taught Ty Cobb," *Collier's,* July 19, 1924, 7.

49. "Spanking Baseball's Baby and Petting Its Paragon," 58.

50. "The Georgia Peach," 966.

51. Ibid.

52. Seib, *The Player,* 2.

53. "Christy Mathewson," *Youth's Companion,* November 12, 1925, 802.

54. Allen, "Christy Mathewson's Glove," 430–33.

55. Eric Rolfe Greenberg, *The Celebrant* (Omaha: University of Nebraska Press, 1993).

56. Eddie Frierson, *"Matty": An Evening with "The Big Six,"* Two Roads Run Theatre, 1995.

57. "Christy Mathewson," *Youth's Companion,* November 12, 1925, 802.

58. "Christy Mathewson," *Playground,* December 1925, 517.

59. Mrozek, *Sport and the American Mentality,* 176.

60. Susman, *Culture as History,* 275–79.

61. Rice, *The Tumult and the Shouting,* 333.

62. Susman, *Culture as History,* 146.

63. Cited ibid., 145.

64. Ibid., 146–47.

65. Drucker and Cathcart, eds., *American Heroes in a Media Age,* 82–83.

66. Boorstin, *The Image,* 57.

67. Drucker and Cathcart, eds., *American Heroes in a Media Age,* 93.

68. Asinof, *Eight Men Out,* 46–47.

69. Evensen, *When Dempsey Fought Tunney,* 49–52.

70. Bent, *Ballyhoo,* 31.

71. Susman, *Culture as History,* 146–47.

72. Koppett, *The Rise and Fall of the Press Box,* 178, 179.

73. Inabinett, *Grantland Rice and His Heroes,* 21–24.

74. Holtzman, *No Cheering in the Press Box,* 71–72.

75. Harper, *How You Played the Game,* 475.

76. Koppett, *The Rise and Fall of the Press Box,* 178–79; Silva, *Baseball over the Air.*

77. Nick Trujillo and Leah R. Vande Berg, "From Western Prodigy to Ageless Wonder: The Mediated Evolution of Nolan Ryan," in *American Heroes in a Media Age,* ed. Drucker and Cathcart, 221–40; Daniel A. Nathan and Mary G. McDonald, "Yearning for Yesteryear: Cal Ripkin Jr., the Streak, and the Politics of Nostalgia," *American Studies* 42, no. 1 (Spring 2001): 99–123.

78. Williams, *The Long Revolution,* 34.

79. Philip Goldstein and James L. Machor, eds., *New Directions in American Reception Study* (New York: Oxford University Press, 2008).

80. Major League Baseball officially banned women from professional baseball in 1952 (Gai Ingham Berlage, *Women in Baseball: The Forgotten Story* [New York: Praeger, 1994], 78).

81. Kirk, "When 'Matty' Was a Boy," 2.

82. "Ty Cobb Remains King of All Batsmen," *Literary Digest,* January 17, 1920, 118; Brunner, "Hero Worship on the Diamond."

83. Stoddard, "What Baseball Has Taught Ty Cobb," 7.

84. Lane, "Who Is the Greatest Player in the History of Baseball," 27–34; Lane, "The Secret of Christy Mathewson's Success," 65–70.

EPILOGUE

1. Lynn Zinser, "Bisher, the Loss of a Legend," *New York Times,* March 19, 2012, onpar.blogs.nytimes.com/2012/03/19/bisher-the-loss-of-a-legend/ (accessed July 17, 2012).

2. Frank Deford, "Sweetness and Light: Jocks Who Fail, and the Fans Who Can't Love Them" NPR, "Morning Edition," March 3, 2010, www.npr.org/templates/story/story.php?storyId=124238044 (accessed May 20, 2010).

3. Factoryville, Pennsylvania, honors Matty with Christy Mathewson Days each August. The weekend event features live music, a parade, an ice-cream social, the Big 6K Run, and, of course, several community baseball games. Meanwhile, Royston, Georgia, celebrates the memory of Cobb with the Ty Cobb Museum.

4. Stanton, *Ty and the Babe,* xii.

Index